T0046318

THE SEEDS OF DISASTER

The Stackpole Military History Series

THE AMERICAN CIVIL WAR

Cavalry Raids of the Civil War
Ghost, Thunderbolt, and Wizard
In the Lion's Mouth
Pickett's Charge
Witness to Gettysburg

WORLD WAR I

Doughboy War

WORLD WAR II

After D-Day
Airborne Combat
Armor Battles of the Waffen-SS, 1943–45
Armoured Guardsmen
Army of the West
Arnhem 1944
Australian Commandos
The B-24 in China
Backwater War
The Battalion
The Battle of France
The Battle of Sicily
Battle of the Bulge, Vol. 1
Battle of the Bulge, Vol. 2
Battle of the Bulge, Vol. 3
Beyond the Beachhead
Beyond Stalingrad
The Black Bull
Blitzkrieg Unleashed
Blossoming Silk against the Rising Sun
Bodenplatte
The Brandenburger Commandos
The Breaking Point
The Brigade
Bringing the Thunder
The Canadian Army and the Normandy
    Campaign
Coast Watching in World War II
Colossal Cracks
Condor
A Dangerous Assignment
D-Day Bombers
D-Day Deception
D-Day to Berlin
Decision in the Ukraine
The Defense of Moscow 1941
Destination Normandy
Dive Bomber!
A Drop Too Many
Eager Eagles
Eagles of the Third Reich
The Early Battles of Eighth Army
Eastern Front Combat
Europe in Flames
Exit Rommel
The Face of Courage
Fatal Decisions
Fist from the Sky
Flying American Combat Aircraft of World
    War II, Vol. 1
Flying American Combat Aircraft of World
    War II, Vol. 2
For Europe
Forging the Thunderbolt

For the Homeland
Fortress France
The German Defeat in the East, 1944–45
German Order of Battle, Vol. 1
German Order of Battle, Vol. 2
German Order of Battle, Vol. 3
The Germans in Normandy
Germany's Panzer Arm in World War II
GI Ingenuity
Goodwood
The Great Ships
Grenadiers
Guns against the Reich
Hitler's Nemesis
Hitler's Spanish Legion
Hold the Westwall
Infantry Aces
In the Fire of the Eastern Front
Iron Arm
Iron Knights
Japanese Army Fighter Aces
Japanese Naval Fighter Aces
JG 26 Luftwaffe Fighter Wing War Diary,
    Vol. 1
JG 26 Luftwaffe Fighter Wing War Diary,
    Vol. 2
Kampfgruppe Peiper at the Battle of
    the Bulge
The Key to the Bulge
Knight's Cross Panzers
Kursk
Luftwaffe Aces
Luftwaffe Fighter Ace
Luftwaffe Fighter-Bombers over Britain
Luftwaffe Fighters and Bombers
Massacre at Tobruk
Mechanized Juggernaut or Military
    Anachronism?
Messerschmitts over Sicily
Michael Wittmann, Vol. 1
Michael Wittmann, Vol. 2
Mission 85
Mission 376
Mountain Warriors
The Nazi Rocketeers
Night Flyer / Mosquito Pathfinder
No Holding Back
On the Canal
Operation Mercury
Packs On!
Panzer Aces
Panzer Aces II
Panzer Aces III
Panzer Commanders of the Western Front
Panzergrenadier Aces
Panzer Gunner
The Panzer Legions
Panzers in Normandy
Panzers in Winter
Panzer Wedge, Vol. 1
Panzer Wedge, Vol. 2
The Path to Blitzkrieg
Penalty Strike
Poland Betrayed
Prince of Aces

Red Road from Stalingrad
Red Star under the Baltic
Retreat to the Reich
Rommel Reconsidered
Rommel's Desert Commanders
Rommel's Desert War
Rommel's Lieutenants
The Savage Sky
The Seeds of Disaster
Ship-Busters
The Siege of Küstrin
The Siegfried Line
A Soldier in the Cockpit
Soviet Blitzkrieg
Spitfires and Yellow Tail Mustangs
Stalin's Keys to Victory
Surviving Bataan and Beyond
T-34 in Action
Tank Tactics
Tigers in the Mud
Triumphant Fox
The 12th SS, Vol. 1
The 12th SS, Vol. 2
Twilight of the Gods
Typhoon Attack
The War against Rommel's Supply Lines
War in the Aegean
War of the White Death
Warsaw 1944
Winter Storm
The Winter War
Wolfpack Warriors
Zhukov at the Oder

THE COLD WAR / VIETNAM

Cyclops in the Jungle
Expendable Warriors
Fighting in Vietnam
Flying American Combat Aircraft: The Cold
    War
Here There Are Tigers
Land with No Sun
MiGs over North Vietnam
Phantom Reflections
Street without Joy
Through the Valley
Tours of Duty
Two One Pony

WARS OF AFRICA AND THE MIDDLE EAST

Never-Ending Conflict
The Rhodesian War

GENERAL MILITARY HISTORY

Carriers in Combat
Cavalry from Hoof to Track
Desert Battles
Guerrilla Warfare
The Philadelphia Campaign, Vol. 1
Ranger Dawn
Sieges
The Spartan Army

THE SEEDS OF DISASTER

The Development of French Army Doctrine, 1919–1939

Robert A. Doughty

STACKPOLE
BOOKS

Copyright ©1985 by Robert A. Doughty

Published by
STACKPOLE BOOKS
5067 Ritter Road
Mechanicsburg, PA 17055
www.stackpolebooks.com

All rights reserved, including the right to reproduce this book or portions thereof in any form or by any means, electronic or mechanical, including photocopying, recording, or by any information storage and retrieval system, without permission in writing from the publisher. All inquiries should be addressed to Stackpole Books.

Printed in the United States of America

STACKPOLE FIRST EDITION

Cover design by Wendy A. Reynolds

Front and back cover photos from *Blitzkrieg France 1940*

Library of Congress Cataloging-in-Publication Data

Doughty, Robert A.
  The seeds of disaster : the development of French Army doctrine, 1919–1939 / Robert Allan Doughty.
      pages cm. — (Stackpole military history series)
  Originally published: Hamden, Connecticut : Archon Books, 1985.
  Includes bibliographical references and index.
  ISBN 978-0-8117-1460-0
1. France. Armie.—History—20th century. 2. Military doctrine—France—History—20th century. 3. Military art and science—France—History—20th century. I. Title.
  UA702.D68 2014
  355'.03354409042—dc23
                              2014019790

For Diane, Mike, and Kevin

Contents

Preface. ix

Chapter 1. The Framework of French Doctrine 1
Chapter 2. An Army of Reservists 15
Chapter 3. The Defense of the Frontiers 43
Chapter 4. The Legacy of the Past 75
Chapter 5. Firepower and the Methodical Battle 95
Chapter 6. Institutions and Doctrine 117
Chapter 7. The Development of the Tank 141
Chapter 8. The Creation of Large Armored Units 167
Chapter 9. Conclusion 185

Notes 199
Select Bibliography 225
Index 233

Preface

It may have been a cool, sunshiny day in Paris in 1922 when Col. J. Roger addressed the assembled officers in a small, dimly lit amphitheater at the *Ecole supérieure de guerre*, France's War College. The hundred or so officers sitting around him were probably exhausted from late-night studying and from an overly full schedule of professional and extracurricular activities. Given a choice, they undoubtedly would have preferred to be elsewhere. But they had to attend Colonel Roger's lecture on artillery. After a long and tedious explanation of the doctrine for the artillery's support of attacks against a defense in depth, the lecturer reached his conclusion. He said, "The loss of control over the attack, which is turned over to the battalion leaders, often renders it impossible for the division commander to intervene by artillery action, the principal means available for meeting unexpected and urgent situations."[1] The students had listened to a familiar explanation of the importance of firepower and centralized control. Thankful for a momentary break, they probably hurried out of the amphitheater, anxious for some fresh air and a few moments of activity.

Beyond the confines of the War College, Paris and France paid little attention to what was said in that lecture hall on that day. Except for those in the army, almost no one bothered to examine the complexities and subtleties of doctrine as it appeared in army manuals or was discussed in lectures. Most believed that such material was the proper concern of military staff specialists, operating within the narrow confines of their responsibilities. And even the students at the War College, who had the study of doctrine as their primary concern, often found its study less rewarding than horseback riding or terrain walks. Almost none of the French recognized the profound effect army doctrine would ultimately have on their fate.

The importance of doctrine has seldom been illustrated as clearly as in the May–June 1940 campaign in western Europe. Few defeats have been as unexpected or as sudden as France's collapse. Few have altered so fundamentally the status or standing of a nation within the community of nations. Despite the swiftness of the defeat, France was anything but unready for war, for she had mobilized numerous units and fielded much advanced equipment. She had devoted more than two decades to preparing for the possibility of a future war against Germany. She was, however, prepared in 1940 to fight carefully controlled and methodical battles that were precisely the type of battles Germany intended to avoid. Under the pressure of war, France simply could not respond to the type of fighting thrust upon her. The resulting debacle swept her from the first rank of world powers.

By focusing on the development of French doctrine from 1919 to 1939, this book seeks to provide at least a partial answer for why French forces failed so disastrously against the German blitzkrieg. To explain the swift defeat, one could attribute the failure to the stupidity of French soldiers, or to the decadence of the entire society. Such explanations, however, fail to describe the difficult situation in which the army found itself, to reveal the choices that were made, or to illuminate why the army chose the path it trod. In seeking the reasons for the debacle, one must search for more profound or fundamental explanations than a failure of intellect or the bumblings of an officer corps dominated by its memories of the last war. And one must look beyond the supposed "genius" of the German officer corps. Such is the purpose of this book.

The story of France's failure clearly illustrates the complexity and difficulty of formulating an effective doctrine. According to French usage, "doctrine" represented the best available thought on what would usually work best on the battlefield. It usually appeared in military manuals, journals, and courses of study and consisted of officially sanctioned concepts for employing personnel, equipment, and units. In the broadest sense, doctrine provided the basis for organizing, equipping, training, and employing military forces.

Correspondingly, this book concentrates on the evolution of doctrinal concepts as they moved through bureaucratic institutions, appeared in official documents, and were applied in field exercises and plans. As it follows these movements, the trail of investigation winds through the historic relationships between doctrine and technology and doctrine and strategy. Since the formulation of doctrine is shaped and deflected by the larger policy of a country, the book also examines the larger issues of military policy as it was affected by questions of politics, economics, and geography. For similar reasons, the book touches upon the effect of military doctrine and policy upon foreign policy. The theme of doctrine provides the vehicle for examining broad aspects of the entire military establishment.

The book also demonstrates the vital role played by doctrine in modern armies. The creation of an effective military force depends upon more than the provision of adequate resources, the building of advanced weapons, or the availability of manpower. Military forces must be organized, equipped, and trained properly. Doctrine is the substance that binds them together and makes them effective. Although a false doctrine can be dangerously suffocating to all innovation, an adequate doctrine can be conducive to creative solutions and is a vital ingredient in any recipe for success. With an adequate doctrine, effective forces can be deployed. With an inadequate doctrine, a military force and a nation are courting disaster. The experience of France testifies to this clearly.

The book is not a study of the German army or the blitzkrieg. Since French doctrinal developments obviously occurred separately from the German effort to create a more mobile fighting force, the book examines German ideas and achievements only to contrast them with what happened in France. The book also is not a study of French air force equipment and doctrine. The air force gained a degree of institutional autonomy in 1928 with the creation of a minister of air and achieved its complete independence from the army in 1933. While its evolution in the interwar period and its role in the 1940 fighting are of evident importance, the air force's development ultimately lies outside the focus of this study. Finally, the book is not an examination of the 1940 campaign. Events in the fighting are mentioned only to illustrate the effect of the decisions made previously in peacetime.

In the course of my research and study I have benefited from the advice and assistance of numerous individuals. I am indebted to Brig. Gen. (Ret.) Thomas E. Griess and Brig. Gen. Roy K. Flint for their confidence in my abilities. I am grateful to Professors Eugen Weber, John Sweets, I. B. Holley, Jr., Dennis E. Showalter, and Henry Snyder for their guidance and constructive comments. I should also thank Jeffrey J. Clarke and Jeffery A. Gunsburg for their comments and suggestions. A special note of thanks is due to the staffs of the libraries of the U.S. Army Command and General Staff College and the U.S. Military Academy, whose interlibrary loan services have always been superb. During my stay in Paris, the staff at the *Service historique de l'armée de terre* and members of the history section at the *Ecole supérieure de guerre* were more than willing to provide assistance. M. Paul Gamelin was also kind enough to allow me to use Gen. Maurice Gamelin's papers. The artwork in the maps is a product of the extremely talented Edward J. Krasnoborski, of the Department of History at West Point.

My greatest debt belongs to Diane, Mike, and Kevin, who ensured that good spirits and great affection have prevailed as "the book" was finished. To them this work is dedicated.

While it is difficult to exaggerate the value of the assistance of those I have mentioned and others, I alone am responsible for the text. The opinions expressed in this book do not represent the official views of the Department of Defense, the Department of the Army, or the U.S. Military Academy. Any errors in fact or interpretation are solely my own.

CHAPTER 1

The Framework of French Doctrine

The fall of France in May–June 1940 astonished the world because of its swiftness and completeness. On 10 May, German forces attacked. On 12–13 May they crossed the Meuse River. By the evening of 16 May, the Germans had ruptured the French front completely. By 20 May, armored columns had reached the English Channel and severed the French, British, and Belgian armies in the north from the French armies to the south. After failing to prevent the evacuation of the British and French forces at Dunkirk, the Germans attacked the French defensive positions along the Somme on 5 June, broke through these hastily established lines on 7 June, and entered Paris on 14 June. An exhausted Gen. Charles Huntziger, whose Second Army had been swept aside at Sedan, signed the armistice before a jubilant Adolph Hitler on 22 June in the same railway car and at the same spot where Marshal Ferdinand Foch had accepted the German surrender on 11 November 1918. It was difficult for experts as well as civilians to understand how the Germans had so quickly shattered a French military previously recognized as among the world's best-prepared forces. It was impossible for the French to accept the shameful defeat without recrimination and accusation.

As the shock of the initial losses swept France, bitter accusations of treason and conspiracy swept the country. The signing of the armistice formally began a search for those responsible for the bloody "second Sedan" in which the powerful descendant of Prussia had destroyed the military power and wounded the pride of France. French soldiers were condemned for lacking discipline and the will to fight; they seemed to differ from the *poilus* of 1914–1918. "Fifth columnists" had supposedly conducted espionage for the enemy, sabotaged bunkers, bridges, and military equipment, and spread terror and panic among the refugees and soldiers. Nazi sympathizers reputedly had infiltrated the ranks of the political authorities and key administrative officials. Other critics perceived the entire society to be at fault. Some Frenchmen thought that their own people had become apathetic if not

1

decadent, their political institutions ineffective if not obstructive, and their schoolteachers unpatriotic if not hostile to national interests. In this floundering morass of accusation, some even believed that God had abandoned France because of her sins and the error of her ways.[1] No explanation was beyond belief.

Charges of incompetence also filled the air. The low point in character assassination came at the Riom trial from February to April 1942, when the Vichy regime conducted an investigation of the military and civil leaders of the Third Republic. A veritable parade of military authorities testified to the inadequacies and errors of such leaders as Paul Reynaud, Léon Blum, Edouard Daladier, and Gen. Maurice Gamelin. After the liberation of France, the National Assembly conducted its own investigation in 1947 and made its own accusations when Marshal Philippe Pétain, Gen. Maxime Weygand, and Pierre Laval were accused of being defeatist, pessimistic, and unwilling to pursue victory. No political or military leader from the interwar period seemed above reproach by the various "schools" of criticism.

France's allies also came under fire in the verbal battle. Numerous observers pointed out that the emergence and initial successes of Nazi Germany were due as much to a failure of Europe as to a failure of France. In that sense, the unexpected loss in 1940 could be considered as much a defeat of the Allies as a defeat of France.[2] The yielding of the Dutch and the flight of Queen Wilhelmina, the surrender of King Leopold III of Belgium, and the evacuation of the bulk of the British forces at Dunkirk were all part of the "battle of France." The improvised coalition, the late and inadequate planning, and the inefficient and faulty coordination at the highest political and military levels sprang as much, if not more, from the lapses of Great Britain, Belgium, and the Netherlands as from those of France.

In comparison to the British, Belgian, and Dutch forces, the French forces were a model of preparedness and modernization. For example, Great Britain had completely failed until March 1939 to prepare any ground forces for use on the Continent, despite her large population and industrial base. The outbreak of World War II caught her in the awkward position of having begun the expansion and modernization of her army too late. When the Germans attacked on 10 May 1940, the British Expeditionary Force was outnumbered in personnel by both the Belgian and Dutch forces. While the Belgians had twenty-two divisions and the Dutch nine, the British had only ten divisions and about six hundred armored vehicles in France. Only twenty-three of these vehicles were equipped with a 2-pounder main gun; the rest carried only machine guns.[3] In comparison, the French had 2,285 tanks with main guns and ninety-three divisions on the northeastern front, including three armored, three light mechanized (*division légère mécanique*), and seven motorized divisions.[4] Had France not been compelled to link her destiny to that of her weaker allies, had the Allies cooperated more closely, or had Great Britain prepared herself more fully, the strategy and its results might have been far different.

But whatever may have been the weaknesses and unpreparedness of the other allies, the crucial disasters occurred in the French sector. The decisive penetrations of the Allies' lines came in the area of the French Second and Ninth armies along the Meuse River, around Sedan, Monthermé, and Dinant. Even if the forces of the other allies were not ready for the challenges confronting them, even though the Allied command structure remained inadequate and obsolete, the final collapse of the Allies began when the French forces crumbled. No criticism of France's wavering allies can obscure this very painful truth. The strength and resolve of the allies may have been illusory; the final paralysis and helplessness of the French army were not.

Some Frenchmen have acknowledged that the key event in the military catastrophe was the collapse of the army. They have recognized that this collapse came not from a spiritual or political failure of the French people but from the fact that the military was overwhelmed on the field of battle by a better-prepared opponent.[5] At the Riom trial, numerous witnesses criticized what they perceived as the inherent weaknesses in the army's doctrine. After the liberation of France, other critics argued that the army suffered from deficiencies as much self-inflicted as due to factors outside the military's control. In recent years, it has become increasingly apparent that the immediate cause of the defeat was that the French army was not ready for the rapid and often tumultuous pace of mobile warfare that it encountered in the dismal days of May and June 1940. The most recently published volume of the French army's official history, for example, admits that the army may have been prepared for mobilization and concentration, but that it was not "ready for combat."[6]

The French army, in short, had formulated a doctrine, organized and equipped its units, and trained its soldiers for the wrong type of war. The framework for this doctrine, and thus for the organization, equipment, training, and employment of French units, came from an emphasis on the destructiveness of firepower, the strength of the defense, the ascendancy of the methodical battle, and the unifying power of the commander. The French firmly believed that the new weapons and greater firepower which had become available to modern armies between 1919 and 1939 had made the battlefield much more lethal than in the past. The great destructive power of the new weapons strengthened the defense, and relatively fewer men could establish a virtually impenetrable barrier of fire. An attacker could overwhelm a defender only by the closely coordinated employment of massed men and matériel.

The doctrine which emerged from this perception of great lethality stressed what the French called the *bataille conduit,* or the "methodical battle." By this term they meant a rigidly controlled operation in which all units and weapons were carefully marshalled and then employed in combat. The French favored a step-by-step battle, with units obediently moving between phase lines and adhering to strictly scheduled timetables. Such methods, they believed, were essential for the coherent employment of the enormous amounts of men and matériel demanded by modern combat. A hastily prepared, impulsive fight was doomed to failure. The focus of decision-making was best kept at higher command levels, because centralized control was necessary to coordinate the actions of numerous subordinate units.

In contrast to a decentralized battle in which officers at all levels were expected to show initiative and flexibility, the French preferred rigid centralization and strict obedience. Their doctrine stressed the necessity of avoiding an encounter battle in which moving armies unexpectedly collided and had to fight in an impromptu and spontaneous fashion. They thus opted for a time-consuming, intricate process that prized preparation rather than improvisation. As a consequence of this approach, French doctrine envisaged first the weakening of an attacker by a defender's fire, and then his destruction by a massive but tightly controlled "battering-ram" attack.

Unfortunately for France, her army was prepared to fight precisely the type of war that Germany wanted to avoid. In the opening days of World War II, the Germans used their tanks, mobile artillery, and airplanes to achieve the short, violent lightning war, famous as the blitzkrieg. They recognized that in addition to firepower, the new weapons furnished shock, speed, and mobility. Instead of "curtains" of carefully regulated fire, they understood the new weapons made possible large mobile formations that could thrust and parry with the enemy. The Germans emphasized offense instead of defense by employing the mobility and mass of armored formations against enemy vulnerabilities. Instead of increased centralization, they wanted lower-level commanders exercising their initiative and adapting flexibly to continually changing circumstances. The German military all too effectively demonstrated the adequacy of their doctrine and of their high command and the corresponding unpreparedness of the French army. The charging panzers seemed to herald the war of the future, while the thinly stretched French lines reminded most observers of wars previously fought.

The complete collapse of the French army in 1940 demonstrated that it had failed to prepare adequately for the demands of modern warfare. Four days of battle, from 12 to 16 May revealed the weaknesses and the errors in the army's preparations more quickly, more clearly, and more painfully than two previous decades of examination and experimentation. Since French army doctrine was unsuited and inadequate for the war Germany thrust upon France in 1940, and since the strategy of rushing forward into Belgium was particularly vulnerable to the German attack through the Ardennes, defeat was virtually unavoidable after the battle began. The army and the army's leaders lacked the proper flexibility and responsiveness to reply to the unexpected.

Despite the army's failure to develop a sufficiently effective and modern doctrine, its leaders between the two world wars never completely closed their minds to fresh ideas and were never simply slaves to previous methods. In peacetime, armies do not prepare for defeat, and the French were no exception. They continued after 1918 to seek innovation and improvement. Above all, the army did not simply take the methods of 1918 and attempt lethargically and unsuccessfully to apply them in 1940.

After World War I, the French army devoted considerable effort to create the best possible and most modern doctrine. It organized a complex and sophisticated system for considering new ideas and new technologies. For two decades, the army carefully analyzed the variety of ways personnel, equipment, and units could be organized and employed. It believed it could identify those methods which had the best chance of success in a future battle, or which enabled the maximum benefit to be obtained from each weapon or unit. The French believed that exercises or tests conducted in a scientific fashion provided the best practical way of determining the feasibility of new concepts or perfecting new methods. They also, however, developed doctrine by the detailed study and comparison of theories offered by military professionals, and by the logical application of lessons of the past to anticipated conditions in the future.

By 1939 the French army had adopted much new equipment and many new ideas, and its doctrine differed distinctly from that of 1918. It had conducted extensive tests with new equipment. It had devoted more efforts and resources to analyzing advanced weapons, such as the tank, than any other army. While numerous advances and changes had been made, the shattering events of May–June 1940 revealed that these advances had been either insufficient or in the wrong direction. What had been perceived as progress or improvement proved to be inappropriate for the unanticipated demands of 1940. Efforts to develop a viable doctrine had failed.

One myth that has emerged about the inadequate French doctrine is that it was the product of a very small group of people. Citing the French use of such terms as "evangelism" or "Bible" for discussing doctrine, some authors have suggested that doctrine in the interwar period fulfilled a role analogous to words of wisdom espoused by followers of a religious prophet. In particular, the notion of evangelic ideas flowing from a single military prophet has identified Marshal Pétain as being the source from whom the initial ideas for the French doctrine flowed. The official history of this period, for example, states, "The doctrine for employment [of the army) will be essentially the work of Marshal Pétain."[7] French doctrine, however, was an eclectic product, influenced by a variety of military thinkers and leaders. While Pétain certainly had great influence, especially through the early 1930s, other well-known officers, including Marshal Ferdinand Foch and Generals Maxime Weygand and Maurice Gamelin, also influenced doctrine.

Gen. Eugène Debeney, another key figure, may have had greater influence over the technical aspects of French doctrine than did Marshal Pétain. As director of the War College and the Center of Higher Military Studies (*Centre des hautes études militaires*) immediately after World War I, he established the educational curriculum and the subject matter that was taught to France's most promising officers during the interwar period. The operations of the First French Army in 1918, which Debeney commanded, provided the conceptual basis for many of the lessons at the War College and for many tactical concepts within French doctrine. As a member of the commission that wrote the important 1921 manual entitled *Provisional Instructions on the Tactical Employment of Large Units*, Debeney played a key role in establishing the foundation for French doctrine in the interwar period. As chief of the General Staff from 1923 to 1930, he was one of the major architects of the basic laws of 1927 and 1928 on organization, recruitment, and cadres and effectives that were to shape the army of the 1930s and 1940. He played a key role in the decisions affecting the design and emplacement of the Maginot Line. The final configuration of the northeastern fortifications were more similar to his initial ideas than they were to the initial ideas of any other leading member of the High Command. While his political and strategic influence may not have rivaled that of Marshal Pétain, his influence over the technical aspects of doctrine was at least as great.

The example of Debeney's influence should not suggest that he was the ultimate source of French doctrine. Other military officers also played crucial roles in the complex process of formulating and publishing doctrine. As will be demonstrated, French doctrine was the work of a large portion of the officer corps rather than the product of a narrow spectrum of the High Command or of a single individual. Simply stated, the process for developing new doctrine was too complex and too vast for any one person to dominate it.

Regardless of its origins, doctrine from 1919 to 1939 represented the best available thought on what would usually work best on the battlefield. Though practices often differed sharply from beliefs, the French believed doctrinal solutions had to be adapted to each solution, and that they should not bind soldiers to an inflexible, prescribed method. Doctrine thus supposedly shaped the actions of military personnel by providing guides, rather than precise formulas, for actions. Doctrine also provided the basis for military education and training; it ensured a uniformity of effort and thought among the numerous and varied units in the army.

In the interwar years, the French considered doctrine especially important, since huge armies required common tactical methods and organizations to assure a unity of effort. General Gamelin, who was chief of the General Staff, vice-president of the Superior Council of War (*Conseil supérieur de la guerre*), and commander of the French army in 1940, argued in 1935 that the military was different from other organizations. Its many layers of "intermediaries" often caused the leader's will to be "deformed," thus threatening the objective of the leader and of the military. To avoid this possibility and to ensure that the many organizations in the military would orient their entire effort toward the same goal, an army required, according to Gamelin, unity of organization and coherent doctrine.[8]

An artillery officer expressed the views of many of his contemporaries when he argued that unity of doctrine imposed on the army "the same tactical and strategic conceptions," "the same discipline of thought," and "the same terminology and mode of expression." The variety of weapons and units in a modern army made it difficult for an officer to understand how to employ all of them, but the various arms had to be coordinated to obtain the best possible contribution from each.[9] Without such coordination, great inefficiencies or even chaos could result.

The methods, organizations, and weapons employed by infantry, artillery, tank, and cavalry units, for example, differed greatly. Yet each had a function to perform in battle. The success of an operation depended upon each arm performing its part of the overall action. The different combat arms could not engage in battle without regard to the methods being employed by the others. The infantry, as a crucial example, had to understand the basic components of artillery doctrine. If every artillery unit had different methods, an infantry unit would have to reconsider its methods every time it operated with a different artillery unit. If it worked with more than one artillery unit, its task of coordination and employment of supporting fires would be overwhelming. Doctrine thus provided common tactical concepts for ensuring that the various arms could work together effectively and efficiently. A mass army required a homogeneity of method to prevent every unit or every commander from trying to fight a war in his own way without regard for or knowledge of the intrinsic capabilities of the units and weapons under him.

The French used the term "harmony" to express the purpose of doctrine, and the analogy of harmony within an orchestra seems particularly appropriate. In the symphonic form, it represents everyone playing his instrument differently but still following the directions of the conductor in order that beauty may emerge from the differences. Without the direction of the conductor, without a unity of doctrine, the variety of instruments being played differently can only result in a harsh cacophony of noise.

Doctrine was also an important vehicle for facilitating communication. With soldiers schooled in the same doctrinal concepts, commanders and staff officers spoke the same technical language when they used such terms as *point d'appui, cloisonnement, bouchon,* etc. Given the wide variety of weapons and people, such a common technical language was essential to orchestrate, or provide harmony to, widely varying activities in an army, and as the complexity of weapons and units increased, the French believed the need for a common doctrine also increased.

In spite of the need for harmony, the officer was not expected to solve his problems by applying doctrine regardless of circumstances. The 1920 *Provisional Regulations on the Maneuver of Infantry* included a report by the director of infantry that stated:

> A solution is never reproduced identically: the state of morale of the troops and the enemy, the terrain, the physical and atmospheric conditions, the means at one's disposal, [and] the dimensions of the assigned zone of action are never the same, on the whole, from one operation to another. Each case must be considered by itself and requires its own solution.[10]

In April 1937, General Gamelin stated that while doctrine did not change, "procedures of combat" did, and added that procedures could be modified during a campaign.[11]

General Debeney emphasized the need for flexibility in doctrine, and explained that the word "doctrine" comes from the Latin word *docere,* which means "to teach." He concluded, "A doctrine . . . includes the essential ideas presiding over the training and employment of the army." An essential part of Debeney's acceptance of a few central ideas "presiding" over the army was belief in the necessity of having leaders capable of "adapting to realities to the exclusion of all dogmatism."[12] Military authors often explained that judgment was a more precious quality for the military leader than memory. Doctrine thus provided a guide for actions on the battlefield, but it did not slavishly bind a leader solely to the doctrinal method.

A variety of sources of doctrinal information existed. Courses at the various army schools enabled officers to acquire a basic understanding of French doctrine, and military journals often contained articles elaborating points of official doctrine. Changes in doctrine were often advertised or explained in these journals to ensure that officers remained current with the latest methods.

Probably the most important sources of doctrinal information, however, were the regulations or instructions published in the format and binding of a military manual. From the turn of the century to 1940, the High Command disseminated the major components of French doctrine through the various instructions or regulations dealing with the tactical employment of large units. These manuals became the prime vehicle for inculcating the main theme of each doctrine during the various periods before the 1940 defeat. The ebb and flow of doctrinal precepts can clearly be seen in them. For example, with the publication of the 28 October 1913, regulations on the conduct of large units, the doctrine of the offensive reigned supreme. Marshal Joseph Joffre later said that he had hoped the publication of new regulations on the eve of the war would result in the emergence of a "central idea" which would bring a "convergence of results."[13] The clear, central idea contained in the 1913 regulation was the dominance of the offensive, and the 1913 manual became the basic document for communicating this doctrine to the army.

Following the terrible losses of World War I, the French shunned the discredited philosophy of the *offensive à outrance*. Excessive stress on the offense was replaced by a more balanced emphasis on the defense, emphasizing the methodical battle and firepower but leaving ample room for the offensive which would deliver the decisive blow. This basic theme also appeared in the two instructions for larger units that were published in the interwar years: *Provisional Instructions on the Tactical Employment of Large Units* (1921) and *Instructions on the Tactical Employment of Large Units* (1936).[14]

Other regulations or instructions pertaining to specific arms followed the lead of these two important manuals. According to General Gamelin, these subordinate regulations emphasized "procedures."[15] Many remained provisional because of the anticipated evolution of weapons and thus of organizations and doctrine. If the manuals disagreed on a technical or specific doctrinal point, the doctrine in the instructions for the tactical employment of large units prevailed.

The 1921 and 1936 instructions remained the documents upon which the French army's methods were based. Since the 1921 edition dominated

French thought for most of the interwar period, it was particularly important. A commission of thirteen officers, with Marshal Pétain as president, wrote the instructions. This group accepted the necessity for eventual revision and emphasized in the foreword of the instructions the requirement to change the methods for employing large units as armaments evolved. A desire to demonstrate the openness of the French army to new ideas and methods led to the selection of "Provisional Instructions" for the title of the work. Despite this title, it remained the "Bible"—as French officers referred to it—of the army from 1921 to 1936.

The major theme of the 1921 instructions was the increasing deadlines and destructiveness of twentieth century warfare. The manual described firepower as the "preponderant factor of combat." World War I battlefields had witnessed the effect of the new lethal weaponry, and the French expected weapons to be even more lethal on future battlefields. While commanders at all echelons were charged with producing the maximum amount of firepower, they could achieve this only by the close coordination of all arms. The immensely difficult task of moving and coordinating the heavy weapons and large units of the twentieth century, however, created an extremely complex problem of command and control. The minister's report for the instructions concluded, "The role of the commander has grown more important."[16]

The primary method for enabling the commander to coordinate developments on the battlefield was seen as the "methodical" battle, which had been frequently used in World War I. This step-by-step process relied upon the tightly controlled movement of men and matériel, usually between phase lines and according to a rigid timetable. It permitted the production of the maximum amount of firepower from every arm, and ensured that higher-level commanders could completely control or direct the battle. It accorded very little freedom or flexibility to lower-level commanders. The 1921 instructions indicated the flow of a methodical battle by describing it as a series of successive actions, beginning with preparation, consisting of movement of men and matériel, and concluding by reorganization.[17]

The 1921 manual did not abandon the offense, but it placed great emphasis on the strength of the defense. It stated that the defense served to "repulse" enemy attacks, while the offense routed him from his positions and destroyed his forces.[18] Contrary to some perceptions, the French did not focus solely on the defense, as they had done with the offense before 1914. In maneuvers, case studies at the War College, and articles in military journals, officers and soldiers gained an understanding of the elements of the offense. While the doctrine may have "tilted" toward the defense, the army retained an understanding of the importance of the offense.

The 1921 instructions remained the most important manual in the French army until 1936, when a new manual was published. The 1936 instructions altered several concepts of the 1921 manual, but readily acknowledged the dominance of the "old" doctrine.

> Without disregarding the importance of the progress realized in this epoch [since World War I] in the means of combat and transport, the Commission . . . affirms . . . that the body of doctrine objectively fixed on the morrow of victory by our eminent military leaders, who had recently exercised high command, ought to remain the charter for the tactical employment of our large units.[19]

Despite the opportunity for fundamental change, the French army willingly chose to remain tied to the previous doctrine and to build any new concepts on the foundation of the old.

The 1936 manual nevertheless included some improvements over earlier methods and identified several areas containing "new ideas": "Fortified Fronts," "Mechanization and Motorization—Antitank Weapons," "Aerial Forces and the Forces of Aerial Defense," and "Communications." An entire section discussed the employment of large motorized units. Another discussed the light mechanized divisions. The inclusion of such ideas marks a clear transition from the methods in the 1921 manual, and in 1946 General Gamelin carefully identified their inclusion as evidence of the High Command's awareness of the changing methods of war.[20] Unfortunately, many of the new concepts were essentially grafted onto older ones. A complete transformation of French doctrine did not occur. Though she had made many improvements, France prepared to go to war with a doctrine essentially based upon the World War I experience, modified to incorporate new ideas about motorization and mechanization. This modified doctrine was anything but radically innovative, since new weapons essentially remained tied to old ideas.

The army also became more inflexible in its use of doctrine. While the theoretical view of doctrine stressed the need for flexibility and judgment, French doctrine before World War II went beyond simply providing harmony. It became something far more restrictive than a loose body of ideas "presiding" over the army, acting as the conceptual basis for adaptive solutions. A lecturer at the War College in 1930–1931, for example, explained to an audience of reserve officers that the manual concerning the tactical employment of large units contained the fundamentals of French doctrine. He declared, "This document, which has hardly more than a hundred

pages, systematically compels every detail of execution."[21] Another audience was told that French doctrine had established the need for a preponderance of fire as "dogma," and that since French doctrine was very near to
being the "truth," it "should only be modified with the greatest care."[22]

As the years passed in the interwar period, the army became much
more protective of its doctrine. The tendency of the military hierarchy to
resist criticism was reinforced by its energetic opposition to the ideas of Lt.
Col. (later General) Charles de Gaulle, which called for a return to the
offensive, the abandonment of the continuous front, and the creation of a
professional armored corps. Although causing a political uproar, his book
Vers l'armée de métier found little or no sympathy among the military hierarchy. His ideas were attacked systematically by its top military leaders of the
1930s, and by every individual who served as minister of war from 1932
through May 1940.

Nor did the publication of de Gaulle's book in the middle of a controversy over the need to increase the term of military service for conscripts
endear his ideas to his superiors. This was especially true after Léon Blum
used the book in the Chamber of Deputies as evidence that the High Command had concealed its ulterior motives and sought to create a professional rather than a conscript army.[23] While military writings thereafter did
not, as André Beaufre has suggested, entirely mirror official doctrine, the
military hierarchy did become more resistant to new ideas after the uproar
subsided over de Gaulle's controversial writings. In 1935 it announced that
only the High Command was qualified to define military doctrine.[24] Even
those such as General Debeney, who had called for a more flexible policy,
found themselves opposing attacks on the fundamental precepts of French
doctrine.

By the late 1930s, French military doctrine had moved from the ideal
of being the basis of military education to the unfortunate status of being
an inflexible prescription. Although the army hierarchy in precept viewed
doctrine as something that should be applied with judgment and accepted
the need for flexibility and improvement, doctrine in practice became progressively more rigid during the interwar years and approached the realm
of a mandatory formula that had to be applied regardless of the circumstances. Rather than providing the harmony that may be essential to an
orchestra or a properly functioning army, doctrine became something to
provide intellectual discipline. The army thus implicitly accepted doctrine
as a substitute for thinking and an alternative to creative, imaginative
actions. And few soldiers questioned the verities uttered in lecture halls or
published in field manuals or official journals.

As seen in the manuals for the tactical employment of large units, French doctrine had evolved in the interwar period, as did the army's view and use of it. The introduction of large numbers of modern tanks and anti-tank weapons, the construction of the Maginot Line, and the adoption of other improvements such as motorization led the French to adjust their methods for organizing and employing their forces. Yet these modifications, which came in increments, did not signal a complete transformation of doctrine. While some progress was made, much remained the same. The French were not ready in 1939 to refight World War I. They *were* ready to fight a war similar to the final phases of the western front in 1918. They were ready to use many methods that had been tested in that war and refined in later years.

Recognizing that the French made only partial changes, however, does not answer the crucial question of why they did not make more fundamental changes, why they did not create a more viable doctrine. The French accepted the need for an adequate doctrine. They organized an intricate system for formulating doctrine and developing technology. They examined an abundance of evidence from maneuvers, exercises, and wars. Despite growing evidence of the need for changes in their tactics, organizations, and equipment, however, the army remained focused upon the advantages of the methodical battle, firepower, and the defense. It also began to view doctrine as a mandatory formula rather than a guide for action. Where sweeping changes were needed, the army remained content with modifications.

CHAPTER 2

An Army of Reservists

Military policy is rarely forged in a vacuum. Governments construct their military system based on an analysis of the requirements of their political system, the demands of their country's unique geographical setting, and the memories of their nation's historical experience with war and with the use of military force. In the interwar period, consideration of such factors also affected the organization and development of the military institutions of France. Careful analysis of her national security needs led France to construct a system of national defense that placed special emphasis on the participation by the entire nation in a future struggle and upon the contribution and importance of the citizen-soldier. By structuring French forces in consonance with these considerations, and by establishing the parameters within which the military hierarchy had to work, political leaders greatly influenced the basic concepts of army doctrine.

The French system of national defense rested upon the philosophy of the nation in arms that had been created in the French Revolution with the "cannonade of Valmy" in 1792 and the *levée en masse* in 1793. The decree establishing the *levée en masse* mobilized the French citizenry for the defense of the country, and the reliance on the military potential of the citizenry became an important part of French republican tradition. Many Frenchmen came to believe that when the country was in danger, a mass of patriotic volunteers would rise and destroy the invading armies. While the details of army organization and employment would play an important role in such a struggle, the concentration of all national energies against an enemy would be morally and militarily sufficient to defend France.

Although France moved away from the armed nation to a professional army after the Napoleonic Wars, she reinstituted the nation in arms after the war of 1870–1871. In that loss, Germany dramatically reminded her that wars were no longer simply quarrels between governments of ruling families, fought by relatively small armies of professional soldiers. Wars were now conducted between entire peoples, fought by armies of completely mobilized nations. In the years after 1871, France responded to the painful lessons of that war by constructing the foundation of her national defenses on an unswerving faith in the massive mobilization of the citizenry in times of national peril. The issue was not whether there should be conscription but how long the term of service should be and who—if any— should be exempted from service. The resulting symbiotic bond between army and nation, in the military view, was well characterized in a 1904 report by a Chamber of Deputies commission: "The modern concept of the army is that . . . it is identical with the nation, draws from it all its resources, and has no separate and distinct existence outside the nation."[1]

Philosophical statements about the identification of the army with the nation, however, did not resolve the important question of how to organize the nation and the army effectively. Among the crucial issues needing resolution were the length of service for conscripts, the organization and function of the High Command, the number and role of the professional soldiers, mobilization procedures, the provision of adequate training and equipment for the reserves, and the organization of reservists and regulars into cohesive, combat-ready units. Unfortunately, decisions about the length of service and the size of the professional components became extremely controversial. The debates in the government over these issues tended to subsume questions of readiness, organizational effectiveness, training, logistical support, and cadre. Despite their concern with questions of military organization and effectiveness, political leaders rarely entered the labyrinth of some of the most complex issues, such as economic mobilization.

With the growing threat of war after 1911, the government reluctantly increased the term of service from two to three years in 1913 and thereby increased the size of the standing army. While the most controversial portion of the 1913 law concerned the term of service, the law also aimed to strengthen the core of professional noncommissioned officers and to provide better training for reservists and regulars. Tragically for France, World War I began before the real effects of the reforms could be felt, and France entered that long struggle with her main opponent having better trained, better-equipped, and better-staffed reserve units. In comparison to Germany, she had woefully neglected her reserves,[2] and she had failed to prepare adequately for the demands of a massive European war.

The traumatic experience of World War I exercised a profound influence over the French perception of the nation in arms. It demonstrated the necessity and the methods for the entire nation to participate in a war against a nation as large and powerful as Germany. The experience of that long total war convinced France that if she were to defend herself successfully against an attacking enemy, she must commit *all* her resources, both men and matériel, to the wartime effort. While she dreaded the enormous destructiveness and numerous deaths of another total war, she believed she had no choice but to endure them should Germany attack. The possibility of an immensely lucky and quick victory always existed for France, but she had little choice in preparing for the "most unfavorable eventuality"[3] of the long total war. She could hardly hope to win the short war without a miraculous series of extremely fortunate events. Preparing for the worst and not having it occur was better than not preparing and then having it occur. She had learned that bitter lesson from her inadequate preparation of 1914.

It was in the sense of total commitment and universal military service that the philosophy of the nation in arms was most widely and obviously accepted in the French nation and the army in the period between the two world wars. The 1928 law on recruitment explained: "Every [male] French citizen owes personal military service, except for duly established physical incapacity."[4] The 1921 instructions on the tactical employment of large units noted the army's acceptance of the nation in arms:

> The very life of the citizenry is associated in an intimate fashion with that of the army, and thus the formula for the nation in arms is realized in every aspect. . . . [This] greatly influences the eventualities of war and consequently the formulation of strategy.[5]

A general officer in 1920 reflected most officers' views of the effect of the nation in arms on the "eventualities of war" when he noted that the French army "could only be an army of national defense." He added, "It can be neither an instrument of conquest nor a constant menace for its neighbors."[6] Such views sprang from the widely accepted belief that an army relying on citizen-soldiers could only be used to defend the legitimate interests of the nation, or would resort to an aggressive act against a neighbor only when it was essential to the defense of the nation. A system of national defense based on conscription was less dangerous to peace than one based on a professional army. The effects of the philosophy of the nations in arms were, however, not limited to a general posture of unaggressiveness in the political or grand strategic spheres; they were to be felt throughout the army.

Immediately following World War I, as in the prewar period, France again focused primarily on the proper term of service, but there were no demands for extremely long service obligations. Marshal Joffre discussed the two extreme views on length of military service which had existed before the Great War and concluded that both sides had "exaggerated" and that "truth" lay between the two views.[7] The brutal and terrible experiences of 1914–1918 had revealed to the military leadership that nineteenth-century models of discipline and training no longer applied. Although doubts lingered about the readiness of reserve units and officers, the conscripted soldier had proved his worth in the trial of fire. Calls for long-term service to "educate" him for military service were no longer recognized as valid.

Notwithstanding this accomplishment, a debate in the Chamber of Deputies over the term of service for the conscription class of 1920 in February of that year demonstrated that even though the citizen soldier had demonstrated his mettle, fundamental questions remained for resolution. Joseph Paul-Boncour, a leader of the moderate left, argued that military organization was "entirely a function of the duration of service," but Col. Jean Fabry, a conservative and leading member of the Chamber of Deputies army commission, contended that military organization was dependent upon "political necessities, diplomatic obligations and foreign policy."[8] While they could not agree on whether duration of service or military organization was more important, both accepted the nation in arms and rejected the notion that the soldier required long-term service to be "educated" for his arduous duties. After all, a professional army had lost the Franco-Prussian War of 1870–1871, but an armed nation had won World War I. Thus, while general acceptance of the principle of the nation in arms existed, major differences persisted over the implementation of policies pertaining to it.

After the Great War, the main discussions by the army hierarchy on the effect of the nation in arms occurred in the Superior Council of War, a body which wholeheartedly accepted the principle of an armed nation and which included the most powerful and experienced generals in the French army. This council had been established by presidential decree on 27 July 1872, with the mission of examining various measures pertaining to the army, especially those dealing with the "armament of the troops, the defensive works, military administration, and tactical marches." It was not extensively used over the next decade, and although subsequently modified by decree, its functions remained largely undefined, with no specific areas of responsibility.[9] It was not until the 1890s that the Superior Council of War became the most important military council in France, concerned (but still not charged) with the direction of military affairs.

Though its exact composition changed slightly over the next five decades, the membership included the minister of war, the chief of the General Staff, and the leading general officers of the French army. The latter included those holding the rank of marshal (after World War I) and the general officers who would be commanding army groups or armies when mobilization occurred. The president of the Third Republic, or the minister of war in his absence, served as the nonvoting president of the council, while the vice-president was the officer designated as the future commander of the army in the eventuality of war. This officer was commonly known as the *Généralissime,* or Generalissimo.

A presidential decree of 23 January 1920, re-established the Superior Council of War. Its responsibilities and organization were similar to those existing before 1914. The council was to be "compulsorily consulted" for its "advice" on the general organization and training of the army, matters affecting mobilization and concentration, and the adoption of new weapons and the perfection of old ones. Other responsibilities were added, including that of furnishing advice on the general organization of the defensive systems for the frontiers. A final broad category was also included; the Council was to be "consulted on all measures able to affect the constitution of the army and the preparation for war."[10] Noticeably absent were the responsibilities for formulating national military strategy or for controlling or directing the entire army.

When the Superior Council of War addressed the problem of duration of service, it stressed the importance of an effective military organization. It did not argue that long-term service was necessary to "educate" the soldier for his duties or to create more cohesive units. During World War I, the conscription class of 1918 had received no more than three months of training, and the council did not suggest or imply that the French soldier had been inadequately educated or trained in the Great War.

Though it steadfastly supported the philosophy of the nation in arms, the Superior Council believed the first consideration in determining the details of France's military organization was to determine the number of divisions needed to ensure France's security, and to accomplish or provide support for her foreign policy. After determining the number of required divisions, the key variables were required size of the army, number of professional soldiers, and number of soldiers to be conscripted. According to the methodology used by Marshal Foch in a May 1920 meeting of the council, the number of required divisions multiplied by the number of men in each division furnished the number of men required in the army. The difference between the required size of the army and the number of professional or long-term soldiers furnished the number of soldiers to be conscripted. When this figure was divided by the number of soldiers in each conscription class, the product represented the required number of classes and the duration of service. For example, if two classes were required, it indicated service of two years, and if one-and-a-half classes were required, it indicated service of eighteen months. The crucial factor was thus the required number of soldiers for active service, not education or training.[11]

The military hierarchy's argument about the size of the army required to accomplish its mission, however, did not prevail, and the ensuing clash with the government revolved around the required number of divisions, the length of service, and the size of the professional component. In June 1920, the council unanimously adopted a resolution stating that the army required forty-one active French divisions, six as part of the army of occupation in Germany and thirty-five on the national territory if it were to ensure France's security. This figure did not include the five Algerian and three colonial divisions, and it assumed France would eventually mobilize eighty divisions if there were a war. In December 1920, the government forced the council to accept thirty-two active French divisions, but discussions continued through 1922.[12] The basic qualification made throughout the discussions by the council was that 150,000 career soldiers were necessary if the active army were to be reduced to thirty-two divisions. In May 1926, the Superior Council reluctantly accepted twenty active divisions, but it added the qualification that 106,000 career military were necessary.[13] Members of the Council often mentioned the lengthy period of time that had been required to prepare reserve formations for combat in 1914. This example underlined the importance of having an ever-ready cadre, with the requisite experience and knowledge for forming cohesive units, that could rapidly be prepared for military operations. A reservoir of knowledge and experience ensured the competence of a fully mobilized army.

Throughout the process of accepting a declining number of active divisions, the council adamantly opposed the decreases, and in December 1921, the minister of war, Louis Barthou, informed it that the Superior Council of National Defense (*Conseil supérieur de la défense nationale*), the country's highest defense policy body, which was little more than the ministers sitting in session,[14] established the number of divisions, not the Superior Council of War; the latter provided technical advice on how they should be established and employed.[15] As demonstrated by subsequent actions, the major consideration for the political authorities was length of service, and the reductions from forty-one, to thirty-two, and then to twenty active divisions corresponded to the reductions in terms of service to two years, eighteen months, and one year in 1921, 1923, and 1928. The 1923 law did not include the requirement for 150,000 career soldiers, but the 1928 law included the requirement for 72,000 to 106,000 career soldiers.[16]

When the Chamber of Deputies discussed the eighteen-month term of service law in 1922, only André Lefèvre, who had served as minister of war from January to December 1920, rose to oppose it and to support the two-year term of service. Lefèvre warned his colleagues that the Superior Council had not agreed to the text of the new law. In June 1922, he proposed an amendment that military service should remain at two years, but when the vote was taken on his amendment, only 8 deputies supported it, while 546 opposed it.[17] Clearly, a longer term of military service was politically impossible. Most military officers were aware of the widely supported demand for shorter military service. When Georges Clemenceau and his military assistant Gen. Jean Mordacq first discussed military problems after the war, they concluded it was only a matter of time before one-year service would become law.[18]

The Superior Council, nevertheless, earnestly and steadfastly opposed the reduction from two years to one year service and from forty-one to twenty active divisions. When it was forced to accept what it called the "degressive" (as opposed to progressive) reduction of service to eighteen months, it warned, "Service of 18 months constitutes a minimum beneath which national defense will be in peril. . . . [I]t is presently inopportune and dangerous to envision a new reduction in service. . . ."[19] The Superior Council did accept each reduction in service and in the number of divisions by a formal vote, but its true feelings were reflected in Marshal Foch's comment in the Superior Council that the reductions did not correspond to national defense needs.[20] Such reservations do not suggest that the army hierarchy objected to the nation in arms or short-term service because soldiers needed longer periods of training. Rather, such reservations indicate that the army believed a shorter term of service would create difficulties for the nation by reducing the number of divisions and the size of the professional component.

Following almost a decade of debate, the government adopted a series of laws in 1927–1928 on the organization, recruitment, and constitution of cadres and effectives for the French army. Rather than represent radical change, the laws represented the fruition under the Third Republic of more than fifty years of evolving military institutions and philosophy. They provided the legal basis for the French army's peacetime operation and for its expansion from peacetime to wartime size.[21] Although the main feature was the adoption of one-year service, the 1927–1928 laws established a military system for France in which the conscript dominated military organizations and the professional soldier prepared the army for mobilization. When General Debeney, chief of the General Staff from 1923 until 1930, discussed these laws, he noted their results: "The metropolitan army, the army of the French territory, organized by the laws of 1927–1928 is entirely oriented toward a realization as complete as possible of the nation in arms." Support within the army hierarchy for these laws can be seen in General Debeney's proud acknowledgment later that he had been "one of the workers" in creating "this solid infrastructure" for the army.[22]

Some grumbling surfaced among the officer corps about the reduction in the term of service and about the new military organization, but considering the sweeping nature of this change and the stakes involved, the relative reticence of the officer corps is remarkable. Public opposition to the short term of service and the new laws was neither as strident nor as convincing as it had been before 1914. Works such as Lucien Souchon's *Feue l'armée française* that criticized the reforms were the exception rather than the rule.[23] General Debeney offered several mild reservations about France's national security policy, but his comments did not have the sharp edge of someone who believed France's security had been eroded substantially. In his comments, he said that France had not erected a militia system for defending herself; she had created a system by which the entire nation could be armed. He argued that if France were to succeed in defending the frontiers, she had to augment the number of the long-term service soldiers and ensure they were adequately furnished with modern equipment and reserve stocks. Despite his acknowledgment that France had not attained the figure of 106,000 career soldiers as stipulated in the 1927–1928 laws, his overall tone was one of positive support for the steps taken by France.[24] Since Debeney was indeed one of the architects of those laws, he presumably had no inclination to attack what he perceived as an important achievement.

General Debeney's comments probably reflected the views of many of his colleagues in the Superior Council of War. That is, they believed that France needed a larger active army but with the 1927–1928 laws providing for the orderly transition of the nation from peacetime to wartime, they saw no need to publicize the critical views of short-term service expressed in their private meetings and thereby to place those laws in jeopardy. If the political leaders were going to demand a small active army and compel it to rely upon short-term service, the 1927–1928 laws provided the structure and methods for organizing, mobilizing, and deploying it in wartime.

In the debate over whether military organization should be a function of duration of service or of "political necessities, diplomatic obligations, and foreign policy," France chose a route emphasizing duration of service, and the decision carried with it fundamental effects on foreign and military policy and on military doctrine. The military leadership had accepted the shorter duration of service with all its attendant difficulties because they believed the necessity for a large, relatively well-organized army in wartime was more pressing than the need for a highly trained, immediately responsive, offensively oriented army in peacetime. Most military officers had evidently accepted the contention that success in a future war could only be gained by a mass army, even if it depended upon relatively short service and hastily trained soldiers. They seemed prepared to exchange a very high level of proficiency and training for a lower level of proficiency and for a sufficiently large army. After all, the victorious army of the Great War had been such a force.

The passage of the laws in the late 1920s had an immediate effect on the army. During the period of one-year service (1928–1935), the army trained approximately 220,000–230,000 conscripts each year, with half being called to duty every six months. As one of the 110,000-man contingents underwent training, the other joined units in the active army. Since a maximum of 106,000 career soldiers were retained in the French army, a figure significantly lower than the 150,000 career soldiers called for originally by the Superior Council of War, the permanent component of the army was reduced to the point where it could handle only a few priority roles, e.g., man the frontier fortifications, operate conscript training centers, and function as planning staffs. In a sense, the peacetime army became nothing more than the skeleton around which the wartime army mobilized. After she removed her forces from the Rhineland, France practically eliminated the capability for independent or limited action in Europe by the peacetime army, and she moved irreversibly toward not being able to conduct any military action without almost complete mobilization. In the bustling but secure period of the late 1920s, however, no real danger or need for a limited military engagement on the continent loomed on the horizon.

Throughout the interwar period, the actual number of troops that could be used immediately to defend the frontiers was much less than the actual number of troops on active duty. In 1920 there were 640,874 soldiers stationed in France and the Rhineland.[25] Following application of the law of eighteen months of service, this number was reduced to 419,000 soldiers in July 1925; 282,000 of these soldiers had more than six months of service and were considered ready for combat service. After the government adopted one-year service in 1928, the major effects were not felt until 1932. In July 1932 there were 358,000 soldiers stationed in France; 232,000 of these were considered sufficiently trained to be usable for the defense of the country. By July 1933 there were 320,000 soldiers stationed in France, with 226,000 having more than six months of service.[26] The French army, in terms of trained personnel, had been reduced to about twice the size of the 100,000-man German army, mandated by the Treaty of Versailles but highly professional and well-trained because of its long-term service.

Although the government relented and adopted a two-year term of service in 1935, the longer term of service did not indicate a change in France's preference for the short-term conscript. Rather, it sprang from the problem of the "lean years," or the *années creuses*. Because of the low birth rate of the war years, the annual contingent of conscripts would have declined from 240,000 to 120,000 during the period 1935–1939. In March 1935, the government announced the implementation of article 40 of the 1928 law. This clause permitted the retention of conscripts beyond a year if circumstances demanded, and it did not require approval of the Chamber of Deputies or the Senate.[27] Implementing the clause also did not alter the system of mobilization established by the 1927 law, and did not change some of the basic readiness problems of the army, even though the number of troops stationed in France in 1938 increased to about 438,000.[28]

Another important aspect of France's resting her defense on a nation in arms concerned the mobilization of her forces. According to the system established by the 1927 law and used until the outbreak of war, the peacetime army had to be transformed into a wartime army before it could be effective in combat. The 1927 law provided for the division of the territory of France into twenty military regions. When the order for mobilization came, each active infantry division (one from each military region) was broken up to form three new divisions. Gen. André G. Prételat, who was a member of the Superior Council of War from 1934 to 1939 and commander of the Group of the Armies of the East in 1939–1940, noted the composition of the infantry regiments within the mobilized divisions. After complete mobilization, less than half of an "active" infantry regiment consisted of active-duty soldiers: 33 percent of its officers, 32 percent of its noncommissioned officers, and 55 percent of its enlisted men. The "series A" divisions had an even smaller percentage of active duty soldiers. Only 23 percent of its officers, 17 percent of its noncommissioned officers and 2 percent of its enlisted men came from active units; all the rest were reservists. With the exception of three divisions, none of the "series B" divisions, according to Prételat, had an active component; they were entirely composed of reservists from the oldest classes.[29] Within the eighteen "B" divisions France mobilized in September 1939, ten were categorized for "battle" and eight for "secondary missions." Additionally, many of the reservists within the "B" divisions had never served in the infantry; they had spent their active duty time as sailors or airmen.[30] Since nearly a quarter of the French infantry divisions consisted of these divisions, the breaking up of the active divisions resulted in the formation of a larger number of divisions of a lesser quality.

The organizational system suffered further from the fact that French law made no provision for the organization of a unit larger than a division in time of peace. Only the Nineteenth Corps, in Algeria, and the three corps that occupied the Rhineland retained their designations as corps; the remainder became identified with the military regions. At mobilization, each of the twenty regions would mobilize a corps of two divisions (three, including the active division), and the regional commander would assume command of the corps. During peacetime, this commander had two staffs, one for the region and one for the corps. Upon declaration of war, the chief of staff of the region became the region commander, and the previous commander became the corps commander. This permitted the corps to mobilize and move without interfering with the regional mobilization. Unfortunately, the designated corps commander and his staff had little or no opportunity, other than the fall maneuvers, to become intimately acquainted with their nonadministrative responsibilities, especially those relating to the movement and employment of the corps as a combat unit. Hence, the corps—not to mention the army—headquarters suffered from the same sort of inexperience as its subordinate units.

France's army thus bore little resemblance to those of previous eras. Despite its eventual large size, it could effectively fight a war against a major power only after calling the nation to arms, and it could not fight a limited war without placing in risk its entire mobilization system and its capacity to fight a total war. France had chosen a narrow edge on which to balance her military policy and thereby greatly restricted her alternatives in responding to a crisis.

Marshal Pétain later observed that the French army was "unfit for beginning [a war] with a strategic offensive, but nevertheless capable of local, tactical offensives."[31] In the opening days of a war, a strategic offensive was impossible, because dismantling the active army would be necessary for the complete mobilization of the nation in arms. The army's mobilization system continued to rely on the twenty active divisions breaking up and forming the newly mobilized army, and the active army for all practical purposes remained little more than a school for soldiers and a framework for mobilization. Despite Pétain's assertion that local offensives remained possible, the requirement for redistributing the regulars after the outbreak of a conflict was a dangerous, if not fatal, flaw in the mobilization system. The French, however, considered the potential of the army for a long total war to be more important than the capability for a limited offensive action. Although its purpose was not expressly defined as such, the system was more appropriate to deter a large-scale war than to fight a smaller-scale battle near the French borders.

By depending upon forces organized (if not created) during a crisis, France's system of national defense also made her borders potentially more vulnerable to an enemy attack, and the military hierarchy acknowledged the difficulty of protecting the frontiers. Discussions in the Superior

Council emphasized the necessity of maintaining forces readily available for use in emergency situations. At a meeting in December 1927 the council unanimously adopted a resolution stating that the success of the forces covering the frontier could not be assured if the units were filled with men from the ready reserves (*disponibles*). Such men could not be brought on active duty fast enough to be used in an emergency situation.[32] Stationing sufficient active-duty units along the frontier could have solved the problems, but the adoption of the 1927–1928 laws and the concomitant reduction in the active army required that *all* active units participate in mobilization by "tripling" themselves. The knowledge and experience of the active forces, according to French military leaders, had to be spread throughout the mobilized army.

Concern for the safety of France's frontiers became more acute as the military witnessed the revival of German military power. As this potential enemy slowly recovered from the war, her apparent growth in strength led French military authorities increasingly to fear the possibility of a sudden unexpected attack. Under the aggressive leadership of Gen. Hans von Seeckt, the German army had molded its 100,000 professionals into an elite, offensive-minded force that might strike without warning against the vulnerable northeastern French frontiers. After grabbing the precious natural resources in that area before either nation mobilized completely, Germany would have an important advantage in matériel over France and could follow her initial gains by employing a huge mass army against the weakened French. Such an attack became known in France as the *attaque brusquée* and was a common theme in military and civilian journals. The threat of such an attack added strength to the argument for reinforcing the *couverture,* or covering forces, along the northeastern frontier to ward off any sudden German strikes and to enable the nation to mobilize successfully. The organization of such forces, however, had to be accomplished by reliance upon the mobilization of reservists.

As France's leaders considered the problems of mobilizing the entire nation, they became greatly concerned about the amount of time required to mobilize the industrial resources of the nation. Although their concerns were heightened by France's difficulties with economic mobilization in World War I, their task was different from what it had been from 1914 to 1918, since they had not only to provide adequate resources and supplies for immediate use in the opening days of a future war, but also to prepare for the complete mobilization of the nation's economic and industrial resources for use in a long war. Their problem was compounded by the fact that France faced an opponent of superior industrial capability and potential, and also an opponent that would probably be the aggressor in any war with France. Germany, if she were the aggressor, had a well-developed industrial system capable of converting rapidly and easily from peacetime to wartime production. Should she initiate a secret industrial preparation for war, she could attack without warning and gain an important matériel advantage by having begun industrial and national mobilization before France became aware of the threat.[33] The question of economic and industrial preparation thus became intertwined with the perceived threat of an *attaque brusquée*, from which the aggressor could gain tremendous strategic, geographic, morale, and matériel advantages.

Within the entire realm of mobilization planning, the French concluded that a two-pronged response to the threat of an unexpected attack was essential, the first the stockpiling of enough matériel to supply the army's needs until the nation's industrial sector could manufacture and deliver sufficient war goods, and the second the organization of the entire nation's industrial capacity for a long war. In the first area, strategic stockpiles served the same purpose as the covering force served for the nation. As the nation mobilized its citizen army and its industrial potential, the covering force of the army and the stockpiles of matériel provided the men and the resources for the beginning period of the war. The battle along the frontiers would consume both as the nation mobilized.

But the cost of creating stockpiles of matériel for every possible military need was prohibitively expensive. At the same time, war-making matériel could rapidly become obsolete, and expensive stockpiles could turn out to be useless.[34] While the possibility of obsolescence did not affect basic supplies, it did affect the choice of weaponry. Constrained by limited financial credits, the French army found it more advantageous to channel its money into weapons that could be more effectively used in the initial defensive period. Weapons more suitable for the offense could be manufactured as the war progressed and as scientific and technical advances permitted the development of more advanced weaponry.

The issue of adequate weaponry became somewhat analogous to the balancing of quality and quantity. For decades France had heard the argument about whether she needed a mass citizen army representing quantity, or a small professional army representing quality. Now she heard a similar argument regarding weaponry. Many Frenchmen believed the antitank gun provided the crucial quality needed to counter the *attaque brusquée* and could be purchased in sufficient quantity—in the French view—to counter this menacing threat. As one military writer pointed out, "One shell . . . costing 150 francs can destroy a tank which costs one million."[35] To counter the threat of an attack by armor, some observers believed France's emphasis had to be on quality antitank weapons of sufficient quantity. France's reluctance to adopt large, costly armored operations was closely linked to this conception, especially since such formations were considered offensive instruments.

The antitank gun, rather than the tank, accorded more with France's approach to national defense, since it was less expensive, was primarily a defensive weapon, and could easily be handled by the citizen-soldier. By 1940 the French possessed an excellent series of antitank weapons. Their 25mm cannon was effective up to 800 meters against heavily armored vehicles (40mm of armor), and up to 1,500 meters against lightly armored vehicles. The 1938 infantry regulations specified that the 25mm cannon, however, was not to be fired at targets beyond a thousand meters because of difficulties with target acquisition.[36] By 1939–1940, the old 75mm cannon was gradually being replaced by the new 47mm cannon, which—except for the German 88mm—was undoubtedly the best antitank cannon employed in the battle of France. General Gamelin, commander of the French army in May 1940, later asserted, correctly, that the antitank capability of France was greater during 1940 than that of Germany.[37] While tactical considerations and technological factors affected the development of reasonably effective antitank weapons, issues pertaining to mobilization had also had an effect.

Returning to the second area of concern, complete economic and industrial mobilization of the nation, French war planners merged the economic aspects of creating the nation in arms with the personnel aspects, and this effort found fruition in the 1927–1928 laws on the organization of the nation for war.[38] Other laws contributed to economic preparation. By the late 1930s the military had arranged for the process of mobilization to be echeloned, with the majority of the resources and men committed as soon as possible and the remaining ones committed as they became available. The military hierarchy recognized that it would take considerable time to call up the reservists, assemble the national army, and organize the industrial capacity of France for military output. They did not naively envisage a magical transformation of the nation from a peacetime to a wartime footing. They devoted great amounts of time to planning and organizing the mobilization of the nation. When war came in 1940, France had an enormously complex and detailed system in place to manage the huge task of complete economic and industrial mobilization. Her planners had prepared thoroughly for everything, from the requisition of trucks and horses to the conversion of plants from civilian to military production. Her failure in 1940 cannot be attributed to too little preparation in this area.

Huge stockpiles of supplies, large numbers of weapons, and excruciatingly detailed planning, however, would not help France emerge victorious unless she had time to complete her mobilization. Hence, the military recognized that the covering forces had to be strengthened if France were to have time to resurrect the nation in arms and to defend against an *attaque brusquée*. In the Superior Council's deliberations on the 1927–1928 laws, Foch and Pétain emphasized the necessity for a stronger covering force whose operations had to be of longer duration, because the concentration of forces behind it took longer under the new laws.[39] As will be discussed in chapter 3, on defending the frontiers, the military leaders had long recognized the advantages and need for prepared defenses along the northeastern frontier, and the Superior Council had discussed the complexities of protecting the frontiers with fortifications as early as May 1920. Other factors, such as the ancient French tradition of fortifying the frontiers, also influenced the decision to build the Maginot Line, but the reorganization of the army in the late 1920s and worries over the difficulties of mobilizing quickly made the construction of permanent fortifications along portions of the frontier even more necessary for the defense of the nation.

The construction of fortifications, however, did not guarantee success, since the outcome of future war could depend upon whether some units and men were immediately ready to fight and others could be made ready to fight fairly quickly. The same factors that made mobilization, stockpiles, and covering forces important made the readiness of units and men important. Yet adequate military training, especially that of the reserves, continued to be an obstacle to better readiness.

A major part of the difficulty with readiness stemmed from the fact that the 1927–1928 laws prescribed rigid limits on reserve training. These limits continued after the reinstitution of two-year service in 1935. After service of one year, enlisted men entered the ready reserve for three years, during which time they had a maximum active-duty period of three weeks for training. During the period of two-year service, enlisted men remained in the reserve for two years. During the sixteen years they were in the first inactive reserve, they had two training periods, one of three weeks and another from two to three weeks. During the eight years in the second inactive reserve, the maximum duration of their training was seven days. Reserve officers could be brought on active duty for as long and as often as the minister of war desired, but the total length of such training periods could not exceed four months. During those years when they were not called to training exercises, reserve officers could request special duty periods of fifteen days, which did not count against the total of four months. Officers and men associated with aviation could also volunteer for special training periods of no longer than thirty days which did not count against their total period of authorized duty.[40] By the eve of World War II, reserve officers underwent twenty-one days of field training every two years. Those officers who voluntarily spent many extra hours each year in military training to supplement these regular biennial maneuvers received a ribbon, *Services volontaires*, in recognition of their diligence.[41]

France's political and military leaders placed great emphasis on ensuring that the reserves received their prescribed training within these limitations. During the period of the gravest effects from the depression, France continued her policies concerning the amount of training required for reservists. This was not accomplished without controversy. Because of a growing deficit and an urgent need for money, for example, the government under Edouard Herriot proposed a supplementary finance bill in 1932 to provide additional funds and to curtail several costly governmental activities. A collision over military policy occurred in July 1932 when the socialists argued that considerable savings could be gained if the training of reservists was suspended for one year. Colonel Fabry, chairman of the army commission of the Chamber of Deputies, opposed the suspension of the training periods and argued that in the initial period of a crisis the fate of the country would rest in the hands of 120,000 recently trained soldiers and 680,000 reservists. He passionately argued that sending men into battle without sufficient training would be a "crime against the nation" and would be the same as sending them to the "butcher." The situation was saved only after an emotional and decisive speech by Herriot, who called for and received a vote of confidence on the measure.[42] Despite the grave financial difficulties of the depression, the government and the majority of the representatives opted to continue the training of the reserves.

From 1932 until 1939, the minister of war made almost no changes in the credits requested by the General Staff for training. The only major change he made in the request for credits for training of the active army occurred in 1934, when he reduced the General Staffs request by 5 percent. In 1938 the minister slightly reduced the General Staffs request for credits for reserve training, but that was the only reduction he made in the 1930s. From 1932 until 1939, the credits for reserve training voted by the National Assembly averaged 87 percent of the credits requested by the War Ministry, while those for training of the active army averaged 93 percent of those requested by the War Ministry.[43] While the General Staff could have been requesting credits that it thought the National Assembly might approve, there seem to have been no demands for greater sums for training, and the relatively minor reductions imposed by the National Assembly could not have seriously disrupted training programs desired by the military hierarchy.

Army leaders attempted to overcome the problem of inadequate training for the reserve by having official regulations rigorously prescribe the subjects and sequence of training. For example, the infantry regulations of 1928 and 1938 described in detail the training to be received by the recruit and by the reserve soldier, who was periodically brought back on active duty. French leaders continued to emphasize the need for additional training after mobilization and tried to make reserve training as effective as possible in peacetime. The 1938 infantry regulations stated that even though officers of the reserve should receive training as leaders, they also had to receive training as instructors to facilitate their conduct of training once their units were mobilized.[44] Special reserve schools provided some peacetime training for officers, but despite their establishment immediately after World War I,[45] attendance was not mandatory until the eve of World War II.

The military took other steps to improve the readiness of the reserves. One of the most important of these, the organization of mobilization centers, was included in the 1927–1928 laws.[46] Before World War I, reserve officers and soldiers reported to a specific regiment for their training sessions and reported to that same regiment in the event of mobilization. The administrative responsibilities of training and mobilizing the reservists remained at the regimental level despite problems of quality control and the occasional resentment of active soldiers toward these duties. Following World War I, training was conducted by units constituted solely for each period of reserve duty. In addition to not creating any cohesion among units or familiarity among soldiers and officers who might actually fight together, the training involved only a portion of the soldiers who could be mobilized, since veterans of the Great War were excused from reserve training periods.

The creation of the mobilization centers, however, changed the entire system and caused the reserve training sessions to occur within, and exercise the same system, as a wartime mobilization. The centers, which functioned essentially as training camps and depots, had more than 11,000 employees, mainly civilian, and had the responsibility for administering the mobilization of units. The active units retained only the responsibility for training. For his periodic training sessions, the reservist reported to a mobilization center, where he would be placed in a nearby regiment for training in his specialty. Should he be an officer, he would receive instructions on his duties, sometimes learning for the first time that he would command a unit. If placed in command of a unit for a wartime mobilization, he would be given a bulky volume, *Journal de la mobilisation,* which provided details on what he was to do and which equipment and how many horses his unit was to draw from storage. He would then accomplish the details of receiving, equipping, and organizing the officers and men of his unit.[47] Although the troops he would command might be of the same regiment if general mobilization occurred, complete units were never present at one time. Training at the mobilization centers did not normally include the active-duty contingent, and included only a few of the reserve classes. No system existed to ensure that officers and men always trained in peacetime with their wartime unit.[48]

In the late 1930s, the High Command also managed to increase the amount of training time for the reservists. The resulting increase came within the time constraints of the 1927–1928 laws. Beginning in 1936, two reserve classes attended reserve training each year, whereas previously only one class had attended. Beginning in 1937, three classes attended each year. By the eve of the war, reserve officers were required to spend twenty-one days in training every two years. At the Riom trial, Daladier triumphantly described the increased numbers of reservists attending training from 1933 to 1938 to defend himself from charges of failing to ensure the proper training of the reserves.[49]

While some improvements had been made before the war, severe deficiencies in providing immediately ready units continued to exist. By 1939, especially after encountering difficulties with the partial mobilization in late 1938, the army had improved the mobilization system and the operation of the mobilization centers, and it did mobilize very smoothly and quickly in September 1939. Although the quality of training and thus the readiness of the reserves undoubtedly improved in the late 1930s, highly trained and cohesive reserve units ready to fight immediately simply did not exist when the French army mobilized for war.[50] France could mobilize quickly, but she was not prepared to conduct operations immediately.

The Superior Council of War often discussed the status of the army's readiness and training, since its members conducted periodic inspections of most army units. Some of its members seriously questioned the readiness of the reserves and doubted that the reservists would have the necessary skills if they were called to active duty in a crisis. In 1935, for example, the director of infantry noted in a letter that many reserve officers did not have sufficient training for their duties. He stated, "In particular, the majority of them have no practical knowledge of the matériel at their disposal."[51] Other members of the council voiced more fundamental objections. Gen. Henri-A. Niessel, the inspector general of military aeronautics, for example, asserted in a December 1927 meeting that he had never met a reserve officer in World War I who was "truly in his place" at the head of an infantry battalion.[52] Even though Niessel's comments were more critical than those of other members of the council, the military hierarchy was clearly concerned with the need for more peacetime training for officers and noncommissioned officers in the reserves.

In September 1934, the army conducted a special mobilization exercise for the Forty-first Division. With General Prételat acting as the main evaluator, the division spent ten days training and two days maneuvering. Although public announcements extolled the virtues of the division and lightly criticized the men's lack of physical fitness, General Prételat's report offered strong criticisms of the division's readiness. Less than 30 percent of the officers and 10 percent of the noncommissioned officers, Prételat complained, had frequently attended schools for the reservists. Most of the division's soldiers had served for only eighteen months and seemed to be weak in the fundamental skills of soldiering. Prételat's report, which was given to the president of the Republic, the president of the Council of Ministers, and the Superior Council of War, concluded that eighteen months of service was not sufficient to ensure adequate training for the reserves.[53] The report could not but raise serious doubts about the army's readiness.

Others voiced concerns about the status of the army's training. In 1930, Georges Clemenceau bitterly complained about the army's training problems. He noted that after one-year service had been established, measures were supposedly taken "to apply it." He added that the adoption of one-year service had rested upon the assumption that 150,000 professional soldiers would be retained and that strong units would be maintained ensuring intensive training of the conscripts. After noting that this had not been accomplished and that only skeleton units had been retained, he said, "All the professional soldiers unanimously acknowledge that under such conditions training is impossible."[54]

Despite Clemenceau's complaint, there were very few public protests from professional soldiers that training was "impossible." Public statements by officers in military journals or books were surprisingly optimistic about being able to train the short-term soldier, even during the period of one-year service. Most authors admitted the difficulty of the task, but went on to describe methods to increase the effectiveness of the training received by the recruit. These suggested methods generally involved intensifying training, having earlier and greater specialization, establishing priorities, and eliminating everything that was not essential. The optimistic comments, nevertheless, concentrated on active duty training of the one-year conscript, not on his retention of what he had learned or on his ability to maintain an up-to-date understanding of new equipment or concepts after leaving active duty.

While most officers had a positive view of the reforms in military training and preparedness, many undoubtedly had reservations about the actual readiness of the reserves. Bitter complaints surfaced after the collapse of France in 1940. At the Riom trial, a parade of general officers scathingly criticized the prewar training of the reserves; they were especially critical of the lack of sufficient training for reserve officers and noncommissioned officers.[55] The postwar criticisms, however, tended to be more vehement than the prewar demands.

Between 1919 and 1939, the High Command evidently accepted the likelihood of ill-trained reserves and did not become overly concerned about it. Few members of the military hierarchy apparently believed that members of the reserves could ever be as knowledgeable or as well-trained as soldiers who were on active duty. The military leadership in the interwar period obviously did not anticipate the mobilization of a well-prepared army, 85 percent of which would be reservists. Most believed, as did Gamelin, that shortcomings in training and preparedness could only be overcome in the initial phases of a future war. Consequently, the military leaders did not allocate or request substantial monetary resources for reserve training, especially since that program ranked below other peace-time concerns in the hierarchy of challenges facing the army. While they had misgivings about readiness, the military leaders nevertheless had few reservations about France's military system. They preferred a system relying upon massive mobilization of the French citizenry and economy, even if the mobilized army were not completely ready for immediate action.

Given the complexity of establishing the covering force and completing mobilization, and given the doubts about the readiness of the reserves and thus of the army, the military hierarchy preferred the simplicity of the defense and the control of the methodical battle in the opening days of a war. At the Riom trial, Gen. Robert-Auguste Touchon indicated that Gamelin had often stressed the need to fight with care in the beginning of a war, for "we will have above all an army composed of very excitable reservists."[56] The 1936 instructions on the tactical employment of large units reflected this belief and stressed the importance of the methodical battle in the early days of a war. It added that "young troops" should only be engaged "methodically" and with the support of all the "necessary fires."[57] General Touchon, who had been president of the commission that wrote the 1938 infantry regulations, stated after the fall of France that those regulations were "a little rigid" for the same reasons.[58] In the absence of the stiffening afforded by combat experience, French military leaders were reluctant to commit their army to an early offensive or to risk an encounter battle in which the French forces would collide with an onrushing enemy. They preferred the control inherent in the carefully orchestrated methodical battle. The first battles, in which the French would rely on the defense, theoretically provided the experience and enabled the creation of the well-trained army that was essential for the conduct of the offense.

One unfortunate result of the desire for greater control was the move toward a more rigid doctrine. In a massive, heavily armed nation, subordinate units had to obey the orders of the commander uniformly without "deforming" them, and similar units had to be "interchangeable."[59] To this end, a clear and coherent body of doctrine was essential, and this doctrine had to be followed closely. The French military recognized that proposing rigid solutions to every problem would "kill initiative," but there is little doubt that it opted for a rigid doctrine. The dilution of quality that was inherent in an army of huge quantity required more stringent doctrine and stronger control by the military leaders. In that sense, the methodical battle became the "logical" accompaniment of an increasingly rigid system.

Another result of the several changes occurring around 1930 was a decline in emphasis on the offense. Until the reduction in service to one year in 1928, the beginning of the Maginot Line in 1929, and the evacuation of the Rhineland in June 1930, the French army placed greater emphasis on a strategic offensive than on a defensive operation. The ending of the clear preference for the offense was an important change in French military thinking, and the shift can be seen most clearly in the various plans for mobilization of the army. Gen. P. E. Tournoux has noted in his study of the plans that all were offensive from May 1920 through May 1929. Until June 1926, all envisaged a rapid advance into Germany. From June 1926 until April 1929, the planners foresaw an offensive advance, but the increasing possibility of an enemy attack on the advancing army's northern wing attenuated the emphasis on a rapid advance.[60] Given the weakness of the German army and the continuation of at least eighteen months of service until 1928, the army perceived the distinct possibility of a war beginning with a French offensive. During this period, for example, lecturers at the War College invariably emphasized that only the offense leads to decisive results, and always began their lectures with an analysis of offensive operations. Similarly, in the annual fall maneuvers before 1930, the French army often practiced pushing light troops forward into Germany and then following them with the main body of the army.[61]

After 1929 the French army slowly began to place a greater emphasis on the conduct of a strategic defense than on an offensive. Again, this can be seen in the plans for mobilization of the French army. General Tournoux has noted that French mobilization plans became defensive in May 1929 for the first time since the end of World War I.[62] The transition can also be seen in the annual fall maneuvers. By the time of the 1931 maneuvers, the French placed a "blue" army (obviously simulating French forces) on the defensive and had a "red" army attack before the blue forces had fully concentrated. Even though the red forces initially met success by pushing back the defenders, the blue forces eventually counterattacked and successfully accomplished their mission.[63] Subsequent fall maneuvers also tended to follow this general model. These changes coincided with the perception after 1930 that a future war would begin with the French on the defensive and then end with a successful counterattack. This transition signals the important beginning of the transition from an offensive focus on the strategic level to a defensive one. The military hierarchy increasingly began to accept the need to defend France rather than to attack an enemy.

The change in military thinking had a direct effect upon tactical doctrine. The introduction to the 1928 infantry regulations, for example, stated that there were three events which required the revision of the 1920 infantry regulations. These included the "enforcement" of the 1921 instructions on the tactical employment of large units, the reorganization of the army through the "approaching adoption" of one-year service and the "considerable reduction" in number of active units, and the increase in firepower of the infantry. As for the effect of the new laws on the organization of the army, the introduction explained that an increasing proportion of the army would consist of reserves on mobilization and concluded, "The result is the necessity to simplify all that can be [simplified] more, to give a restricted feature to programs of training, and to create more rapid means for forming noncommissioned officers among the [conscripted] contingents and the future career soldiers."[64]

One area that was "simplified" was the number of possible infantry formations for the squad, platoon, and company. The regulations explained, "It is more and more suitable to prescribe a limited number of obligatory formations and to explain their methods of employment by stating rules and not tactical considerations that the executants would be tempted to interpret diversely." Since most of the small units would be commanded by reserve officers or noncommissioned officers, it was necessary to "indicate habitual combat formations." In the absence of two-year service and more thorough training while on active duty, the French army opted for simpler combat formations in its small units and for less flexibility in their application.

The 1928 infantry regulations also placed a greater emphasis on fire than on maneuver. The introduction explained the importance of placing a "sufficient number of projectiles" on specially selected enemy positions, instead of trying to move around them by "subtle" maneuvers.[65] Part of the underlying reason for this was the adoption of the model 1924 automatic rifle. Another was that it was simpler to train the short-term conscripts in the firing of their weapons than it was to train them in "subtle" maneuvers. The platoon was the smallest unit, according to the regulations, that was capable of performing an "elementary maneuver." The regulations noted, "The knowledge and employment of their arms are, for the small units of infantry, the essential object of their training."[66]

The adoption of one-year service in 1928 thus directly affected infantry doctrine, causing it to place greater emphasis on fire and on less flexible combat formations. When the 1920 infantry regulations had been published, the *Revue militaire générale* asked B. H. Liddell Hart to make a critical study of them. Interestingly enough, one of his major criticisms was their tendency to "paralyze the spirit of mobility and initiative."[67] Clearly, the 1928 infantry regulations placed an even smaller premium on mobility and initiative than the 1920 edition. Given the limited amount of training that was possible with the one-year conscript from 1928 to 1935, the French army preferred simplicity and a greater emphasis on fire. This tendency existed before 1928, but it was even greater after the changes in the late 1920s.

The cumulative effects of the changes in France's system of national defense were touched upon in a lecture at the War College in 1932 by Gen. Lucien Loizeau, who addressed the necessity for the defense during the early phases of a war. He noted that it would be necessary for France initially to conduct an economy of force operation to permit the rearward concentration of war means. Progress in matériel and in armaments favored the assumption of this initial attitude, for the increased capability of weapons of war permitted a smaller force to engage a larger enemy effectively. For those who criticized his scheme as lacking the spirit of the offensive, General Loizeau answered that France had to "win the first battle," if she were to avoid "a debacle worse than 1914."[68] While only the offensive gained decisive results, an initial defensive was essential for France's mobilization of her war potential. A premature offensive, he argued, might result in disaster. Under exceptional circumstances the initial defensive period could contain limited or methodical offensive battles, but the French army had to be exposed carefully to the rigors of combat if it were to win the first battle.

The military hierarchy's recognition of the effects of France's national defense system on the capabilities of her armed forces directly affected planning for an intervention in German affairs. According to General Tournoux's study of French war plans, France had contingency plans for an offensive movement into the Rhineland until April 1935. Such an advance could be used to support France's allies in eastern Europe. But with the repudiation in March 1935 of the clauses in the Versailles Treaty intended to keep Germany disarmed, and the subsequent rapid build-up of German armed forces, France abandoned that possibility and offered instead what the General Staff described as "an immovable front" from Mézières to Basel

(the northeastern frontier), and "a solid front" covering the national territory north of Mézières (the northern frontier).[69] The perceived need to
establish a successful covering force, to mobilize France's war potential, and
to engage inexperienced troops methodically also affected the decision to
establish an "immovable front" along the Maginot Line from Mézières to
Basel. Reliance on the nation in arms thus negated any possibility of "graduated deterrence," or of a limited thrust into Germany. France could partially
or completely mobilize to protect her frontiers, but an initial offensive was
considered beyond the capability of the newly mobilized army.

The successful remilitarization of the Rhineland by Germany was at
least partially the unfortunate result of this emphasis on a defensive nation
in arms. The failure of the French to act was directly linked to the unpreparedness of the French army for an immediate offensive. Without an army
capable of conducting a limited offensive operation, the nation lacked a
"graduated deterrent" capability and possessed only a capacity for total war.
In other words, the French had a "total war or nothing" capability. When
the French cabinet discussed the Rhineland crisis on 7 March 1936, the
minister for the League of Nations, Joseph Paul-Boncour, and the minister
for colonies, Georges Mandel, declared themselves in favor of immediate
action.[70] The foreign minister, Pierre Flandin, also wanted to act before the
British had a chance to withdraw their already reluctant support.[71] But the
willingness of the Sarraut government to countenance immediate action
was not seconded by General Gamelin and his associates. The leaders of
the French army insisted that a general mobilization was necessary before
army elements could be deployed into the Rhineland.[72] If general war
erupted, the commitment of the active army into the Rhineland would seriously hamper complete mobilization.

In a note sent to the minister of war, General Gamelin later stated,
"The idea of rapidly sending a French expeditionary corps into the
Rhineland, even in a more or less symbolic form, is unrealistic." General
Gamelin explained why this was true.

> The immediate launching of such an operation is able to be real
> ized only by troops in the condition of acting at any moment and
> constituting some sort of an *expeditionary corps* . . . always ready to
> fulfill, outside the frontiers, its eventual mission.
>
> But our military system does not give us this possibility.
>
> Our active army is only the nucleus of the mobilized national
> army. . . . None of our units are capable of being placed instantly
> on a complete war footing.[73]

Gamelin was reluctant to take any action without mobilization. When the government asked the military leaders to propose some low-risk, limited measures that might be accomplished without mobilization, the General Staff suggested two alternatives. The first was to occupy a narrow strip of the Saar from Saarbrücken to Merzig, an area that was about twenty-five miles long and no more than eight miles deep. The second alternative was to occupy Luxembourg to protect it from possible German invasion. Neither of these operations could be accomplished until eight days after the order had been given; they were also *not* low-risk alternatives, according to General Gamelin. On the contrary, they required establishing the covering forces along the frontier, mobilizing at least 1,200,000 men, expending twenty million francs each day, beginning the manufacture of war goods, and preparing to launch complete mobilization.[74] Though the French greatly overestimated the size of the German forces involved in the Rhineland operation, the organization of the army and the mobilization plan limited their alternatives dramatically by giving them little choice but to mobilize completely, even if the German forces were relatively small. The political leadership wanted to chase the German military forces from the Rhineland, but they did not want to do this badly enough to call for complete mobilization—particularly if this were to be done without British support.

France had constructed an army of national defense designed not for limited but for total war. The events of March 1936 demonstrated that her army was neither capable of nor willing to countenance an initial offensive operation. Despite the results of March 1936, no real progress was made in mobilization procedures. When the Permanent Committee of National Defense (*Comité permanent de la défense nationale*) discussed the possibility of intervening in the Spanish Civil War, it reached the same conclusion. Mobilization of at least a million men for the covering force would be necessary, but even this would be insufficient. Even though the decision against intervention was not based on military considerations, the High Command had not envisaged a separate mobilization for the Spanish frontier.[75] At the end of September 1938, during the Munich crisis, France mobilized her covering forces along the northeast frontier, but this action required calling more than 750,000 men and 25,000 officers to duty.[76] The mobilization, however, was nothing more than a precautionary measure during the period of tension, for the mobilized soldiers were fortress troops serving with the covering forces along the Maginot Line. As in 1936, France could not and would not act against Germany without complete mobilization. And even then, her forces could only conduct limited operations before the nation became completely ready for total war. Simply put, with the choices being total war or limited operations followed by total war, she refused to raise the stakes and answer Hitler's challenge in Czechoslovakia.

The events of the late 1930s clearly demonstrate that France could effectively respond to a crisis only with a total war based on the resources of the entire nation. Even the precautionary measures taken during the Munich crisis required three-quarters-of-a million reservists. The chance of responding to a threat in Europe with a limited conflict was not a possibility under the French approach to war. In a practical sense, the choice between military policies of "total war or nothing" meant that France always chose "nothing" until she finally was assured of support from her ally, Great Britain.

Despite the absence of a graduated deterrent capability or a rapid reaction force, the French military continued to defend its doctrine and its organization. In the October 1936 issue of *Revue des deux mondes*, General Weygand attacked the idea of forming a special corps that was always ready for the offensive. He declared, "Nothing pertaining to that [force] has to be created, for it already exists."[77] Weygand said this even though the events of March had all too obviously demonstrated the woeful state of the offensive in the French army. In June 1936, the General Staff of the army reaffirmed the task of the mobilized army as being the strengthening of the covering forces. This included "Assuring without withdrawing, the absolute integrity of the fortified front which extends, at the moment, without being interrupted from Longuyon to Basel, as well as in the Alps." The task also included "Halting the maneuver of the enemy that may be executed around the wings of the fortified front."[78] This mission, the instructions of 1936, and the philosophy of the nation in arms coincided completely.

General Charles de Gaulle's concept of a mobile, professional army was an attack on this method of national defense erected on the nation in arms, though de Gaulle did not propose the abolition of the nation in arms. He foresaw the need for a rapid reaction force that could be used before the nation completed its mobilization. Since war was becoming more and more technical, he did not believe a massively armed populace would have great military power simply because it was armed. He was particularly disturbed by the inadequate training the conscript received. The increase in the technical level of war, in de Gaulle's view, demanded more highly trained troops, not simply more troops.[79] The short term of service, he believed, provided little opportunity for in-depth and comprehensive training for the citizen-soldier.

Opponents of de Gaulle's ideas argued that the creation of a special armored corps would tend to split the national army into two armies, thereby causing the second-line army to suffer. This was not a theory solely constructed to counter de Gaulle. General Debeney had offered the objection as early as 1930 when he described the problems and limitations of a professional army for France. After de Gaulle proposed his theory in 1934, Debeney's argument resurfaced[80] and became a continual theme in the works of the military hierarchy attacking de Gaulle's professional army as a siphon that would progressively act to drain resources from the legitimate needs of national defense. According to these critics, the special armored corps would attract the best personnel and the best equipment, to the detriment of the larger and more important second force. Therefore, its existence would make the winning of the final victory by France more improbable, if not unlikely.

As General Weygand argued, France most of all had to "fear an abrupt attack, unleashed without a declaration of war." She had to have an army with enough strength in manpower and matériel to stop the initial attack and enough potential to expand its size for the long total war. De Gaulle's professional army, he declared, detracted from both these capabilities. It could possibly be checked and shattered in its initial aggressive assault, leaving France ill-defended during national mobilization. Furthermore, resources allocated to it would seriously detract from the potential for molding an effective national army. As General Weygand asserted, the second-line army would quickly "fall to the state of a resigned militia, without pride, without life."[81] And it would be this "resigned militia" that would have to fight the final battle for the defense of France. In sum, his criticisms of de Gaulle included strong support for the existing methods and institutions of the military establishment.

The French thus firmly believed in the principle of an aroused nation valiantly defending itself, and the military leaders willingly constructed their army's organizations, equipment, and doctrine upon the precepts of that principle. By virtue of her beliefs and her actions, France chose to build a force structured solely for total war in Europe and limited in its alternatives for response to an international crisis. When the army accepted the complete implementation of the nation in arms, it agreed to a less flexible military force and a significantly limited readiness for immediate action. The adoption of the nation in arms also affected army tactical doctrine, causing it to give greater emphasis to the methodical battle, firepower, and the defense, as well as causing the doctrine itself to become more rigid, rather than more flexible.

Despite the reservations of the army's leaders about the number of divisions, the size of the professional component, and the adequacy of the reservists' training, the political and military leaders remained relatively content. Since France had fought and won World War I with a similar but not as adequately prepared system, almost all of them believed the 1927–1928 laws provided a firm basis for the military organization of the nation. Ironically, the extensive preparations for a total war did not deter the outbreak of such a war or contribute to France's emerging victorious. Instead, those preparations made France pursue a less flexible and hardly vigorous foreign policy, and contributed to the creation of an army that could not respond effectively to the type of warfare it encountered in 1940. More importantly, the efforts did not prevent France from losing the "first battle." Tragically for France the question of her losing the first battle or what she should do if she lost it was not sufficiently addressed before the dismal days of May–June 1940.

CHAPTER 3

The Defense of the Frontiers

In the interwar period, France's military and civilian leadership confronted the enduring challenge of determining how to defend her frontiers. This challenge was driven by more than patriotic verve or by an emotional attachment to "sacred" French soil. In comparison to the much larger population and natural resources of Germany, France possessed a relatively small potential for mobilization and conduct of a war. She faced a potentially more powerful enemy, one that she could repel successfully and defeat only by employing every resource. Much to France's misfortune, a major portion of her natural resources and of her industrial capacity was located near her frontiers and thus within easy striking distance of the Germans. This vulnerability contributed to France's adoption of a strategy emphasizing defense of this crucial war-making capability. She accepted the need for a complete mobilization of the nation in arms, but that mobilization would be seriously hampered if her frontiers were lost to an invading enemy. Strategy and doctrine formulated by the French military had to be functional within this important constraint.

The experiences of World War I had demonstrated the importance of protecting France's vulnerable natural resources. Even though wartime requirements vastly increased demand, production of many important resources dropped significantly from 1913 to 1915—coal by one-half, raw steel by three-fourths, lead ore by five-sixths, and iron ore by a staggering 97 percent.[1] This dramatic decline in the production of critically needed resources occurred primarily because the Germans occupied several crucial areas along the frontier. Following World War I, France's resources were dangerously exposed to enemy action. Since she believed that the increasing scope of modern warfare demanded an even greater consumption of resources and matériel, she perceived this vulnerability to be more critical than ever before.

Two clear examples of the threatened resources are coal and iron ore. The total coal reserves of France before World War II were estimated to be only 18 billion tons. In comparison, Germany had approximately 423 billion, while England had 190 billion. Within France, the most important coalfield lay in the departments of Nord and Pas-de-Calais, not more than twenty-five miles from the Belgian border. During World War I, heavy shelling and deliberate flooding of the mines by the Germans in 1915–1916 severely damaged these coalfields. The French did not regain full production from the damaged mines until some ten years after the end of the war.[2]

By 1932, 63 percent of the coal produced in France came from this frontier region, and another 11 percent came from the department of Moselle within Lorraine. These Lorraine deposits were also located along the German border, and thus almost 75 percent of French coal production was exceptionally vulnerable to a minor German penetration of the frontier. Since France had to import about 25 percent of her coal and coke,[3] crucial imports were also subject to the whims and changing politics of foreign powers.

French iron ore was even more vulnerable. After the war of 1870–1871, Germany acquired control of most of the iron-ore-producing area of Lorraine, but France still retained a portion of that region. By 1913, 83 percent of the iron ore produced in France came from that part of Lorraine still under French control. When the war began in 1914, the German seizure of the remainder of Lorraine almost completely halted the production of iron ore. To make matters worse, military operations also closed other mines that had produced 9 percent of the prewar production. Consequently, wartime production of iron ore in France never exceeded even 10 percent of that produced in 1913.[4] After the war, with the restoration of Lorraine to France, nearly 95 percent of the iron ore produced in 1932 came from Lorraine.[5] In the interwar period, these iron fields were the largest in Europe, the second largest known in the world, and the most economical of all to work. Yet the great iron fields lay in some places as close as a quarter of a mile from the border. In short, although the iron fields were immensely important to the French economy and to any war effort, they were still located dangerously close to the potential enemy.

The problem of oil was different, since France possessed little or no known petroleum resources. Most of the oil fields were in Alsace, and these had been controlled by Germany from 1870–1871 until the end of World War I. When Alsace was returned to France, production immediately jumped to some 47,000 metric tons in 1919 and reached 67,000 by 1926.[6] Unfortunately, this was only 1.8 percent of the petroleum consumed by France in that year.[7] Access to sufficient petroleum for national defense depended upon foreign policy and naval power. The protection of her own minuscule oil reserves had little effect on planning for frontier defenses. Other than increasing her storage capability, France could do little more than hope that her needs would be met if war came. Even then, the problem would not necessarily be the threat of German naval power. A shortage might result from differences in foreign policy with petroleum suppliers to France and thus might come from a shut-off of supplies for diplomatic and political, rather than military, reasons.

The Germans also threatened a major portion of the French manufacturing industry. Since manufacturing plants tended to locate near the major sources of coal and raw materials, especially iron ore, many factories were located around the Pas-de-Calais and Nord coalfield and near the Lorraine iron fields and coalfields. Paris was another important manufacturing area, largely because of highways, railroads, water communication routes, highly skilled labor, and reasonably easy access to the requisite coal and other raw materials. During World War I, a massive build-up of industry had occurred in and around the city, but Paris represented more than an industrial or commercial center. In many ways, the metropolitan area was the heart of France. In the 1930s, one out of every seven Frenchmen lived in Paris, and the other six were greatly influenced by what went on in that city. It was the seat of government, the center of French industry, the hub of the communications system, and the focus of its will, thought and opinion. Yet Paris was only a scant 110 miles from the Belgian frontier and a mere 125 miles from Sedan, where Gen. Heinz Guderian crossed the Meuse in May 1940.

Clearly, misfortune had placed a significant portion of French economic wealth and potential dangerously close to the German threat. Within a triangle formed by Dunkirk, Strasbourg, and Paris, France had about 75 percent of her coal and 95 percent of her iron-ore production. And most of her heavy industry lay within that same triangle. Drawing another triangle between Paris, Lille, and Rouen would encompass nine-tenths of the factories producing French cloth in the 1930s and four-fifths of the factories producing woolen goods. In that same area France produced most of her chemical products, all her automobiles, and all her aircraft. France recognized that coal, iron, and factories are the basis for the matériel side of total warfare. She also knew that her war-making capability would be seriously threatened even if she managed to hold the enemy along the same lines where the Germans had been halted in 1914.

At the same time a major portion of France's population resided near the natural resource and industrial centers. The problem of manpower for the French armed forces had long been a source of gloom. From the time of the Franco-Prussian War of 1870–1871, the ratio of Frenchmen to Germans progressively declined. In the late 1860s, the Germans slightly outnumbered the French in numbers of men aged twenty to thirty-four who were in the prime period of their lives for military service. By 1910 the Germans had increased their advantage to a ratio of 1.7 to 1. By 1939 the Germans had more than twice as many men of military age.[8] For manpower reasons as well as patriotic ones the Frenchmen living along the frontiers could not be relinquished to the enemy.

The desire to prevent the Germans from seizing any part of France exerted a strong emotional influence over the military. France had suffered four invasions (1814, 1815, 1870, 1914) over the past century, and wanted to avoid another such incursion. On numerous occasions politicians lectured the Chamber of Deputies and the Senate on the terrible effects of the German occupation during World War I. One of the most emotional of these presentations occurred on 10 December 1929, during the debate over the concept of the frontier defenses. Albert Meunier passionately described to the Chamber of Deputies the horrors perpetrated by what he described as the "brutes," "barbarians," "Germanic hordes," and "inexorable enemy." He painted a vivid picture of the rape of the occupied areas and pleaded that no Frenchman should ever again come under German control. He repeated the sometimes exaggerated tales of villages burned and destroyed and their inhabitants shot. He argued that animals and all sources of support should be destroyed rather than allow them to be used by the enemy.[9] Although such tales were sometimes more myth than fact, they continued to have an impact on France. The perception of the brutality of the Germans was more important than the reality. Against this consuming dislike and fear of Germany, France sought defenses to shield her countrymen from the Germanic pestilence.

France's need to defend the frontiers in the interwar period clearly differed from that prior to the Great War. After having lost Alsace and Lorraine to Germany in 1871, France concentrated in the years immediately after that loss on constructing her northeastern defenses—the area which she believed had the most likely and dangerous avenue of attack—along a line between Verdun and Belfort. Under Gen. Raymond A. Seré de Rivières' tutelage, after 1874 she built a primary defensive line between Verdun and Toul along the Meuse, with the largest and most modern fortifications centered around those two cities. Another defense line began at Epinal, ran along the Moselle River, and stretched across the Vosges Mountains to Belfort, with the main fortifications being centered around Epinal and Belfort. The unfortified area between Verdun and Luxembourg became known as the Stenay "gap" and the area between Toul and Epinal as the Charmes "gap." General Seré de Rivières believed an attacking German army would channel its main forces toward and through these natural avenues, and the defending French army—by holding the shoulders of these gaps—could then counterattack and destroy the invaders. An attacking French army could also pour through these gaps for an attack into Germany.

As for the northern frontier, the French military in 1874 did not believe that the Germans could or would cross Belgium. Consequently, they did little more than reinforce or modernize the forts in such areas as Maubeuge, Lille, and Dunkirk. They did recognize the need to defend in depth and proposed a second line of defense running through Dijon, Langres, Rheims, Laon, and La Fère. In the northeast they planned on building several forts in the Stenay and Charmes gaps along the railway lines an invader would have to use in these areas. By 1885 the French had built or modernized eighty-nine forts and twenty smaller defensive works along the frontier between the Pas-de-Calais and Switzerland. Some of these forts, such as Douaumont and Vaux, would play extremely important roles in the fighting around Verdun.[10]

In the two decades after the 1871 defeat, the frontier covering forces consisted primarily of troops stationed in close proximity to the northeastern border, most being active-duty infantry and cavalry units with some reinforcement from the reserves. The covering forces initially would occupy positions forward of the fortification line. Their mission was to delay an attacking enemy until the remainder of the French army could be mobilized and brought into action. They would fight forward of the fortifications as long as they could to gain the required time for the mobilization of the armed nation. Utilizing their thorough knowledge of the terrain, the covering forces would destroy as many of the enemy as possible and then slowly withdraw before the probable enemy superiority. After several days of fighting in the thirty to forty kilometers between the border and the fortifications the covering forces would reach the protection of the fortified system of the upper Moselle and the Meuse. The covering forces thus traded space for the time required to mobilize the French army.

After 1890 French strategy became "less timid," to use Marshal Joffre's phrase,[11] and the army became much more offensively minded. The publication of the notorious Plan XVII in February 1914 signaled the complete change in thinking which had occurred since 1890. The French abandoned their reluctance to attack and resolved to assume the offensive as soon as the mobilized forces assembled. The fortifications played a smaller role than they had in the past, since Joffre and the other army leaders expected a short battle and wanted to concentrate all the nation's strength in the climactic, decisive battle that would begin and end the war. They dreamed of leaving the fortifications to the rear, as they led their forces in a massive thrust into the heart of Germany.

As France became obsessed with the offensive on the eve of the war, the covering forces were also relegated to a lesser role, though plans still existed for their employment. If mobilization delays or railway accidents occurred, the covering forces, reinforced by the first units arriving on the frontier, would defend along the line of forts established by Seré de Rivières in the 1880s and delay the invaders from crossing the Meuse and Moselle rivers. The 1913 regulations on the tactical employment of large units explained that the purpose of the covering forces was to permit mobilization along the frontier and to protect the debarkation and concentration zones for the mobilizing French army. The regulation said that the covering force has to "assure the protection of lines of communication, engineering works, telegraph lines, and provisions in the frontier zone."[12] There was no mention of protecting natural resources or industrial capability.

After 1918, however, the problem changed. The 1914 covering forces had been able to trade French territory in order to gain the critically needed time for the mobilization of the army. If France were to win a future total war, she would no longer have that "luxury." The vulnerable natural resources, industrial capability, and population would be vital to France's successful participation in a long and terribly destructive total war. By the early 1930s, northwest France and the reacquired areas of Alsace and Lorraine had become far too important to a future war effort to contemplate abandoning them to an enemy or not defending them.

Given the need to protect the frontiers, the military hierarchy's task after 1918 became one of determining how the frontiers were to be defended. Throughout the evolution of the frontier defenses between World Wars I and II, the Superior Council of War played a decisive role in the entire process—from the initial concept to the final strategy. The decree of 23 January 1920, which reestablished the council, specifically stated that it had to be consulted on the "general organization of the defensive systems for the territorial or coastal frontiers."[13] This phrase had not appeared in the pre–World War I list of subjects on which the council had to be consulted, and its inclusion indicates the widespread interest among French civilian leaders after World War I in protecting the frontiers against another invasion. Its inclusion also gave the council greater influence over the protection of the frontiers than over almost any other task.

When the council met in May 1920, it addressed the question of the "defense of the national territory." The session demonstrated the lack of a clear consensus among the generals and marshals on the best method for defending the frontier. Marshal Foch's comments are particularly

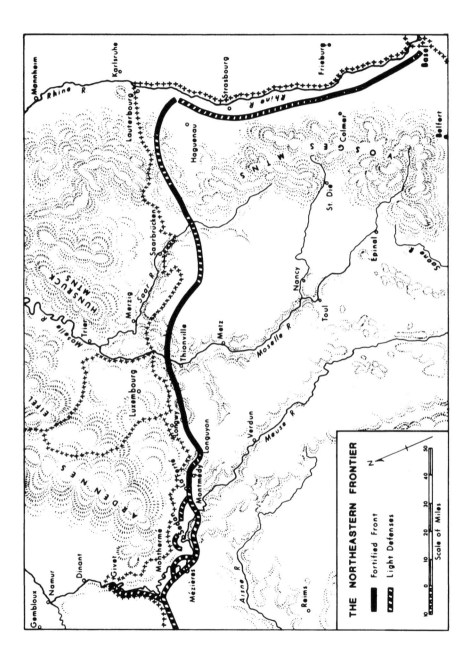

THE NORTHEASTERN FRONTIER

Fortified Front
Light Defenses

Scale of Miles
0   10   20   30   40   50

interesting, for he argued that fortifications are "inert matter which has value only to the troops that put it there." He argued that before fortifications could be built, one must know the plan of operations, the object of the war, and how the war would begin—Germany attacking or France attacking. When Marshal Pétain asked whether the defenses "should henceforth depend upon prepared battlefields for the operating armies," Foch objected to the "epithet" of preparing the battlefield upon which one might fight. Gen. Edmond A. L. Buat, the chief of the General Staff, said he could see not one but four fields of battle. When General Debeney noted that the defenses had to be organized differently if France could not count on Belgium, Pétain seconded his comments, and Foch observed that Belgium remained the major route of invasion. The only conclusion from the meeting was that members of the council would continue studies on the defense of the frontiers. These defenses had the purpose of "halting the enemy," and "organizing a base permitting the development of an offensive maneuver into the enemy country."[14]

The council again addressed the problem of the frontiers in May 1922, and several major issues appeared. When it discussed the question of whether the defensive organization should assure the "inviolability" of the national territory, Foch stressed that such an approach had to be examined thoroughly, since French territory had been defended in the past by the maneuver of armies. Marshal Joffre supported Foch and said that too great an emphasis on fortifications would be "doomed to defeat for seeking to establish a new wall of China."[15] In a study entitled "Note on the Defensive Organization of the Frontiers," published in 1921, Pétain had strongly supported the need to ensure the "inviolability" of the territory,[16] but Foch and Joffre clearly rejected such a proposal.

When the council addressed the need to establish a "continuous battlefield" along the frontiers, Pétain noted that fortifications were necessary only where the French army would defend, and that the remainder of the frontier should be prepared to permit maneuver. Joffre objected to creating a continuous front from Dunkirk to Basel (the Franco-Swiss border). In the discussions that followed, Generals Debeney and Frédéric E.A. Hellot (the inspector general of the engineers) emerged as the major proponents of creating a prepared battlefield with permanent fortifications. But the council's only action was to form a special commission to study the problem of the frontiers.[17]

The first phase of addressing the issue of the frontier defenses thus ended inconclusively. Through both meetings in 1920 and 1922, however, the military hierarchy did not concentrate solely on defensive operations, and major reservations appeared as to the validity of a continuous front or a prepared battlefield. The first meetings also demonstrated that no single individual was going to dominate the planning for defense of the frontiers. By mid-1922, two clear but conflicting concepts for the defense of the frontiers existed. The first suggested building a continuous line of defensive works along the frontier, reminiscent of the trench and barbed wire system of World War I. Its major proponent was General Buat, the chief of the General Staff. Although Marshal Pétain apparently supported Buat, his comments in the meetings of the Superior Council demonstrated that he was not an inflexible advocate of a continuous line of defensive works. Opposing this view were those led by Marshals Foch and Joffre who supported the concept of fortified regions acting as centers of resistance to facilitate offensive actions by an army. Such armies maneuvered around the centers of resistance, seeking the proper time and most favorable conditions for launching an attack. The centers of resistance were associated with the offensive and defensive maneuver of armies, while the continuous line of defensive works was associated with a relatively static defense.

By late 1922 supporters for the two concepts became more obvious, and most members of the council apparently preferred a system that could be used offensively *and* defensively. Marshal Joffre was appointed in 1922 as the chairman of a commission to study the territorial defenses, but he resigned his position shortly thereafter when a letter from the minister of war, André Maginot, appeared to intervene in the deliberations of the commission. After General Marie L.A. Guillaumat, who commanded the French Army of the Rhine and who was a firm supporter of Joffre and Foch's ideas, replaced him in August 1922, the commission heatedly debated in 1922–1923 the best method for defending the frontiers. Buat led those supporting a continuous line of defensive works; Guillaumat led those preferring the centers of resistance.[18] With the occupation of the Ruhr in January 1923, however, the work of the commission faltered and did not begin anew until the spring of 1925. Meanwhile, fate intervened, for the death of General Buat in late 1923 removed the most powerful and vocal opponent of the centers of resistance from the commission. The new chief of the General Staff, General Debeney, supported Guillaumat's ideas, but he preferred that the centers of resistance be defensive rather than offensive.

In December 1925, the commission presented its report to the Superior Council of War. As expected, it questioned the validity of creating a continuous front and supported the need for centers of resistance. A deputy chief of staff also read a 16 March 1923, report from the deceased General Buat, which strongly supported the necessity for preparing a continuous front. When the president of the Republic, Gaston Doumergue, posed a question on whether a defensive system should be constructed on the frontier from Basel to the English Channel, Foch objected that it was necessary to specify the objective of the defensive system. Pétain replied that it would "guarantee the inviolability of the territory." Foch exclaimed, "Fortifications should not have the purpose of security, [of guaranteeing] the inviolability of the territory, but the protection of the concentration of forces in the face of the enemy."[19]

To conciliate both sides, Doumergue divided the question into two parts. When he asked whether a defensive system should be created for the frontiers, the council responded unanimously that it should. The council decided, however, not to address the question of whether fortifications should extend to the Franco-Swiss frontier. When Doumergue asked whether the fortified system should be conceived under the form of a continuous battlefield, the council responded unanimously that it should not. It affirmed unanimously that the defensive system should be constructed with fortified regions which were not arranged in the fashion of a continuous front. The council also recommended that the system be prepared during peacetime, and that technical studies be performed on the best methods of fortifications.

The meeting was thus an important one; the council advised the creation in peacetime of a discontinuous system of fortified regions. Other than recommending the formation of a special commission to address the problem of the frontiers, that was all it recommended. The council had not yet decided upon the actual purpose, the technical form, or the extent of the fortifications. It had also not yet decided whether the fortifications could be used offensively or defensively. Much remained to be done.

Shortly after the December 1925 meeting, the minister of war, Paul Painlevé, followed the advice of the council and created the Commission on the Defense of the Frontiers, with General Guillaumat as its president. The commission's responsibilities included determining the best design and choice of locations for the fortified regions, selecting the required equipment and supplies for the frontiers, and defining the program of field tests to determine the best engineering works and the armament to be used in the fortifications.[20] Although formation of the commission may have been an attempt to overcome disagreement within the Superior Council of War, the selection of Guillaumat as president of the new commission ensured that it would follow the ideas of the previous commission under him. The selection of Guillaumat also illustrated that Pétain did not have sufficient power to dominate completely the deliberations of the Superior Council or the War Ministry.

The commission worked for almost a year and submitted its report to the minister in November 1926. On 17 December 1926, General Guillaumat explained to the Superior Council how the commission envisaged the defenses for the northeastern frontiers. Throughout the discussions, there was little or no disagreement on the need to place strong fortifications in three areas: Metz-Thionville-Longwy, Lauter, and Belfort. The Metz region had long been identified as a major invasion route, since the Moselle River valley ran through its center in a north-south direction. Additionally, the commission believed that fortifications in the Metz region could protect much of the industrial basin and natural resources of Lorraine. The Lauter area included the farthest corner of the northeast frontier bordering on Germany, and covered an obvious invasion route flanking the Rhine. When it discussed the extent of the fortifications in the Lauter area, the commission saw no need to extend the fortifications along the Rhine. The commission considered the river a difficult obstacle for an attacking army and believed the Vosges Mountains stood in the path of any invader moving from east to west. The commission recognized that the Germans could only concentrate forces along the Rhine with great difficulty because of the low density of railroads in that area.[21] The French army could defend the Rhine, a natural obstacle, with less peacetime preparation, so no major defenses had to be erected along it. Since the commission considered Strasbourg indefensible, it recommended that fortifications in that city be abolished. The third area was near Belfort, which bordered on the Swiss frontier and stood astride a possible route of invasion. The Rhine partially protected Belfort, but the open avenue of approach on the western bank invited an enemy attack through the area.[22]

In terms of priorities, the commission placed the greatest emphasis on the Metz region and the least emphasis on Belfort. The Metz and the Lauter regions provided protection for Alsace and Lorraine in the most likely avenues of invasion along the northeastern frontier. Fortified regions in these areas also protected important railway and communications centers that were essential for the frontier defenses. At the same time, fortifications in those two areas could provide some protection for the crucial resources located along the northeastern frontier, and could also act as the supporting base for an offensive thrust into Germany. Protection against an *attaque brusquée* emerged as the major consideration, because the commission feared Germany might attempt to overrun the Metz and Lauter regions with a limited objective attack before covering forces could be placed in position. Such an attack could seize the areas containing the natural resources and industrial basins that were essential for France's defenses. Placing fortified regions in the Metz and Lauter areas thus accomplished the dual purpose of protecting France's war-making capability and blocking the two most likely avenues of invasion on the northeastern frontier. There was little or no disagreement on the primary areas to be fortified. The council accepted the recommendations and priorities of the commission for the Metz, Lauter, and Belfort regions.

Strong opposition emerged, however, when the Superior Council addressed other recommendations of the commission. A crucial point of disagreement had surfaced on 15 December during one of the preparatory meetings by the council on the report from Guillaumat's commission. The issue was the technical design of the fortifications. The commission favored building large concrete fortresses in the Metz and Lauter regions, which had to be strong enough to withstand the heaviest artillery concentrations and gas attacks. In the areas between these large fortresses, the commission proposed building a defensive system consisting primarily of smaller concrete bunkers, linked together by a network of command posts, observation points, and communications lines. In the preparatory session, Pétain had criticized the large fortresses and stated, "It is necessary to find a more economical system." He suggested a "blockhouse" system, similar to the one the Germans supposedly used. Several members of the commission, according to the reporter, "energetically attacked" Pétain's system, for they had already considered and rejected it unanimously. Those objecting to Pétain's system included Marshal Joffre and Generals Debeney and Guillaumat.[23]

The divergent points of view again appeared in the official meeting of the council on 17 December. Pétain criticized the proposed system by noting the failure of fortresses in World War I. He observed that the best method was the prepared battlefield, with positions arranged in depth. While fortresses were an easy target for large-caliber weapons, trenches and underground defenses offered less expensive but greater protection. Although the council did not formally accept Pétain's suggestions, he had created enough doubts for the council to decide to have the commission complete another study on the technical design of the fortifications.[24]

The council meeting of 17 December also encountered continuing disagreement on whether the fortifications could facilitate offensive operations or act as a base for the projection of power into the heart of Germany. Pétain observed that while France desired to employ an offensive for "carrying" the war into the Rhineland, the situation would no longer be the same after her eventual withdrawal from that German area. He also argued that fortifications must be "above all" defensive before they could "permit" an offensive. Guillaumat replied, apparently rather testily, "Fortifications do

not impede the offensive."[25] Their comments reveal the continuing disagreement over the basic purpose of the fortifications, and the minutes of
the meeting reveal that support for their offensive employment was slowly
dissolving.

One of the most important reasons for the loss of support for the
offensive employment of the fortifications was the emerging recognition of
the effect of the 1927–1928 laws. During the debates in the council on what
were to be those laws, the military hierarchy concluded that any war against
Germany would necessarily consist of two phases: the period of the operation of the covering forces, when the frontiers were defended and the
nation mobilized; and the period of national struggle, when the entire
resources of France were brought to bear against the enemy. Given the
specter of the army having to endure a complex process of breaking up
active peacetime units to form the wartime army, the military leadership
concluded that the covering forces had to be strengthened.

As early as April 1925, Marshal Foch had stated that the period of cov-
ering-force operations had to be lengthened, since the concentration of
forces behind it took longer.[26] The mission of the covering forces had
never been more crucial, for France had to have time to resurrect the
nation in arms. And after the national forces were mobilized, they were
more suited for defensive operations than for offensive operations. The
coupling of the lengthy mobilization period with the lack of confidence in
the army's offensive capabilities in the opening phases of a war slowly dis-
solved much of the support for using the frontier fortifications for offensive
operations. When the threat of an *attaque brusquée* appeared, the argument
for reinforcing the covering forces became even more insistent. Considering the complexity of mobilizing the nation, fortifications could strengthen
the covering forces, which needed all the assistance they could get to
ensure the successful completion of their mission.

In December 1926, the Superior Council of War concluded its second
phase of deliberations on defending the northeastern frontiers, after having agreed only on the general location of the fortified regions and after
having witnessed a slow erosion of support for using the fortifications in an
offensive operation to project power into the heart of Germany. It had not
yet agreed on precisely where the fortifications should be located within
those regions, nor had it agreed upon the technical design of the fortifications. The points of disagreement involved crucial doctrinal issues, which
had to be addressed and which involved the entire organization and role of
the fortifications. After studying the problem of defending the northeast
frontier from May 1920 to December 1926, the council still had some very
important decisions in front of it.

In the next phase of deliberations, the need for depth in the system of fortifications became a crucial point of discussion. This was one of the most important operational "lessons" of the war, for a defense organized with successive obstacles, lines of fire, etc., could absorb the massive fires and strong thrust of an attack by slowly grinding it to a halt. When an attacker faced several defensive lines, he had to conduct a series of actions, beginning with an attack, followed by a consolidation and regrouping, followed by another attack. Such attacks consumed great amounts of time, men, and matériel. Fighting a battle in depth, however, necessarily required the relinquishing of crucial areas to enemy control as the defender moved backward. In France's case, this meant that defending forces might permit an attacker to capture valuable resources along the frontier.

The Guillaumat commission did not ignore the requirement for depth, but its solution obviously placed the greatest emphasis on the strength of the fortresses themselves. When it again presented its recommendations, in 1927, on the technical design of the fortifications, the commission, supported by General Debeney, continued to support the use of fortified regions, with large fortresses in the most important positions and smaller concrete bunkers between them. It recommended placing the defensive line close enough to the frontier to provide protection for industrial centers and natural resources. While the combination of the large fortresses and the smaller concrete bunkers provided an unbroken line of fire in the fortified regions, there was very little depth between any forward positions and the final line of resistance at the fortresses. The commission believed that only strong fortifications located near the frontiers could protect crucial resources, as well as provide the best defense against the *attaque brusquée.* Permanent fortifications provided continuous protection, whereas a prepared battlefield provided protection only when it was completely manned.[27] The commission's initial concept envisaged depth only in the sense of providing protection to the rear from cavalry or tank raids. Also, if an attacking enemy forced the French army to pull back and fight a delaying action away from the fortifications, the commission believed the fortified regions could defend themselves until the French army returned.

The commission's concept of depth clearly differed from that of Marshal Pétain. At the preparatory session of the Superior Council of War on 2 July 1927, Pétain counterattacked, and noted that a strong defensive position consisted of two major systems: a forward position, and a final barrage or barrier of fire. He noted that the system suggested by the commission only foresaw a forward position, but it still cost more than twenty-five million francs per kilometer. In doctrinal terms, the commission viewed their system more in terms of the final line of resistance (which was located near the frontier), than as a forward position. The council understood Pétain's main point: if the enemy penetrated through the single barrier, there were no other prepared positions for halting them. Pétain's criticisms found support in an alternative offered by Gen. Jean M. J. Dégoutte, who suggested a system of small defensive works consisting of machine-gun positions echeloned in depth. He stated the price of this system was approximately five to eight million francs per kilometer, and it did provide depth.[28]

In a regular session of the Superior Council of War on 4 July 1927, the commission presented its recommendations, and the council formally addressed the problem of depth. General Fillonneau, who was the inspector general of the engineers and a member of the commission, argued passionately that the recommended fortifications provided a powerful system of defense which was virtually impenetrable and which protected the crucial areas near the frontier. He described the long work of the commission and explained how it had received suggestions from a wide variety of sources. Pétain replied by again emphasizing the need for depth, and to illustrate his point, he used the example of General Debeney (who supported the commission's recommendations) who had halted the Germans in March 1918 by reconstituting a front with fresh divisions. The debate continued, but Pétain emerged the victor when the council approved a resolution supporting the need for depth in the frontier positions. His opponents saved themselves from a complete route by having the council approve a resolution stating that the technical design of each fortified area should be the design most appropriate for that area. Geographic diversity ruled that some areas could be more easily defended than others or required different types of fortifications; similarly, the requirement for depth did not eliminate the need to protect crucial industrial basins and natural resources.[29]

Pétain supported the concept of a prepared battlefield, reinforced by small concrete defensive works, but his concept also had several weaknesses. One of these was the dilemma of providing depth while also protecting critical areas. The other was the requirement for larger numbers of personnel. During the council's deliberations on 4 July 1927, Gen. Charles Nollet, who had served as minister of war during the Herriot government, noted that before the council adopted a system requiring large numbers of men, it was necessary to know whether France had enough personnel for such a system. Pétain lamely replied that that was a question for the General Staff. The Guillaumat commission had noted in its first studies that a prepared battlefield required large numbers of personnel, and this requirement eventually forced Pétain to drop his plans for a prepared battlefield consisting of small defensive positions. Pétain's "victory" of 4 July 1927 in the Superior Council was thus only a temporary one.

Ammunition to use against Pétain's concept came from a technical study on fortifications. When the military governor of Belfort conducted a test on the requirements for frontier defenses consisting of the small infantry positions, his conclusions provided strong evidence against the employment of such a system. According to the study, such a position needed at least four concrete bunkers per kilometer, required emplacing machine guns in protected bunkers, could be controlled only with great difficulty, and could not be protected adequately against gas attack. More importantly, such positions required a battalion of infantry every two kilometers, rather than every five kilometers, which was the previously established planning figure.[30] Since the effects of the 1927–1928 laws were dramatically clear by the middle of 1927, such evidence could not be ignored by Pétain. France required a system that enabled its comparatively fewer soldiers to fight more effectively. Dégoutte's system of small fieldworks required more men than did larger fortifications, and Pétain soon did a rapid about-face.

In a preparatory session of the council on 11 October 1927, Pétain explained his new conception, which was remarkably similar to the original one of Debeney and the Guillaumat commission. The meeting began with General Fillonneau describing the two major systems before the council: the commission's concept of large concrete fortresses interspersed with smaller fortresses, and General Dégoutte's concept of small infantry fieldworks on a prepared battlefield. Pétain followed with a pointed criticism of large, above-ground fortresses, again using the example of World War I fortresses to illustrate their vulnerability. He then suggested using a new type of underground fortification consisting of small turrets, bunkers, and fighting positions which protruded slightly from the ground but which were linked to a central underground fortress by tunnels.[31] This system dispersed the fighting positions, ensured protection for communication lines, and could be protected against massive artillery and gas attacks. As the commission had suggested earlier, Pétain wanted his web of fortifications placed relatively close to the frontier. Since there was little hope of actually creating a defense in depth, the fortifications protected more of the crucial resources of Alsace and Lorraine when they were placed near the frontiers. Pétain saw his solution as being midway between that of Dégoutte and Guillaumat. Actually, it was closer to Guillaumat's idea, except that it was essentially an underground system which had small infantry positions armed with cannon or machine guns linked to the main fortress by tunnels.[32]

On 12 October 1927, the Superior Council of War adopted Pétain's concept of the fortifications, which was eventually to become the major system within the Maginot Line. The approval of the council was neither automatic nor unconditional. Gen. Joseph-L.-M. Maurin, for example, argued that the suggested design of the fortifications was too expensive and would cause numerous delays in construction. He also believed that the fortifications would be completely immobile and might remain as useless as those at Toul and Epinal in 1914. Such reservations, however, did not receive sufficient support from within the council to reject Pétain's concept. The council concluded the discussion by stating it had a "favorable" view of Pétain's concept for establishing large fortifications in the important points along the frontier. Lighter infantry defensive positions with protective cover would be established in the intervals between the major fortresses.[33]

When the fortifications were built, they were placed generally along the line approved by the council in December 1926. The only major changes came about as the result of suggestions made by Pétain after a detailed reconnaissance in the summer of 1927.[34] Even though Pétain continued to say the fortified regions had depth, the positions actually had little or no more strategic depth than the initial concept of the Guillaumat commission.[35] They were, however, vastly more expensive than the prepared battlefield initially suggested by General Buat. While Pétain's greatest influence was over the technical design of the fortifications and their exact placement within the fortified regions, the final defensive system for the northeastern frontier was much closer to the initial concept of General Debeney than anyone else. From the beginning, he supported the idea of large fortified systems organized in regions as close to the frontier as possible. In contrast to the Guillaumat commission, he also conceived of the fortifications as being more important for the defense than for the offense.[36]

The decision of October 1927 thus resolved the issues of technical design of the fortifications, the precise location (within the context of being closer to the frontier), and the requirement for depth. At the same time, it was now possible to say that France was erecting a continuous front of defenses along the northeastern frontier. When General Debeney noted that fortified regions enabled France to use her personnel more efficiently, Pétain said, "The organization of the fortified regions, in creating the possibility of economizing with personnel, actually permits the realization of a continuous front."[37] The frontier defenses, however, were a continuous front only in the sense of having *some* defenses (rather than strong defenses) along the entire frontier. The defenses to the west of the Metz fortified region and between Metz and Lauter were never as strong as the fortified regions, since the military hierarchy sought to concentrate the fortifications in the most vulnerable areas or in the areas most valuable to the military effort. Considerations of excessive costs also undoubtedly influenced the decision. Only a limited number of the expensive fortified regions could be completed, and relatively weaker areas had to exist between the strong points.

In a June 1928 meeting of the Superior Council of National Defense, Marshal Pétain described in detail the Superior Council of War's concept for fortifying the frontiers. His introductory remarks explained that modern war required the resources of the entire nation, and that if a battle destroyed France's industrial or agricultural areas, this would be a "disaster" whose consequences would endure for decades. He explained, "Assuring the inviolability of the national soil is thus one of the major lessons of the war."[38] He described the proposed system with its fortified regions, and assured the members of the council that plans existed for creating a permanent system of defensive works between the fortified regions of Metz and Lauter.

When Pétain concluded his remarks, the president of the council, a civilian politician, stressed the need to extend the fortifications between the regions of Metz and Lauter in order to provide needed protection for those areas.[39] His comments illustrated a common demand among political leaders to ensure a continuous line of fortifications for the areas along the frontiers. When General Debeney had appeared before a joint meeting of the Senate finance and army commissioners in 1926, he found it necessary to reassure the senators that steps would be taken to protect the unfortified areas. Stronger opposition later emerged in the Chamber of Deputies. Pierre Cot, momentarily lacking the postwar wisdom that would enable him to charge the military hierarchy with a "lack of intellectual power and scientific training" because of its preference for the continuous front,[40] became the spokesman in the chamber for those seeking fortifications providing a continuous line of fire. Since Cot's group preferred the building of smaller defenses along the entire frontier, their concept closely coincided with the initial one of General Buat. André Maginot eventually stated in the Chamber of Deputies that political opponents of the centers of resistance had intervened successfully in the military question by forcing the army to strengthen the defenses in the intervals between the fortified regions. The minister of war explained that in consonance with the lessons of the war of 1914–1918, the first objective of the frontier fortifications would be to establish a "continuous line of fire."[41]

The fieldworks that were ultimately constructed along other portions of the frontier, however, bore only a slight resemblance to the massive fortifications of the three fortified regions in the northeast: Metz-Thionville-

Longwy, Lauter, and Belfort. And to credit or blame the politicians for the erection of the defenses is to ignore the long process of discussion which occurred in the Superior Council of War. Those discussions reveal a clear desire from the beginning by the military to establish fortifications. After a long debate, they concluded that given France's system and problems of national defense, only a system of frontier defenses could strengthen the covering forces and protect France's crucial resources in the northeast. While fortifications provided greater strength to covering forces whose soldiers had only a short term of service, the Superior Council of War accepted the need for fortifications long before it was forced to accept eighteen-month or one-year service. Even without the shorter terms of service, the military hierarchy would probably have sought frontier fortifications. In that sense, the acceptance and design of France's frontier fortifications were far from being a "compromise"[42] between the political and military leaders for the army hierarchy's acceptance of one-year service. If there was a compromise, it was on the technical design of the fortifications and the role they were to play in a future war.

Although some disagreement existed over the nature of the northeast fortifications, very few doubts appeared about the Ardennes. In the Superior Council's debates and in the war plans, the Ardennes was treated as an area of secondary concern. When in 1927 the Guillaumat commission addressed the question of the Ardennes, it assumed the area could easily be defended. The narrow, winding roads and the heavily forested, rugged hills could be blocked with sufficient felled trees, minefields, and roadblocks to prevent a large force, especially a mechanized one, from crossing rapidly.[43] The Ardennes was not necessarily impenetrable, but the combination of natural and man-made obstacles would make any penetration a slow and arduous operation. If the enemy were able to make his way through the Ardennes, he still had to cross the Meuse River, whose depth and width made it a reasonably strong obstacle. Even if an enemy were to pass through the Ardennes and cross the Meuse, such an operation required such extensive resources and preparation that the French were confident they could reinforce the threatened area before a major penetration occurred.[44] They assumed the Germans would require nine days to cross the Ardennes, thereby giving them plenty of time to reinforce if necessary. Unfortunately, they overestimated the required time by more than six days.

Throughout the 1930s, the French perception of the Ardennes remained unchanged. When Pétain appeared before the Senate army commission in March 1934, he reflected the views of the military when he emphasized that this sector was "not dangerous."[45] When General Gamelin discussed in 1936 the coordination of French and Belgian defense efforts with the Belgian chief at staff, General Cumont, they concluded that as long as the shoulders of the region were held by the Belgians at Liège and by the French at Arlon (near Longwy), the Ardennes was not dangerous.[46] In comparison to the vulnerable resources on the northeastern frontiers and the absence of easily defensible terrain on the northern frontier, the Ardennes seemed to require less defensive preparation. From beginning to end, the French High Command treated the Ardennes sector as simply the connecting sector between the northeastern and northern frontiers.

Of all the sectors, the question of defending the northern frontier remained probably the most controversial and complex. When the Superior Council considered the defense of the frontier between Luxembourg and Dunkirk, it viewed the defense of that sector as being intimately related to that of the northeast and recognized that the two areas could not be approached as two separate issues. The High Command believed that building the Maginot Line permitted the economizing of forces along the northeastern frontier and the concentrating of larger forces along the northern frontier. Yet it also believed that the methods employed on one frontier were not necessarily the proper ones to employ on the other frontier. While fortifications could assist in protecting the vulnerable resources of the northeast and could be reinforced by natural obstacles, the absence of such obstacles in the flat, open countryside on the Franco-Belgian frontier argued against the erection of extremely expensive fortifications in the north. Terrain considerations alone dictated that any fortifications would have to be more extensive than those in the northeast, and the problem of the high water table meant they would have to be constructed differently. Also, the existence of the large industrial region surrounding Lille and Tourcoing, and the location of several crucial railway lines and junctions nearby, interfered with building in peacetime an extremely deep, prepared battlefield with barbed-wire entanglements, entrenchments, and tank obstacles. Perhaps more importantly, building fortifications at Belgium's back would create doubts in the mind of that wavering ally about France's intentions. Another method of defense had to be used in this most likely area—in the High Command's view—of enemy attack.

In its May 1920 meetings, the first deliberations after the war on the problem of the frontiers, the council believed that Belgium remained the major route of invasion. The French assumed that the construction of fortifications on the northeast would encourage the Germans to divert their attack toward Belgium, and thus to attempt another version of the 1914 Schlieffen Plan. In the minds of the French, the likelihood of that occurring was heightened by the previous German violation of Belgian neutrality, the absence of geographic obstacles, and the location of a large network of roads and railways running directly toward Paris. Throughout the interwar period, the High Command did not deviate from this perception and demonstrated an unswerving preference to fight on Belgian soil in the north, rather than on French. The French leaders vividly remembered the disastrous destruction of precious agricultural, industrial, and mining resources in the World War I fighting. None wished for that to occur again.

In September 1920, France moved decisively toward a strategy of defending her northern frontier by rushing into Belgium. General Buat, chief of the French General Staff, and Gen. Henri Maglinse, chief of the Belgian General Staff, signed a military accord ensuring close cooperation between their two armies. In a period of international tension, Belgium would ask for aid and France would dispatch an army to Belgium's border with Germany. The German border thus became the principal line of resistance to a German attack.[47]

As the French considered alternatives in the following years for implementing this strategy for forward defense, they concluded that the forces charged with establishing those defenses would have to be highly mobile if they were to reach the previously selected positions before the Germans did. Despite their mobility, these forces would fight a defensive battle, rather than an offensive one. The motorized transportation would serve only to carry the units forward to their fighting positions. And they would bring enormous amounts of barrier and defense materials with them to strengthen their positions and impede the advance of the attacking enemy. To move massive amounts of matériel into Belgium, the French army created mobile fortification parks, which were reserves of war matériel organized to be carried forward by trucks and railroads.[48]

If the Belgian army collapsed under an overwhelming German attack, the French risked having to fight a perilous encounter battle in the not easily defended countryside of central Belgium. They recognized this danger and repeatedly emphasized that they did not want to fight a war of movement or risk an encounter battle in which they and an onrushing enemy would collide. They wanted to avoid fighting a decisive battle while they were still trying to move forward, since they did not wish to repeat the ill-advised and reckless rushes of 1914. But they would move forward, since, above all, they did not want the battle to occur in France.

In subsequent years, the French military hierarchy frequently discussed the strategy of forward defense but remained faithful to its basic tenets. When the Guillaumat commission presented its recommendations for the first time on the technical design of the fortifications for the frontier to the Superior Council in December 1926, General Guillaumat asserted that the

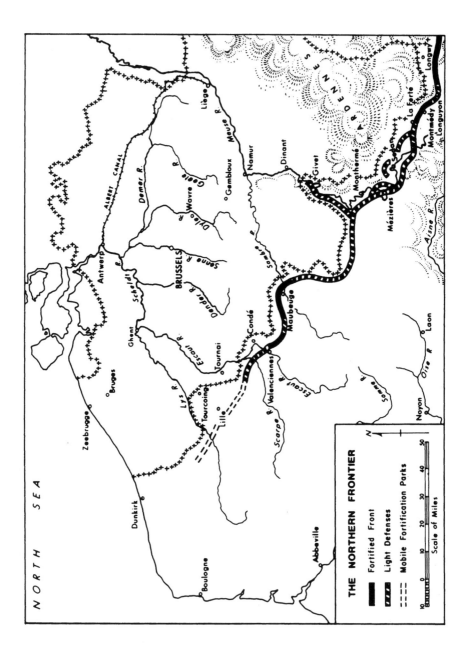

THE NORTHERN FRONTIER

▬▬▬ Fortified Front
▨▨▨ Light Defenses
- - - - Mobile Fortification Parks

Scale of Miles

defense of this region could only be obtained by penetrating into Belgium. The council agreed, and Pétain noted, "The situation will be such that we will have to go forward. . . . *A priori*, the defense of the northern frontier consists . . . essentially of seeking a stopping line in Belgium."[49]

In January 1927, the council addressed in detail the problem of defending the northern frontier. Though it never wavered from its preference to fight in Belgium, the council recognized that France might have to fight along her own northern frontier, rather than along the more favorable and easily defended river lines of her neighbor. Should the German army attack without warning and rapidly overrun the surprised Belgians, should the French army fall back on its own or be driven back to the Franco-Belgian frontier by the invaders, or should the Belgians unexpectedly elect to be neutral and allow the Germans to pass through their territory unopposed, France would have to defend herself along her northern frontier. While the council continued to prefer the option of going into Belgium, most of the debate concentrated on the contingency of having to defend France at the frontier rather than going into Belgium.

The problem of defending Lille illustrated the council's dilemma. Even though the area contained crucial industries, the council reluctantly concluded that the city could not be defended and had to be forward of any defensive line if France had to defend along her borders. The army could mobilize reserves from the city, but after mobilization, the soldiers had to move to areas that could be defended. When the council considered establishing fortifications along portions of the frontier, Foch insisted, "A partial barrier serves no purpose. If you want to make a barrier, it is necessary to build it from Luxembourg to Dunkirk." Pétain agreed but asserted that some parts of the frontier were more important than others.[50] Though it was not implemented until several years later, the eventual solution for the contingency of defending the northern frontier emphasized the establishing of fortifications in the most likely avenues of enemy approach. When it made these improvements in the late 1920s and early 1930s, the French army built additional fortifications at Maubeuge and Valenciennes, with those at Maubeuge stronger than the others but none as strong as those on the northeastern frontier. The fortifications at Maubeuge impeded movement along the valley of the Sambre River, while those at Valenciennes did the same along the valley of the Escaut River. Both defensive areas, however, were considered security areas to be used by French forces that might be pushed out of or not permitted to enter Belgium; they were not intended to be a primary line of resistance.

The reluctance of the High Command to improve the northern fortifications surfaced markedly in May 1932, when the Superior Council met to discuss the defenses of the northern frontier. The president of the Senate army commission had sent a letter to General Gamelin, requesting that the use of fortifications be considered anew. He explained that the Germans had greatly increased the motorization of their forces. While he did not "renounce" the idea of fighting the battle in Belgium, he believed "precautionary measures" were necessary to protect the northern frontiers. General Weygand, the vice-president of the council, admitted the possibility of the Germans rapidly overrunning the Belgian defenses and suddenly appearing on the French border. In that case, he noted, it would be necessary to conduct a strong defense along the frontier. The council continued to oppose a system of fixed defenses along the northern frontier, and Weygand concluded, "The military frontier of the northern provinces is on the German-Belgian frontier." When the discussion turned to whether defense of the northern frontier was "possible" with fortifications, the minister of war finally concluded that the council was hostile to fixed fortifications on that frontier.[51]

When the president of the Senate army commission sent another letter, this time demanding that fortifications be constructed, the council met in June 1932 and again considered the problem of the northern frontier. The reaction of the council was somewhat different this time. The demand for fortifications had been accompanied by an offer of 250 million francs to pay for their construction. Gamelin explained that the suggestion of the minister of war was to accept the offer. The ensuing discussion ranged over a number of topics, including the deplorable status of the Belgian army and the condition of the French tank and antitank program. The council believed the problems of defending the frontiers could not be artificially separated from discussions about the potential ally or the weapons that might be used. The council finally concluded that if the additional credits were made available, they should be spent on accelerating the tank program, increasing the number of antitank weapons, and reinforcing the fortified regions in the northeast. They should be spent on these requirements before they were spent on additional fortifications along the northern frontier.

The council then considered what should be done if the government refused to abandon the fortifications project. When Weygand posed the question within the context of whether the council favored moving forces forward for conduct of a defense in Belgium, or organizing a system of permanent fortifications in France, the council voted seven to six that French forces should move into Belgium. Ironically, both Weygand and Gamelin, who were more sensitive to political whims than most of their colleagues, supported building permanent fortifications in France if the government insisted.[52] Despite the clear opposition of the council to the extension of fortifications across the northern frontier, the minister of war, Daladier, decided to devote 250 to 300 million francs to the defense of the north. Although the improvements were not begun for another year, their impending start did not alter the High Command's preference to go into Belgium.

In 1934, France began Daladier's complementary program, which was designed to strengthen the northern frontier defenses but not to frighten the Belgians into thinking they were being abandoned to the Germans. Additional fortifications were added to the previously strengthened Valenciennes and Maubeuge sectors in the valleys of the Escaut and Sambre rivers, and the Maginot Line on the northeastern frontier was extended around Montmédy from Velosnes to La Ferté. Light fieldworks were begun along most of the northern frontier from near Sedan to a point east of Lille. Mobile fortification parks extended from the end of the light fieldworks, to the west toward Dunkirk. While the army intended to rush the barrier materials in the parks forward into Belgium, it recognized that they could also be used along the northern frontier, probably more easily than they could in Belgium. If an emergency need appeared, the combination of prepared fortifications and pre-stocked barrier and defensive materials could ensure a stronger defensive effort than otherwise would have been available. Nonetheless, the military hierarchy continued to focus primarily on preparing the army to rush forward and conduct a position defense along the river lines in Belgium. From their perspective, the improvements on the northern frontier were probably little more than a momentary diversion to satisfy the civilians and permit the army to get on with its other preparations.

Throughout the 1930s, the council often discussed the risks of the Belgian maneuver. In January 1933, Gamelin noted the problem of having to wait for the Belgian government's approval before the French army could enter Belgium.[53] In May 1933, Weygand remarked that if the French army did not have time to reach the German-Belgian frontier, he would be happy to have fortifications along the French-Belgian frontier.[54] In March 1939, Gamelin said that after entering Belgium, the first task of the French army would be to "collect the remnants" of the Belgian army. Later, it would assume the offensive with the British.[55]

The May 1933 meeting of the Superior Council summarized the major problems encompassed in defending France's frontiers. When Weygand formally posed the question of whether the French army should establish a continuous front along all its frontiers, thereby "guaranteeing the integrity of the national territory," a lively discussion ensued. Generals E.F.X.L. Hergault and H.J.E. Gouraud noted that France did not have a continuous front on the northern frontier, and Weygand observed that this was also true of the northeastern frontier. When Daladier attempted to define the term "continuous front" as the establishing of covering forces along every frontier in order to permit mobilization, General Gouraud complained, "This can only result in establishing a linear front." Pétain observed that it was impossible to have a continuous front if one were to have depth, but "the defensive battle cannot be conducted without depth." The council finally approved unanimously the question originally proposed by Weygand, but only after the term "continuous front" was deleted and replaced with "defensive front." The council also approved unanimously the need to go into Belgium. Gamelin explained that the German-Belgian frontier was only eighty kilometers long, while the northern French border was two hundred kilometers long. If there were any doubts among the members about the wisdom of going into Belgium, they were not expressed in this meeting.[56]

Throughout the 1930s, the requirement for moving forces rapidly into Belgium played a prominent role in French war plans. Plan D, which was in effect from April 1933 to April 1935, foresaw the movement of forces into Belgium as soon as the order was given. Since the French army could not move forward until the Belgian government issued an invitation and the French political leadership agreed, crucial decisions remained completely outside the control of military leaders. Even though the French military leaders recognized the difficulty of obtaining such permission, the conviction that French forces *had* to enter Belgium overcame their fears. When the Germans announced in late 1934 their withdrawal from the disarmament conference and their intention to withdraw from the League of Nations completely, France rewrote her war plans (Plan D *bis*, which was in effect from April 1935 to January 1938) and organized her forces for an even more rapid movement into Belgium. Following the retreat of the Belgium government into neutrality in 1936, after the remilitarization of the Rhineland and an apparent shift in the balance of power, the problem of entering Belgium became still more complex and more influenced by political uncertainties. The High Command, nevertheless, clung to its original intention to rush forward into Belgium.[57]

The issue that was not resolved, however, was how far and where to go into Belgium, and it became particularly problematic when that uncertain ally defected from her alliance with France. In the 1920s, the French and Belgians had agreed that French forces would relieve the Belgians along the border facing Luxembourg and Germany between Arlon (near Longwy) and Liège. The French would move another army forward to act as a reserve for the Belgian army defending a line beginning at Liège and following the Albert Canal to Antwerp. After the evacuation of the Rhineland, the Belgians altered the agreement between the two allies so that French assistance would not come automatically but would depend upon a Belgian request. The French altered their plans, since they foresaw the possibility—should the Germans launch an *attaque brusquée*—of their being summoned too late and thus being unable to reach the Belgian-German frontier. Consequently, they prepared to halt along a line short of that frontier; the new line ran from Givet along the Meuse River to Namur, through the open terrain of the Gembloux gap from Namur to the head of the Dyle River at Wavre, and along the Dyle to Antwerp.[58]

The picture changed dramatically when Belgium renounced her alliance with France. If Belgium appealed for aid prior to a German invasion, French forces might be able to join the Belgians in defending their frontiers. If not, the French had three other lines along which they might defend. The first of these, which was the farthest forward and the one mentioned above, ran from the French border at Givet along the Namur-Dyle River-Antwerp line. The plan for placing troops along this line eventually became known as Plan D, or the Dyle Plan. The second alternative was to defend farther to the rear along the French frontier to Condé, through Tournai along the Escaut River to Ghent, and then either directly to the North Sea, at Zeebrugge, or along the Scheldt River to Antwerp. The plan for placing troops farther to the rear along the Tournai-Escaut River-Antwerp lines eventually became known as Plan E, or the Escaut Plan. The final alternative was to defend along the entire French border to Dunkirk. Of these three alternatives, a defense along the Namur-Dyle River-Antwerp line would be about seventy or eighty kilometers shorter than the other two.[59]

By September 1939, the broad outlines of France's military strategy had been drawn and had been decisively influenced by geographic and resource considerations. While holding on the right, she would push forward on the left. How far she would push forward, however, depended upon luck and circumstances beyond her control. In the opening weeks of the Phony War, Gamelin preferred to be cautious and followed the Escaut Plan. Not until November, when he had evidence suggesting the Belgians intended to resist a German invasion, did he adopt the Dyle Plan. He chose the more ambitious strategy despite the suggestion of caution from Gen. Alphonse Georges about the importance of reaching the Dyle line before the Germans attacked. Georges's comment was not new, since the High Command had discussed the point on several occasions in peacetime. While the British initially expressed reservations about *any* move into Belgium, Gamelin discussed his plan with their top-ranking officers in early

November and managed to gain their consent. The formal adoption of the Dyle Plan came on 17 November, when the Supreme Council for the allies approved Gamelin's plan for a forward defense along the Dyle River, if time and circumstances permitted the allied army to move that far forward.[60]

The most severe criticisms of the plan concerned the possibility of linking up with the Dutch forces along the Scheldt River, or pushing across the river into Dutch territory. As early as 23 November, Gamelin mentioned the possibility of moving into the Netherlands toward Breda. Subsequent studies by French headquarters elicited strong objections from several high-ranking French officers, but none were as prophetic as those voiced by General Georges. He emphasized the danger of committing most of France's mobile forces against a "diversion," when the main German attack might come through the French center.[61] Despite these objections and others, Gamelin decided about a month before the German attack that the Dyle Plan would include the "Breda maneuver." In making this decision, Gamelin personally took the final step in the long evolutionary process by which the military hierarchy decided how to defend France's frontiers.

Except for the improvement of fortifications in the early 1930s and the final choice of plans, the major decisions about the defense of the frontiers were made by 1929. The need to protect crucial resources along the northern and northeastern frontiers, coupled with the effects of the 1927–1928 laws, led the military hierarchy to construct a defensive system, as General Debeney explained, which relied upon the French army at the beginning of a conflict "adopting a clear defensive attitude."[62] The Maginot Line provided additional strength to the forces along the northeastern frontier while furnishing protection to critical industrial and natural resources, but the initial post-World War I concept, potentially offensive, had been methodically molded into one of the defense. The Maginot Line was not designed to facilitate the offensive maneuver of large units as initially envisaged by Marshals Foch and Joffre. It was designed to protect the northeast, to canalize the Germans toward the northern frontier, and to permit the concentration and movement of large French forces into Belgium.

After World War II, Jacques Mordal argued persuasively that France had little choice but to construct a continuous front along the northern and northeastern frontiers of France. According to him, the "myth" of the continuous front was the belief after 1940 that France could have avoided defending along the frontier. With critical industrial and natural resources concentrated along the frontier and with the routes of communication all converging on Paris, Mordal saw no real alternative other than the construction of the continuous front.[63] His perception agreed with that of many members of the military before World War II, most of whom could not conceive of a defense of France that was not conducted along the frontiers. While they did not necessarily accept the idea of a continuous front, they believed France had to have every ounce of coal and iron and every factory she possessed to defeat Germany. Few doubted that frontier fortifications and the plan to dash into Belgium would fail to provide protection to France's vital industries.

The Maginot Line and the forward defense in Belgium were the result of the need to defend the frontiers, as well as being a logical product of French doctrine. Specifically, the concept for the Maginot Line emerged from a wide-ranging and complex assessment by the military hierarchy of the best method for defending the vulnerable frontiers. In that sense, the Maginot Line was a result and a reflection of French thinking, not a "cause" for military leaders to think the way they did. The army's faith in firepower, the methodical battle, and the strength of the defense coincided completely with the defensive system which evolved in the 1920s and came into fruition in the 1930s. The mission of the army evolved into one of initially protecting the integrity of the national soil and later gaining the final victory. This was incorporated into French war plans after 1935, which stated that the mission of the mobilized army was to maintain the "absolute integrity of the fortified front" and to "parry the maneuver of the enemy" around the "wings of the fortified front."[64] Unfortunately, the final step in France's planning—the Breda maneuver—depleted France's reserves and left her with little to parry a thrust through her center.

Had there been no requirement to protect the critical resources along the frontier, the organization of the French army and the final strategy may have been very different. The army may have found the potential of large, mobile, mechanized formations more appealing. With the obvious vulnerability of the resources close to the border, however, large armored formations seemed inappropriate. They could not create an impenetrable barrier, and their very mobility promised that crucial areas could pass to and fro from friendly to enemy hands. From the French perspective, the main advantage of large formations, especially those proposed by Charles de Gaulle and Paul Reynaud, lay in their ability to act as "an instrument of political intervention,"[65] not in their ability to protect the frontier regions. Moreover, the idea was reminiscent of the infamous Plan XVII, for the armored forces might charge into Germany without a clear objective.[66]

Unfortunately, the requirement to rush forces forward into Belgium also did not favor the development of armored forces. Rather than seeing a need for tank units, the French foresaw a need for much greater motorization of the infantry and artillery units that would be moved forward. They consequently led the world's military in motorizing their forces. Cavalry units also received special consideration. The High Command considered them ideally suited for moving rapidly into Belgium, providing security for the remainder of the force, and fighting against superior enemy forces. The cavalry could accomplish an economy-of-force mission and guard the infantry-heavy forces as they occupied their positions. Since it could fulfill an important defensive mission, its modernization was easier and its adoption of modern tanks was much more rapid than other French forces. Though they had the capability, the French did not plan on using their cavalry as an offensive force.

A large armored corps with numerous tanks, especially a professional unit, was thus almost superfluous from a strategic viewpoint. It could not maintain the integrity of the national territory, and its maneuvers would unavoidably yield critical regions to an attacking enemy. Motorized infantry and mobile cavalry received a higher priority. The crucial resources and the frontier could best be defended by relying on the doctrine of the defense, the methodical battle, and firepower. Covered by an impenetrable curtain of fire, the industrial resources could continue to serve the voracious wartime needs of the military.

In comparison to the argument for mechanized forces, the argument for fortification along the northeastern frontier seemed more logical and appropriate to the French military. Ironically, while the popular perception is one of futility, the fortifications performed reasonably well in the actual fighting and much better than the armored divisions. Except for the piercing on 13 May 1940 of the defenses along the Meuse River near Sedan (which consisted only of casemates and no major fortresses), the first attack by the Germans against the Maginot Line itself occurred on 16 May. It was directed against the isolated fortifications at La Ferté on the extreme western end of the line. The defenses at La Ferté consisted primarily of two blockhouses, which had been built as part of the 1934 program and were not as strong or as extensive as the earlier generation. The configuration of the terrain also made it difficult for one blockhouse to cover the other. Despite this inferior construction, the Germans managed to capture the blockhouses only after three days of hard fighting, from 16 to 19 May, and with the support of large amounts of heavy artillery and high-velocity 88mm fire. Having witnessed the strength of the forts, the Germans did not continue their attacks on the Maginot Line until almost a month later. Nevertheless, they did attempt to exploit the propaganda value of having captured one of the fortresses.

Less than a week before the French surrender, the Germans renewed their attacks on the Maginot Line but concentrated on the relatively weakly defended portions. On 14 June, they attacked into the interval along the

Sarre River, which consisted primarily of blockhouses and casemates. Except for the extremely dry summer, much of this area would have been inundated and made impassable with water. Similarly, many of the French defenders who would have fought in this interval had been moved south by the High Command to reestablish defenses. On the second day, the Germans broke through the French defenses and rushed south. Similar events occurred with the 15 June crossing of the lightly defended Rhine, and with the rush on the same day through the plateau of Marville (near Longuyon) when the defenders retreated. In contrast to these successes in the lightly defended sectors, the Germans failed miserably in their attempts to seize the fortresses at Fermont (east of Longuyon), Michelsberg (northeast of Metz), and Haguenau (in the eastern portion of the Lauter fortified region). At Haguenau and the other fortresses in the Lauter sector, the Germans concentrated overwhelming infantry, artillery, and aerial forces. Although they directed 88mm fire at the apertures, massed heavy 355mm and 420mm artillery on the fortresses, and employed numerous Luftwaffe attacks on the defenders, the Germans accomplished little from 19 to 23 June. They finally ceased their ground attacks but not their artillery fire on the defenders. Despite surrounding the defenders and despite the use of massive force, the Germans failed to capture a single major fortress before the armistice on 25 June. They succeeded only against the lighter defenses.[67]

Similar results occurred on the Italian frontier. Although fortifications in this area had been neglected in the interwar period and were much less extensive than those in the northeast, Mussolini accomplished little after declaring war on 10 June in an attempt to exert some influence over the armistice ending the war. The Italians suffered thousands of casualties and captured only a few advance posts.

In June 1940, the last units to surrender in the French army were those occupying the fortifications in the northeast and in the Alps. In the northeast the fortress troops continued to resist, despite being surrounded and having little or no contact with the High Command. After suffering heavy casualties while attempting to capture the fortresses, the Germans informed the French government (which had surrendered) that if this resistance continued, they would bombard the city of Lyon. General Georges sent three officers forward to arrange the surrender of the Maginot Line, and a week after the cease-fire the fortress troops lowered the French flag and marched into captivity.[68] Had the troops defending along the Ardennes done as well, the fate of France might have been different.

Admittedly, a Maginot Line complex did emerge in France before World War II. The psychological security gained from the existence of the

fortifications provided comfort to many Frenchmen who believed themselves secure behind the supposedly impregnable line. Such misplaced
faith, nonetheless, did not detract from France's security, for the errors
occurred in strategic thought and tactical doctrine, not in protecting the
frontiers. The northeast fortifications simplified France's problems of
defense because greater attention could be paid to the unprotected areas
of the frontiers. Whereas France had previously feared an attack anywhere
along her frontiers, she now had relatively strong defenses along the most
vulnerable portions, and she had reduced the number of German options.
In that sense, there is little or no evidence to support the contention that
the Maginot Line weakened the French army, although it may have promoted a false sense of confidence.

The Achilles' heel of France's defenses was the vulnerability of her natural resources along the frontier, not the presence of the fortifications. Her
mistake was not building the Maginot Line on the northeastern frontier;
her mistake was preparing inflexibly and stubbornly to charge into Belgium and the Netherlands, while failing to prepare adequately for the possibility of a rapid enemy move through the Ardennes.

CHAPTER 4

The Legacy of the Past

As the French organized their military forces for the possibility of war, they could not escape the legacy of World War I. Few of them could forget the powerful emotions and traumatic losses associated with the 1914–1918 years, and neither the nation nor the army could separate their examination of current issues from their past experience. Even though they did not prepare from 1919 to 1939 to refight the Great War, they prepared to fight a war surprisingly similar to the battles of 1918, which had been more mobile than the static ones of previous years.

The effect of World War I on France is difficult to overestimate or overemphasize, since the terrible losses of that war scarred her very soul. With a male, military-age population of 13,350,000, she mobilized an army of 8,410,000, including North African and colonial forces. Of these, 1,122,400 were killed or died during the war, 3,594,889 were wounded, and 260,000 were missing. Hence, 1,382,400 French soldiers, or 16.4 percent of those mobilized, were dead or missing in the war. Of those killed or missing, 36,600 were officers, and of the 100,600 infantry officers mobilized, 29,260 (or 29 percent) died. Furthermore, 6,000 of the 17,000 graduates of the military academy, St. Cyr, who served in the war were killed. Since most were junior officers, more than half of the most recent graduates fell in the war.[1] These terrible losses were written indelibly into the minds and memories of the military; the scars of the war could not be forgotten.

After 1918, France's leaders believed that many of the losses occurred because of her unpreparedness in 1914 for a long war. She had entered the war virtually as a novice in the organization and conduct of modern mass warfare; she left a veteran. As a consequence of her great suffering at the beginning of the war, France became convinced that she had to make elaborate preparations for another long total war and that she had to use her every resource if she were to emerge victorious. Implicit within these convictions was the recognition that her success had come not so much from the excellence of her equipment and doctrine as from the scale and scope of her effort. The experience of World War I thus became a crucial factor— as explained in chapters 2 and 3—in her postwar efforts and in her decisions about relying on reservists and conscripted forces, about mobilizing her entire national economy, and about protecting her frontiers.

The wartime experience also left an indelible impression on the French about the nature of battle. The change in view is evident when one compares the 1913 and 1921 instructions on the employment of large units. French military leaders no longer believed they could achieve a swift, relatively painless victory. The 1913 manual emotionally asserted, "Studies of the past have borne their fruit: the French army, returning to its traditions, admits in the conduct of operations no law other than that of the offensive."[2] Reflecting the trauma of the war, the 1921 instructions contained numerous adjectives that are bluntly descriptive of modern battles but are not to be found in the 1913 regulations. Such words as "annihilating," "crushing," and "irresistible" simply do not portray the view of war or perception of firepower that existed in 1914 but pervaded the military after 1918. France's generals after 1918 may not have been "peace-loving" in the negative sense some writers have suggested, but they were definitely not "warmongers." Nor were they as anxious for war as they had been in 1914.

The brutal experiences of the Great War convinced the military leaders that the errors made in that war should never be repeated. Most officers agreed that one of the most terrible mistakes had been excessive emphasis on the offense. Before World War I, French doctrine had been greatly influenced by questions of morale and by the perception that the army had lost the Franco-Prussian War because it was too passive and unaggressive. Following the defeat in 1871, many officers and soldiers carefully read the writings of Col. Ardant du Picq, which emphasized the will to fight. His writings influenced many to view morale as more important than matériel. On the eve of the war, the French army molded its men and units for offensive action and extended the ideas of du Picq to their most extreme point in the *offensive à outrance*.[3] According to the aggressive doctrine, commanders were to break the enemy's will to fight by a ferocious infantry assault. The attacking French troops would supposedly gain a superiority of fire with the rapid and intense fire of the 75mm cannon and with a hail of bullets from the charging soldiers. When they closed with the enemy, the infantrymen would throw themselves into his ranks and finish the fight with the bayonet and with superior courage.

After the war, military authors and lecturers often noted how officers had bravely but senselessly stood fully erect under enemy fire in the initial clashes. Although the supposed creator of the offensive doctrine, Col. Louis Loyzeaux de Grandmaison, had never suggested such foolishness, numerous officers had often disdained the seeking of cover, even though they were in the full view of the enemy. And they had wasted their lives and those of their men in romantic but senseless charges against strong enemy defenses. A German near-victory and huge casualty lists soon revealed that more than courage and audacity were needed; officers began employing their units more carefully and seeking cover and protection. They had learned a not easily forgotten lesson about the difficulty of overcoming a strong defense.

If personal experiences were not enough, statistical data from the war demonstrated the safety and strength of the defense. Among others, Gen. Frédéric Culmann compiled the losses from selected battles in World War I from July 1917 to November 1918 to illustrate the strength of the defense. Using English, French, and German losses on the western front, he concluded that in a strongly conducted defense, casualties would be much lower than those suffered in an offensive battle (about 35 percent as compared to 65 percent).[4] While General Culmann's main purpose was to demonstrate the importance of artillery, his data clearly reflected the ability of a defender to extract a heavier toll from an attacker. Such data could be used to disarm any critic who argued for a return of the offensive spirit, and many officers did not hesitate to use the data in this manner or to accept conclusions drawn from it.

From their analysis of the war, the French concluded that increases in firepower had greatly altered conduct on the battlefield. They reflected this belief in the oft-quoted slogan "*puissance du feu*," or "firepower," and its corollary, coined by Marshal Pétain, "*le feu tue*," or "fire kills."[5] The maxim of the killing power of fire became a truism piously repeated by practically every French military writer. Again and again, one reads, "The great lesson of the war of 1914–1918 was the pre-eminence of fire."[6] The maxim also appeared in military manuals. In the 1921 instructions on the employment of large units, the report to the minister of war by the committee charged with writing the new manual stressed the importance of firepower. It emphasized the crushing nature of that fire and its almost "irresistible" nature. The committee believed the basic nature of the offense and the defense had changed because of the overwhelming destructiveness of fire on the battlefield, and the instructions stated, "Fire is the preponderant factor of combat."[7] While the 1913 instructions had claimed that battles were above all contests of morale,[8] the emphasis on morale was no longer supreme in the 1921 instructions. The French firmly believed that firepower kills. This belief differed from that of 1913 as night from day.

Other important lessons came from the war, especially those relating to the use of the methodical battle for concentrating massive fires against the enemy. General Gamelin, for example, derived several conclusions which— not surprisingly—supported his strongly held belief in the necessity for centralized control. When queried in 1936 about the major lesson of the war, he responded that the war had demonstrated the need for the higher commander to keep a "firm hand" on the conduct of the battle.[9] That observation reflected his own experience as an aide to Marshal Joffre at the battle of the Marne and his exemplary performance as a general staff officer. In the 1930s he applied those lessons toward ensuring an even greater amount of authority for larger unit commanders.

The tactical and operational methods used by the French in the methodical battle had evolved throughout the war and had been the product of numerous innovations and adjustment. In contrast to the almost frivolous wasting of lives and matériel in the beginning of the war, the carefully controlled, methodical battles in the final phases of the war saved lives and concentrated overwhelming matériel superiority against the enemy. They enabled the French to use a series of strong hammerblows against an enemy without exposing the attacking troops needlessly, and to attack by moving from one defensive position to another. They also enabled them to maintain artillery supremacy in the counter-battery struggle and in the massive employment of indirect fire against an entrenched enemy force. By the war's end, the advantages of the system were apparent to almost everyone. The perfected methods that came out of the war, particularly those used in 1918, thus had the compelling logic of success behind them. In the safety of peacetime, another reason for emphasizing the methodical battle became evident. While a stabilized or fairly static fight might appear after the opening days of a war, victory could be obtained only by concentrating forces for an attack and by driving the enemy into an untenable position.

Throughout the interwar period, authors constantly reminded the army of the nature and the methods of the Great War. For example, military journals were saturated with articles on the Great War. The *Revue d'infanterie* is an excellent journal for analysis of focus, since its contents before World War I and those before World War II can be compared. Using the contents from January 1928 to December 1938 to define historical subject, one finds that sixty-five articles analyzed battles in the war of 1914–1918, twenty-three covered colonial campaigns, one reviewed the war in Ethiopia, one described the Spanish Civil War, and nine discussed ancient campaigns (meaning not in the twentieth century). Of the nine articles discussing ancient campaigns, five were devoted to the Foreign Legion, three to sieges or blockades, and one to historical passages of the Rhine River.[10]

This widely circulated and highly influential military journal thus devoted about 60 percent of its historical studies to discussions of World War I or campaigns similar to those of that war. Since the articles on colonial campaigns and the Foreign Legion were concerned with "colonial" rather than "total" wars, there was practically no discussion of battles in "total" wars that were dissimilar from the pervasive model of the Great War. The resulting historical distortion contrasts sharply with the contents of the *Revue d'infanterie* before World War I. Despite the army's concern with the battles of Napoleon as it focused upon maneuver and the offensive, less than 2 percent of the historical articles in that journal from July 1905 to July 1914 actually dealt with the era of Napoleon. Over 41 percent discussed the Russo-Japanese War, and 32 percent discussed the Franco-Prussian War of 1870–1871.[11] The contents of the journal were strikingly more balanced in that era than in the interwar period.

While there were some exceptions to military thinkers concentrating on the Great War, dramatically different conceptions did not emerge from these studies. For example, in the 1930s General Loizeau, of the War College, lectured and wrote on "maneuvers of the wing" and analyzed such great captains as Hannibal, Frederick II, Napoleon, Moltke, Schlieffen, and Joffre.[12] Nonetheless, his tactical methods envisaged little more than a set-piece battle in which a mass of French troops swept around an enemy flank into his rear. This is precisely what Pétain envisaged in his conception of a strategic maneuver from behind the Maginot Line, and remarkably similar to what Gamelin tried to do in the opening days of World War II. Loizeau's studies offered no real alternative to the many others available, for he parroted the common belief that the rupture of an extended front "will always be a difficult accomplishment and will exact heavy losses." At the same time, Loizeau saw the maneuver of armies as being possible only in the first encounters of war, before enough manpower and matériel had been mobilized to "permit the immediate establishment of strong, unbroken fronts in the principal theater of operations."[13] Whether he was conscious of the similarity or not, his conception of mobile battles bore a remarkable resemblance to those of August and September 1914 on the western front.

World War I thus provided innumerable lessons to the French about the nature of modern warfare and the methods most appropriate for its conduct. Needless to say, veterans of that war dominated the hierarchy of the army after 1918. The commonalty of their experience in the trenches on the western front ensured fairly widespread agreement on the main lessons to be drawn from the war. In comparison to the Germans, who had fought mobile battles in eastern Europe and who had used somewhat different methods on the various European fronts, the French army did not have as diversified an experience.[14] Had they been willing to look beyond their own experiences, the French might have been able to discern other techniques at variance with those used on the western front, but they preferred to concentrate on the methods that had provided them victory in 1918.

The supreme irony in the military's misuse of history after 1918 springs from the scathing criticism of pre-1914 thinkers for having misused history.[15] Much of the criticism in the interwar period focused on the performance of the War College, which had had great influence over prewar doctrine. Critics of the disastrous 1914 offenses sometimes identified several instructors who had served at that institution from 1880 to 1900 as the initiators of the fallacious thinking which distorted French military doctrine. Col. Louis A. G. Maillard, a professor of tactics at the War College from 1881 to 1890, supposedly began the distortion with his great focus on maneuver in the Napoleonic battle.[16] Col. Henri Bonnal, Maillard's successor, also relied strongly upon history and preached the importance of maneuver and the offensive. He was a prolific writer, and he reacted sharply to those who dared to argue that modern combat, such as that between the Boers and the British in South Africa from 1898 to 1902, offered new lessons about firepower that rendered the lessons of the Napoleonic campaigns less useful.[17] When the future Marshal Foch taught at the War College as the successor to Bonnal, he too followed the lead of Maillard and elaborated on the importance of manuever and the advantages of the offensive. Although he acknowledged the destructiveness of modern firearms and artillery, he misunderstood how their effect had strengthened the defense and instead stressed the importance of the decisive attack.[18] Despite the effect of these ideas, Foch was rarely criticized after 1918 by military writers, obviously because of his esteemed and powerful position in the French military. In the eyes of numerous observers after the war, the ill-fated efforts of Maillard and Bonnal at the War College had led France to disaster. Many believed that the improper study and use of history had produced a false doctrine and that proper study of other pre-1914 battles would have yielded better results.

After 1918, the French sought to avoid misusing history again. The military formally emphasized their avoidance of a doctrine based solely on principles derived from historical studies. At the War College and the Center of Higher Military Studies, they made special efforts to prevent the appearance of another Maillard or Bonnal, even though they did not publicize their efforts. The organization of the curriculum was altered from its prewar form to ensure a balance between historical studies and practical exercises. After the War College reopened, General Debeney, as part of his commandant's duties, cancelled the course in military history, strategy, and applied tactics, and replaced it with two different courses, one in military history and the other on the general staff, strategy, and tactics.[19] This change agreed with the idea that historical studies broadened the intellectual perspective of officers, and that practical exercises demonstrated specific concepts or teaching points. Thus strategic and tactical doctrine supposedly would not be based on unchanging lessons of history but would be deduced from evidence existing in the present, not the past. Historical studies could contribute to the development of doctrinal concepts, but they would not be the main method used.

Within its classrooms, the War College relied after 1919 on a balanced program of practical exercises and historical studies. The practical exercises, which were essentially case studies, were designed to develop the military judgment and understanding of the student officers and also to expose the student to the theory or basic concepts of certain operations. As General Loizeau told the students at the War College in 1932, practical exercises were not intended to provide the student with a "stereotype, a staunch mandarin theme or a model solution, that one could apply to every circumstance. . . ."[20] The students were told that if they considered numerous examples in which the mission, situation, terrain, enemy, and friendly forces available varied, this would develop their "qualities of decision, judgment, and initiative . . . , and would lead them to think as a leader, with their good sense, their character, and their personality."[21] The practical exercises were designed to develop these qualities through a consideration of numerous case studies, and solutions to tactical exercises often included the disclaimer "The enclosed orders are given only as examples. They constitute neither the sole possible solution for the situation studied, nor a scheme applicable to every analogous situation."

At the same time, historical studies remained important. The French recognized that exposure to theory was insufficient, and that the officer needed to learn how to think and decide for himself before he was placed in a combat environment. Military history contributed to this endeavor. In order to create a sense of realism and to illustrate the complexities of the battlefield, most of the exercises at the War College and the Center of Higher Military Studies were based on historical problems. The fear, the confusion, the unknown, and the disorder of the battlefield could not be duplicated in the classroom, but the student could gain a sense or a flavor of these complicating factors through an exposure to history.

Military history also served as a vehicle to illustrate the nature of change in warfare. One lecturer at the War College described history as a "precious source of education."[22] Another officer, who was also a historian, stated, "Military history is able to furnish, in times of peace, a base that permits the building of a strategic or tactical doctrine, and then defining the changes that must be accomplished if new conditions are going to appear."[23] In short, the French viewed military history as a useful tool for introducing the officer to the problems and realities of war, while also exposing him to the dynamic changes that occur during war. By understanding the events of the past, the officer might be better prepared for the events of the future.

As one surveys the lectures given at the War College, however, it is evident that the separation of history from the present did not always occur. Virtually all the examples used in lecture halls were those of World War I. When Lt. Col. René J. A. Prioux (the commander in 1940 of the cavalry corps in the Gembloux gap and, later, of the First French Army) gave his lectures on the cavalry at the War College, he relied on historical examples as the models for the conduct of particular types of operations. Most of his examples came from World War I. When he studied offensive operations, all his examples came from that war. These examples were not used to illustrate the limitations of the cavalry but to prove that the horse had played an important part in World War I and would therefore continue to play an important part in the future. When Lieutenant Colonel Touchon (the commander in 1940 of the Sixth Army) gave his lectures on the infantry, every operation he discussed was illustrated with a historical example from World War I. When Col. Paul M. J. de la Porte du Theil gave his lectures on artillery, he separated his historical examples from the major portion of his lectures, but he still frequently used comments about operations in the recent war to support the points he made in his lectures.[24] The same methods used by these three men were used widely by other instructors in the War College throughout the period. The separation of historical studies from practical exercises theoretically continued, but the historical example often provided the evidence to "prove" the validity of the practical exercise or of the point being made by the instructor.

At the same time, the French utilization of history yielded unintended results. For example, an unfortunate distortion occurred when pre-World War I thinkers were criticized, since such criticisms emphasized the failures of the past and failed to question whether similar errors of a different type might be happening again. Military lecturers and writers in the late 1920s and 1930s often identified the 1815–1870 era as a period of "decadence" crowned with the ignominious defeat of 1870–1871, the 1870–1895 era as a period of reflection and accomplishment, and the 1895–1914 period as the unfortunate era of the offensive. They stressed the failure of the *offensive à outrance* thinkers to understand the effects of firepower on the battlefield and meticulously pointed out the mistakes made by the pre-World War I High Command with history. In a lecture at the War College, Lieutenant Colonel Touchon quoted the commission that wrote the 1875 regulations for the infantry: "The commission admits, as a veritable *axiom, the preponderant importance of fire.*" He then explained that the understanding of the preponderance of fire became "increasingly blurred" in subsequent regulations, and that this "terrible mistake" resulted in a "nearly absolute contempt for enemy fire" in August 1914. The error had been made in the past, and the officer concluded that current regulations correctly recognized the preponderance of fire. In the same series of lectures he railed against those whose "scorn for fire is no longer punished with death . . . ," and he cautioned the student officers against letting considerations about fire intervene into their work and study only as an abstraction.[25] He failed to recognize that he had permitted the concepts of maneuver and audacity to become abstractions.

Military instructors or authors also criticized specific techniques used before World War I, and often included these criticisms in supposedly nonhistorical lectures. They especially emphasized the misuse of artillery. The French recognized that their artillery's effectiveness had been decreased during World War I because they had not made adequate efforts before the war to gain the maximum benefits of indirect fire and to enable the fires of several batteries to be massed on a single target. Instead of developing techniques of indirect fire and methods of coordinating fires from separate batteries, the French had concentrated before the war upon the close support of the infantry during the attack with rapid fire from closely following artillery units. Their doctrine foresaw no need for lengthy preparatory fires before an attack.

In a 1925 course in artillery tactics at the War College, the lecturer stressed the failure of prewar thinkers to understand the proper role of artillery. He commented favorably on the 28 May 1895 manual on the *Service of Armies on Campaign*, the field service regulations, which emphasized the necessity for counter-battery fire against enemy artillery, but which also recognized the absolute need to prepare the objective being attacked by the infantry. After discussing the evolution of French thought on artillery over the next decade, he harshly criticized the manual of 21 December 1913 on the *Service of Armies on Campaign*: "There was no PREPARATION BEFORE the attack; there was simply SUPPORT DURING the advance."[26] In 1930, another lecturer observed that the disastrous operations of 1914–1915 demonstrated the erroneous approach of the 1913 manual.[27] Without artillery preparation, the enemy would simply hide in their trenches until the initial artillery fire ceased; then they would emerge and direct withering small arms and machine-gun fire against the attacking troops. In his explicit defense of existing artillery doctrine, the lecturer neglected to question whether technological advances might have altered the World War I methods for preparation or support by artillery.

Lecturers at the War College and writers on artillery techniques described the numerous improvements made during the war, including a growing emphasis on preparation by the artillery, an increasing capability to gain surprise and accuracy because of technological and methodological improvements, and the growing importance of heavy artillery in the destruction of enemy trenches and fortifications. At the same time, they usually noted the superiority of the Germans in heavy artillery and the superiority of the French in light artillery when the war began. One lecturer observed in 1925 that the number of heavy artillery pieces had increased in the French army from 308 in 1914 to 5,340 in 1918, eighteen times larger than the earlier figure. He concluded, "The present doctrine . . . is based upon this dominant idea: the importance in combat, in the defensive as well as in the offensive, of the SURPRISE concentration of the fires of POWERFUL ARTILLERY."[28] There was little doubt, the lecturer suggested, that the only way the "powerful artillery" could be sufficiently concentrated was through the methodical battle and centralized control, and that this conclusion had come from the hard lessons learned during the war.

The implication is clear. Historical studies immediately prior to World War I, according to postwar thinkers, had supposedly ignored the true lessons to be learned from history. Members of the French military reassured themselves that they would not make the same mistake again, that they had learned the "correct" lessons. Such assurances became an integral part of most lectures presented at the War College and Center of Higher Military Studies. Unfortunately for France, harsh criticisms of the past and reassuring praises of the present failed to substitute for rigorous dissection and analysis of past and contemporary methods. In a sense, the French were victims of their own history. They had tried mobile methods in 1914 with disastrous results; they were not going to try them again without having abundantly clear evidence of their effectiveness.

And the best examples of effectiveness came, in the French view, from the Great War. Despite the intention to separate the study of military history from the teaching of theory or doctrine, the models for military operations, as they were taught at the War College and the Center of Higher Military Studies, invariably came from the World War I experiences of France. The most widely used example of offensive operations was the battle of Montdidier, in August 1918, where the First French Army, commanded by General Debeney, delivered one of the final and most important blows of the war to the German Army. Occurring on what Gen. Erich Ludendorff termed the "black day" of the war for the German army,[29] the August attack represented a turning point in the conduct of French operations and inaugurated the form of open warfare that characterized the last months of the war. At the same time, the First French Army was composed primarily of French units, with only the American First Division making an indirect contribution to the

French success with its capture of Cantigny in June 1918. As such, the battle represented an extremely important achievement of French units and demonstrated to student officers the glorious French achievements during the Great War. Additionally, since General Debeney reestablished the curriculum at the War College, the inclusion of a successful and important battle fought by the army he commanded obviously added to the influence he held over the students.

For those studying tactics and battlefield command, the battle demonstrated important features of planning and execution. General Debeney commanded a force of fifteen divisions (divided into four corps), supported by more than sixteen hundred pieces of artillery and two battalions of light tanks.[30] The initial concept was for a limited offensive by the French First Army to support an attack by the Fourth British Army under Gen. Sir Henry Rawlinson, but the First Army commander recognized that his army had an opportunity to strike a deadly blow at the Germans to his front. Rather than make a massive frontal assault, Debeney resolved to strike suddenly, with a French corps on his army's left flank (near the Fourth British Army's area of attack), and seize key terrain that would destroy the equilibrium of the enemy's defenses. This attack would be followed by a second attack in the same general area and would encourage the Germans to reinforce those threatened areas. As the enemy reinforced his units on the First Army's left flank, the French would attack with two corps from the right flank of the First Army.[31] As Debeney had planned, the battle began with four French corps on line, and despite difficult resistance, the attackers soon swept aside the enemy defenders on the French left. The sudden commitment of the two corps on the army's right flank caught the Germans off guard, and they could not respond to the unexpected maneuver. The result was a major defeat of the Germans.

To study this battle, students at the War College used a book written by Maj. Marius Daille, an assistant professor of military history at the War College. They often spent four days at the end of May in their second school year walking the Montdidier battlefield and studying the details of the attack.[32] Major Daille's analysis of the battle warned the students that Napoleonic methods no longer applied to twentieth-century warfare. For Napoleon, the object had been to bring decisive fires and forces against a single point, to make a break in enemy lines, and to destroy the cohesiveness of the enemy force. In the Great War, the French had tried similar methods but had taken enormous casualties at Artois, Champagne, and Verdun. Such methods had never achieved a breakthrough. To explain this failure, Daille argued that despite initial successes, an attack would eventually slow as the direction of attack became apparent and enemy reserves came into action. Instead of becoming larger, the breach would progressively become smaller as the attacking forces pushed forward, and the friendly line ultimately would resemble a "narrow triangle" on the terrain, pointing into the enemy's position.[33] Within this triangle, concentrated enemy fire from the flanks would preclude movement and eventually the attacker's advantage would dissolve. Repeated and powerful attempts to punch through the enemy's defenses could only lead to the creation of "pockets," or salients, which were vulnerable to concentric artillery fires and enemy counterattack. Daille concluded that success in breaking through an organized defensive position would remain for a long time beyond the ability of an attacking army.[34]

For Major Daille, the offensive by the First Army in 1918 demonstrated a new method for overwhelming an organized defensive position without attempting a breakthrough. He identified the new method as juxtaposing separate and powerful attacks along converging lines. The enemy could not reinforce one area without weakening another, and thereby could not prevent the attacker from pressing forward. While attacking across a broad front might appear to be a linear attack, it actually consisted of concentrating powerful means along several areas in a defender's line and then attacking. This type of operation ensured that the attacker was always stronger than the defender, and that the defender could not mass sufficient forces to halt the attack. Clearly, this had been Debeney's method at Montdidier, and it had succeeded beyond his wildest hopes. While Daille preferred the broadly based attack, he did not reject completely the straightforward attack in which a new action was superimposed on top of another as it faltered. The single-axis attack sought depth. According to Daille, it could be used in the opening of a campaign before a strongly organized defensive front had been established or in striking at the boundary between different armies or the armies of different nations.[35] The main theme of Daille's study, nevertheless, was that the battle of Montdidier provided the formula for future success—attacks across a broad front with concentrated efforts at selected points.

As a model of the methodical battle, of centralized control, and of effective planning and execution, the battle of Montdidier became the common basis for officers to study and learn doctrine. For the instructors, the battle provided a clear model of a relatively mobile attack against an enemy in prepared defensive positions. At the same time, the attack was divided into three operational phases, and the battle illustrated the successive steps of preparation, attack, and exploitation. Within the planning for the divisions and corps in the battle, several bounds and phases had been foreseen for the operation. These controlled the forward movement of the divisions and prevented accidental bombardment of French units by friendly artillery. The step-by-step execution of the plan for what was in fact a complicated operation had enabled the French to achieve success despite being faced with excellent German forces commanded by Gen. Oskar von Hutier. Following World War I, the official doctrine on how to conduct an attack bore a remarkable resemblance to the battle won by General Debeney in 1918. In every sense the battle had tremendous influence over the army's thinking.

Similarly, the battle of La Malmaison in October 1917 was recognized widely as the model for attacks with limited objectives. Even though the French preferred a less restrained attack, they believed a limited attack could serve useful functions. Such attacks could improve an unfavorable situation, could gain objectives the enemy could not recapture except by a concerted and costly effort, or could destroy enemy forces without using the enormous means normally required for a more extensive attack. The battle amply demonstrated the problems of counter-battery fire and the difficulty of infantry and artillery coordination, but instructors at the military schools rarely noted the exceptional nature of such a tightly controlled operation as La Malmaison.

Thus, while accusing their predecessors of improperly using history, members of the French military after World War I committed the same error. They selectively gleaned examples from the historical evidence and thereby improperly used history to support previously formed conclusions.[36] Remaining tied to a historical method which continued to seek and cite infallible lessons or models from the 1914–1918 war, the army could not see beyond those lessons or models. The primitive level of historical analysis by the army is surprising, but the evidence is clear.

One interesting result of the ill-fated attempt not to misuse history and of the reaction against pre-World War I thought was a temporary backing away from the idea of principles of war. Though France never condensed her principles into a terse list of single words, each comprising or suggesting a larger concept, she did include in her 1913 regulations on the conduct of large units a list of "fundamental ideas." The list included:

"The conduct of war is dominated by the necessity of giving a vigorous offensive impulse to operations."

"It is necessary to mass initially and to act offensively as soon as the forces are massed."

"The battle, once begun, should be pushed completely, without reservations, to the extreme limit of the forces."

"In war, all the command decisions should be inspired by the will to take and to keep the initiative in operations."[37]

Clearly, these "fundamental ideas" embodied the doctrine of the *offensive à outrance*. With that theory in disrepute after World War I, the commission charged with the writing of the 1921 instructions decided not to furnish a list of principles of war. Its introductory report explained its hesitation to offer "vague formulas" too far removed from reality.[38] The commission did not reject principles or "fundamental ideas;" it simply avoided the issue.

By 1936 principles were no longer avoided and were again included in the new instructions, but they differed remarkably from the 1913 list. The instructions explained that the commander should be inspired by "directing principles which, by their generality and permanence, are the foundation of all operations in war." The instructions then explained that the commander should:

> "——impose his will on the enemy . . . ";
> "——conserve his liberty of action . . . ";
> "——divide his forces between diverse missions according to the rules of a strict economy [of force]. . . ."[39]

While the earlier list strongly emphasized the offense, the list in 1936 emphasized principles that might apply to the offense or defense but that supported the methodical battle and placed the greatest emphasis on the role played by the commander. Ironically, the 1936 principles proved to be as fruitless as those of 1913.

Having convinced herself that she had extracted the proper lessons and principles from the war, France did not zealously search for new ideas or methods from the experiences of other nations. The best example of this concerns the misinterpretation of German infiltration tactics. The essence of these new tactics, which were created in 1917,[40] was rapid advancement and infiltration by small infantry groups. The tactics emphasized maneuver more than fire, but they also relied on recent improvements in artillery which permitted the artillery to work more closely with the infantry. Specially trained "storm" battalions led a division in the attack. To increase the offensive capabilities of the handpicked and well-led soldiers, they were armed with light machine guns, light trench mortars, and flamethrowers. In the attack, they usually bypassed enemy strongpoints, leaving their destruction to succeeding waves of attacking infantrymen.[41] The objective of the "storm" battalions was not destruction of enemy soldiers; rather, it was to seek penetration by attacking the weak spots of the enemy's resistance. The new tactics could result in a breakthrough of enemy lines, but France saw no special value in rapid penetration and continued to place the greatest value on fire.

French military thinkers did not believe the German tactics had had a major effect in the final phases of the Great War. In a 1925 lecture at the War College on the evolution of artillery, an instructor discussed the German attacks in 1918 but ignored their tactical innovations. He argued that the most important reason for the return of the war of movement in 1918 was the newly regained ability to mass artillery fires suddenly and without warning. According to him, when the Allies went on the offensive in July 1918, the Germans no longer had the capability for surprise, because they had great losses in equipment and personnel.[42] Thus, the lecturer concluded that the German attack failed because they had lost their capability to maneuver fire, and that the Allies had won because they had been able to regain the initiative by reestablishing their fire superiority.

A military historian at the War College found another weakness in the German tactics. He was extremely critical of General Ludendorff's forming of special shock units for rupture and maneuver. The remaining units supposedly diminished in fighting value, strength, and morale as the struggle continued. He concluded that this loss of quality throughout the German army, for which Ludendorff bore responsibility, explained the eventual military defeat.[43] Lt. Col. Gaston C.G.A. Duffour, who was later to become the commandant of the War College, also argued that the initial German successes came from the employment of elite "gladiators," but that their final defeat came from the inability of the remaining portion of the German army to maintain the pace of the battle and to extend the gains made by the elite soldiers.[44] The segregation of the German army into elite and non-elite units may have resulted in initial gains, but over the long term this separation had seriously weakened its fighting capability.

The French understanding of German infiltration tactics and their relation to the breakthrough during World War I was thus distorted by the French preference for fire rather than maneuver, their rejection of elite or specially trained units, and their reaction against pre–World War I thought. They did not notice how the Germans let the small units set the pace of movement, and they continued to prefer having a higher headquarters restrain any units moving forward too rapidly. They interpreted the German methods of World War I from the perspective of their own doctrine and failed to see anything fundamentally different from their own tactical methods. Hampered by their misinterpretation of this important advance in tactical methods, the French went blithely on their way. They spent little or no time studying the 1917 battle of Riga on the eastern front, even though no less an authority than General Buat, chief of the General Staff, had argued in several books that the tactical "formula" used in France in 1918 was first applied in this battle.[45] The artillery officers who did study and cite the battle emphasized the importance of the surprise use of artillery in the battle, rather than the infantry tactics or the closer infantry-artillery coordination. They believed the pace of forward movement had to be set by the artillery and by the higher headquarters, not by the infantry. Similarly, in their historical analyses of the campaigns of 1918, almost all studies analyzed the Allied defensive effort from March until July and the offensive effort from July until November. Comparatively little effort was expended in the study of the German experience with mobile warfare on the eastern front in World War I, or in its offensive methods on the western front from March through July 1918. By failing to grasp the significance of the German tactical innovations and the different German experience in the war, the French misunderstood one of the most important advances in twentieth-century tactics, one that was to be an essential link in the evolution and creation of the blitzkrieg concept.

The great focus on their own experience in World War I also led the French to overlook evidence from other wars that may have suggested alternative methods. In the twenty years from 1919 to 1939, soldiers of France fought in more battles than those of almost any other country. Ironically, the circumstances of the largest of her limited wars outside the continent of Europe—the Rif campaign of 1925–1926—proved to support a methodical, massive approach.

For France, the Rif war began in April 1925, when dissident tribesmen under the leadership of Abd el Krim in Spanish Morocco and northern French Morocco attacked French outposts along the boundary of the mountainous and almost inaccessible region known as the Rif. This area lay mostly in Spanish Morocco but extended south into the French zone. The North African tribesmen numbered over 100,000 regular and irregular soldiers and possessed numerous modern artillery pieces, machine guns, and rifles. They apparently had a small number of European mercenaries or French army deserters as advisers. Between April and July, the Rif contingents overwhelmed the few French defenders, and hardly a day passed that France did not lose a post or some terrain.

Marshal Louis Lyautey, the resident general of French Morocco, initially planned on sending two "mobile columns" against the attacking tribesmen. These columns were the main elements in the traditional French approach to colonial warfare: a heavily armed, highly mobile force that could rush into enemy territory to seize key terrain or important enemy leaders and thereby end the fighting in a swift, sure strike. The forces could operate in converging columns to conquer specific objectives or in parallel columns to sweep a large area, or could conquer successive zones of an area with either converging or parallel columns. The mobile column usually consisted of professional soldiers and French Legionnaires and had been the standard tactic used successfully against lightly armed, hostile tribesmen for almost a century. That such methods might work against the well-armed Rif, who had a nearly European capability for battle, was unlikely. When Marshal Pétain was consulted on the problem, he recommended a more careful approach in which a large, heavily armed French force—in close cooperation with the Spanish—would halt the enemy's gains and would then push forward "methodically" until the enemy's vital centers were menaced.[46]

The French government responded to Pétain's recommendations by placing him in charge of military operations, by withdrawing troops from the Rhineland and transferring them to Morocco, and by providing Pétain with the requisite air, tank, and artillery support. The presence of conscripted soldiers and the units from the Continent who had not been trained in the ways of colonial warfare contributed to Pétain's preference for a tightly controlled battle. Before long, the outgunned tribesmen found themselves being subjected to massive amounts of fire from airplanes, tanks, armored cars, artillery, and machine guns. Despite the emphasis on massive fire support, the battles were not simply a replay of those of World War I. The mobile rebel forces had the huge Sahara territory in which to operate, and the French had to rely on their own mobile forces. Their two tank battalions were divided into independent tank companies, and the platoons, reduced to three tanks, became accustomed to operating by themselves. The operations, nevertheless, were vast affairs in comparison to the traditional mobile columns.[47]

By the end of October, the French had recovered all territory lost to the tribesmen, and the Spanish had captured Ajdir, the former capital of Abd el Krim. After the rainy season began, the French halted their offensive and Pétain returned to France, having turned the tide and confident of victory in the near future. During the final battles in 1926, the Rif tribesmen proved to be as helpless and vulnerable as before when faced with the overwhelming French firepower.[48]

Thus the Rif campaign witnessed the emergence of no new lessons that might have suggested new methods of warfare. If any new ideas did emerge, they met the automatic response that the war had had a special character and that its methods were not necessarily transferable to the European continent. Instead, the war had demonstrated that Continental methods, with some adjustment because of terrain and enemy considerations, could be applied successfully in limited wars. One French officer said that even though this was somewhat analogous to using "a hammer to crush a fly," no one could doubt its success.[49]

The success in Morocco in 1925–1926 did not prevent the French from using mobile columns in other colonial areas. Even in the Rif campaign, the French had continued to use widely separated defensive posts, supported by mobile groups to rescue or resupply them. During the fighting in Syria in the early 1920s, the French relied strongly on mobile columns. In the 1931–1933 campaign for the pacification of Morocco, the French did not use the methods of the Rif campaign but returned to their traditional mobile columns. Methods designed for the European continent obviously required heavy, unwieldy columns that lacked the mobility of the native tribesmen. Against the scattered and lightly armed dissident tribesmen, mobility obviously had greater value than firepower, since lightly armed Europeans probably still possessed more firepower than their opponents.[50]

Consequently, the various colonial conflicts exercised little or no influence upon the French approach to war. The colonial experiences did not suggest that French doctrine was inappropriate for a massive struggle against Germany. Instead, it suggested that methodical techniques could be applied outside Europe. The French nevertheless recognized that such methods might be pointless against a more lightly armed enemy or at a different time. The key lesson seemed to be that the methods had to be adapted to the circumstances. The French thus gained combat experience from the several campaigns and demonstrated the tenacity and courage of their soldiers, but they did not acquire new insights into more advanced or different methods.

Had they pursued the topic energetically, the French could have gained some important details about mobility and training from the Sino-Japanese War that began in 1937. One retired general officer analyzed this war for the *Echo de Paris*, a conservative newspaper that often covered military developments. After describing the weaknesses of China and the better preparation, equipment, and leadership of Japan, the officer observed that victory usually goes to the best prepared. After considering tactical lessons, he concluded, "More than ever, an attack badly prepared and insufficiently supported by fire is bound to fail."[51] As with the various colonial campaigns, France did not detect any evidence suggesting her methods were not the most advanced and best possible.

The Spanish Civil War of 1936–1939 might have been the proving ground to demonstrate the inadequacy of the old ideas and of France's concept of war. Of all the wars after 1918, it represented the greatest opportunity for gleaning new ideas, since aviation and tanks played a key role in several battles. The military recognized this and showed a keen interest in the events and developments of that war. Nevertheless, the reader can almost sense a feeling of relief in the French military community when the

Revue d'infanterie was able to announce in November 1938 that Gen. J.C.M.S. Dufieux, the inspector general of infantry, had concluded:

> The Spanish experience has confirmed the lessons of the Great War on two important points: (1) Tanks should be employed in mass and on a front as extended as possible . . . ; (2) They [tanks] are not able to fight without the support of the artillery and the support of the infantry, which is alone capable of clearing and occupying terrain.

The *Revue d'infanterie* could only remark, "Note the return to classic ideas. . . ."[52] For France, the "classic idea" remained the model of the tightly controlled battle derived from World War I, developed in the 1921 instructions, and strengthened in the 1936 instructions.

Within France's concept of total war, the methodical, deadly battle survived. No new method or counter-evidence could overturn or replace that concept. Vacillation on the nature of future warfare, which had been common in French thought in the early 1930s, subsided in the late 1930s. In the opinion of many in the military, French doctrine had been corroborated by the Spanish Civil War. In addition, their careful study of the French experience in World War I reassured them of the correctness of their approach, and their analysis of other wars seemed to demonstrate support for their methods, rather than to refute them or cast them in doubt. Very few members of the French military questioned the carefully designed and logically constructed doctrine. Doubts about the doctrine emerged after rather than before the defeat.

Despite the disastrous results from improperly using history to reinforce preconceived beliefs, the French did not set out to use history to "prove" their doctrine and did not create a conscious, directed program to make historical studies the servant of those seeking data to protect their assertions. The failure was more one of preoccupation than of commission—or even of omission. Of all the accusations made against the French military hierarchy, however, perhaps none is so devastating as this one, that the leadership was unable or unwilling to disassociate its thinking from the perceptions of the past. Part of the roots of the failure to modify completely the concept of war is to be found in this tragic error. By overreliance on the historical example as the correct model for the conduct of operations, the French doctrine for the methodical battle was molded more by past experiences than by technological or conceptual advances, or by careful analysis of more recent wars.

CHAPTER 5

Firepower and the Methodical Battle

In formulating their doctrine, the French military placed the greatest emphasis on the requirement for firepower. This preference came not only from the recognition that the army was unready for a war of great movement in the beginning of a war but also from the demonstrated efficacy and destructiveness of modern weapons during and after the Great War. Additionally, the reliance on firepower supported the need for the methodical battle, fought offensively or defensively. The vast "curtains" of fire could only be coordinated and delivered through tightly centralized, successive actions in which the artillery played a large role. The doctrine resting upon these beliefs may ultimately have been inadequate, but it possessed a logic and coherency rarely found in modern armies' thinking.

Both the 1921 and 1936 instructions stressed the importance of firepower. In its description of firepower as the "preponderant factor of combat," the 1936 edition repeated verbatim the 1921 manual but added the phrase that fire "destroys the enemy or neutralizes him."[1] The 1936 instructions repeated another sentence which had appeared in the 1921 edition: "The attack is the fire that advances, the defense is the fire that halts [the enemy]."[2] Fire permitted the maneuver or movement of infantry which remained the "queen of battle." Whether from tanks, aviation, artillery, gas canisters, or the infantry, supporting fires assisted the infantry with the "principal mission of combat."[3] Thus the machines of war appeared as the auxiliaries of the infantryman.

While the French had complete faith in the destructiveness of firepower, they did not ignore the importance of morale. Both the 1928 and the 1938 infantry regulations stressed that matériel forces alone were not sufficient; they argued, "Among the survivors, it is morale which determines success."[4] Morale remained important, but it was not envisaged as blind or foolhardy courage in the face of the enemy. The French believed the commander had to impose his will on that of a demoralized enemy. Once this occurred, victory could not be far away.

The army continued to accept the possibility of an offensive. The 1921 and 1936 instructions emphasized the decisive nature of the offensive and the protective nature of the defensive.[5] A commander could impose his will on the enemy on either the defensive or offensive through the wise use of firepower. By assuming the defense, French forces could furnish themselves a protective shield behind which they could bleed an attacking enemy and prepare themselves for the final victorious offensive. The killing fires of the defense would be used to repulse the attacks of the enemy or to inflict heavy losses, while the offensive would chase the enemy from his position, rout his combat dispositions, and destroy his combat potential.

Military thinkers and writers often mentioned the importance of the offensive. General Loizeau, director of instruction and then assistant commandant at the War College from 1930 to 1932, described the defense as a "necessary form of operation, so long as it contributes at the least cost to the success of the offense."[6] For Loizeau and almost the entire French army, the defense could contribute to the success of an operation, but only an offensive could gain final success. Numerous officers castigated the idea of an army prepared solely for the defense. In one instance, a July 1936 note from the chief of the military cabinet of the war minister labeled the charge that the army had assumed a passive, defensive attitude as "nonsense."[7]

The recognition of the importance of the offensive, nevertheless, did not mean that the French army always preferred to attack rather than to defend. The perception of an immense amount of fire available on the battlefield contributed to the army's belief that the defense was stronger than the offense. The employment of automatic weapons and artillery permitted the establishment of "curtains" of fire that would extract a terrible toll from any attacker. For an attack to succeed, France believed a larger number of troops and matériel were required than for the defense. The 1921 instructions argued that the offense was favored only after the "massing of powerful matériel means, artillery, combat tanks, munitions, etc."[8] A hasty attack against a well-prepared position would probably lead to failure, since the defender had the advantage and could inflict heavy casualties on an attacker. The only way an attacker could penetrate a deadly curtain of defensive fire would be to create a much greater concentration of fire with "three times as much infantry, six times the artillery, and fifteen times the ammunition."[9] Obviously, the complexity of such an effort limited the possibility of maneuver dramatically, and its coordination could most effectively be done through the use of the methodical battle.

The step-by-step approach to battle became a vital part of French doctrine. In its analysis of the "Characteristics of Battle," the 1921 manual stated:

The offensive battle thus presents itself under the form of successive actions of force, preceded by indispensable delays for their preparation, and followed by periods of movement more or less long.

This concept was repeated almost verbatim in the 1936 manual, except the wording was changed from "presents itself under" to "assumes."[10] A certain "eclipse of the offensive sense" had occurred, for the army considered the offense to be the advancing of fire on the battlefield.[11] The advancing of the infantry by itself would be wasteful and useless.

Similarly, an eclipse of the maneuver sense also occurred. The French perceived maneuver, at any stage of a campaign, predominantly in the sense of moving units in order to have them deliver fire or of moving fire without moving units. They rarely emphasized the advantages of moving units to gain something other than an advantage in firepower over an enemy. That is, the doctrine stressed the physical destruction of the enemy's soldiers and equipment to destroy his will to fight, not the movement of a unit so it could have a decided advantage over the enemy, thereby weakening the morale and the cohesion of his units. For the French, the word "maneuver" did not necessarily mean movement. They often used the word to indicate the ensemble of actions by a unit in a specific period, or to outline the schema for the employment of an entire force, even if no movement occurred.

Reliance on firepower, according to the French, ruled against subtle maneuvers on the battlefield because of the difficulty in massing and controlling the matériel means. The 1936 instructions made the contradictory assertion "[A]udacious solutions . . . should be executed methodically."[12] This limited view of maneuver dominated their doctrine.

In the late 1930s, emphasis on the methodical battle and centralized control by higher-level commanders increased. The minister's report in the 1936 instructions explained, "The attack is the work of the army commander, applying the maximum means, strongly centralized in his hands, toward the desired direction." The manual added, "The concentration of efforts obtained by the centralization of command is the distinctive characteristic [of the attack]. . . ."[13] The battle remained a sequence of successive steps, and the tight control of the commander provided essential coherence and cooperation in every phase.

One apparent change in the 1936 manual appeared in its description of the relationship between the offense and the defense. It stated, "The offensive is the pre-eminent mode of action. . . . Only the offensive permits the obtaining of decisive results."[14] This sentence had not appeared in the

1921 manual, and Gamelin later asserted that Pétain had removed it from an earlier draft of the 1936 manual.[15] Despite the inclusion of the sentence in the 1936 instructions, and despite the implications of Gamelin's claim, the army's leaders had not become more offensive-minded and had not substantially modified the basic components of the 1921 doctrine. The change in wording did not entail a fundamental shift in the army's thinking. If anything, the greater firepower, larger logistics support, and more unwieldy units described in the 1936 manual made the argument for greater centralization and coordination even more compelling. A limited view of offense and maneuver continued to dominate French doctrine.

The introduction of new technology for motorization and mechanization also did not alter the doctrine substantially. The 1936 instructions explained that the new advances permitted a "certain acceleration of the rhythm of the battle."[16] The commission which wrote the manual, however, did not believe that the accelerated rhythm required the army to change its philosophical approach to command and control. Tragically for France, as the increased pace of warfare in the 1930s threatened to dissolve the ability of commanders to influence every action on a battlefield, the army remained committed to imposing order and regulating the disparate actions from above. The methodical approach continued to occupy its pre-eminent position in army thinking.

Throughout the interwar period, the key to the methodical battle and its frequent phases was the role to be played by the artillery, since the "successive actions" were necessary to permit the forward displacement of the artillery during an attack. In World War I, artillery had caused the greatest number of casualties, and the French believed it would provide by far the greatest amount of support for the infantry in a future war. The control of the artillery's fires and their coordination with the movement of the infantry became the most obvious and compelling raison d'être for the methodical battle. The infantry had to operate under an umbrella of supporting and protective fires.

Having an effective artillery assumed a large importance, and following the Great War, the French army conducted several studies on the proper organization and role of the artillery on future battlefields. The confidence of the artillery in its having gleaned the important lessons from the recent war, however, is perhaps illustrated by the fact that it was the first to publish a regulation after the war. The 15 June 1919 regulation on the *Service of Artillery in the Field*[17] was a clear synthesis and distillation of the methods recently employed. The technical studies, however, envisaged several major changes.

One of the most important studies was done by Pétain's staff at the headquarters of the Armies of the East and was published on 24 February 1919. An important assumption of the study was that in a future war in which the opposing armies would be supplied with modern armaments and equipment, "[O]ne will not likely see reproduced the long period of stabilization which characterized the major part of the war of 1914–1918." The study noted that the strategic mobility of French artillery, or the "ability to make rapid displacements of important masses of artillery from one theater of operations to another," had been satisfactory in the war, and that this had been clearly demonstrated in 1918. As for tactical mobility, or the "ability of artillery to be displaced on the battlefield itself," the study found major problems, especially in the inability of the artillery to follow attacking units closely. The report noted that the cooperation of the various arms, which should provide the initial successes on a future battlefield, would soon deteriorate because of problems with the artillery's tactical mobility, and this would prevent complete exploitation of the initial gains. An offensive would lose momentum, and subsequent attacks would be made under less favorable circumstances than the initial attack because of the difficulties inherent in moving artillery forward. These observations reflected the World War I difficulties of transporting artillery across heavily damaged terrain on which recent battles had occurred.

The report suggested that future artillery weapons be able to move and be resupplied, "whatever may be the weather and state of the terrain." It offered the solution of mounting artillery on tracked vehicles. This weapon system would be especially appropriate on the more mobile battlefield foreseen for the future, since tracked artillery would have better tactical and strategic mobility.[18] Such weapon systems, however, were intended to accompany the infantry, not function as division or corps artillery.[19] Consequently, they would have been only a small part of all the artillery available in a large unit. The recommendation to create mechanized artillery eventually fell victim to budgetary problems, as well as to a loss of confidence in such weapons. A series of dramatic budget cuts into ambitious armaments programs for 1921, 1922, and 1923[20] seriously reduced any hopes for major improvements in mechanization of the artillery.

Ideas about creating a mechanized artillery, however, did not disappear completely. When the army tested the B-1 tank in 1931, the commission charged with studying the practical uses of the new tank concluded that it needed special artillery protection that was immediately available. Such protection could only come from artillery that closely followed the attacking tanks. The 1931 commission recommended a special "protective tank" for the B-1 tank that actually would have been a highly mobile, armor-protected, self-propelled artillery piece.[21] In the late 1930s, the same problem was addressed in another report on field exercises for tanks. This time the report was not so favorable, for it said such a vehicle must be "armored itself, in the manner of a veritable tank." It suggested that the best alternative was to provide an echelon of tanks to protect the artillery,[22] and it therefore completely reversed the 1919 recommendation that artillery be made more mobile so that it could follow moving forces. According to the study, the mobile tanks would be tied to the less mobile artillery. Though studies continued until the eve of the war, the army never seriously pursued the move toward mechanized artillery after the early 1920s. By the late 1930s, such support as existed in the army for increased mechanization had almost vanished.

The army made several attempts to increase the use of automotive equipment and to improve the mobility of the artillery. In 1928 it conducted a test in which a motorized and a horse-drawn artillery battalion competed to determine which method of conveying the artillery was most rapid. The two battalions were required to displace about ten kilometers and then open fire. The winner was the motorized artillery, which opened fire one-and-one-half hours before the horse-drawn battalion.[23] In subsequent years, the French converted an increasing number of artillery units to be either carried by truck or drawn by truck or tractor. A vast transformation, nonetheless, did not occur. When the army mobilized in September 1939, more than two hundred artillery regiments were formed, but only forty-four of these regiments were motorized or drawn by truck or tractor.[24] The great majority were drawn by horse. While there were some improvements in motorization and mechanization of French artillery, the recommendations of the 1919 report from Pétain's headquarters were not followed. Dramatic improvements were not made in tactical mobility.

The failure to improve mobility might have been overcome by the development of more modern artillery pieces. The replacement of the 75mm cannon with the long-range 105mm howitzer, especially the 105L-model 1936 Schneider with a range of 16 kilometers, could have permitted increases in mobility simply because its greater range reduced the number of artillery displacements. The long-range 105mm had essentially the same mobility as the 75mm, but the target effect was better, since shell fragments from its exploding rounds scattered over a larger area. Though the older, short-range 105mm had about the same range of the 75mm (7–9 kilometers), the long-range 105mm clearly was technically better with greater range and target effect.

The 1919 report from Pétain's headquarters, however, downplayed the advantages of the 105mm. It acknowledged the greater range and effect on target, but it added that two 75mm projectiles weighed the same as one 105mm projectile and that two projectiles had a better chance of hitting and destroying a target than did one. The report also noted that a soldier would be more "impressed" by a hundred rounds of 75mm than he would by fifty rounds of 105mm. A final comment was that the rate of fire of the 75mm was twice that of the 105mm piece.[25] The report clearly favored the 75mm over the 105mm artillery piece. When the Central Committee on Artillery, under General F. G. Herr, discussed the merits of the 105mm howitzer, it considered the 105mm as a possible replacement for the 155mm howitzer in the artillery battalions with the division. The committee did not consider it as a replacement for the 75mm cannon.[26]

In subsequent years, the 75mm gun retained its dominance, especially in the division's artillery. General Maurin, who had been inspector general of artillery after World War I, explained in a meeting of the Superior Council of War in 1936 why the Germans but not the French could adopt the 105mm howitzer. "The situation of the German army," he said, "can be explained by the fact that it began at zero. We have major quantities of the 75[mm], and moreover this gun proved itself from the beginning to the end of the Great War."[27] The 5,412 pieces left over from World War I could only serve to underscore the validity of retaining the 75mm as the major artillery piece with the division. By May 1940, the French army had 5,667 such cannon.[28]

Discussions occurred in the Superior Council of War on wider use of the 105mm piece, but the council did not consider replacing the 75mm with the 105mm howitzer. In February 1936, the council recommended that a 105mm battalion with the short-range howitzer be placed in each infantry division, while one 155mm-howitzer battalion from the division be sent to the general reserves and one 155mm and three of the 75mm battalions retained at the division. In 1938, the council decided to withdraw the 105mm battalion with the long-range model guns from the light mechanized divisions and the cavalry divisions. It argued that the longer-range 105mm howitzer should be with the corps rather than the division.[29] The result of these discussions was to place the shorter-range 105mm howitzers with the division, but to retain the longer-range 105mm howitzer at the corps. Throughout these debates, the 105mm was not designed or intended to replace the 75mm cannon in the French army. As the Herr report had suggested, the shorter range models of the 105mm howitzer actually replaced the 155mm howitzers.

The short-range, flat-trajectory 75mm cannon remained the major artillery piece at the division, while the 105mm howitzer normally operated under corps control for counter-battery or long-distance missions. In a December 1938 meeting of the Superior Council, Gamelin argued that the 75mm was superior to the 105mm howitzer for employment in armored divisions, since it was more mobile and could follow movement better.[30] When the first French mechanized cavalry divisions were formed, they were equipped with two 75mm battalions and one 105mm battalion with the short-range howitzers. As far as the French were concerned the 75mm cannon was completely adequate, but the events of 1940 were to demonstrate that the greater range of a modern 105mm was essential on a rapidly moving battlefield.

By the beginning of the battle of France in May 1940, the number of 105mm howitzers in the French arsenal had increased. According to the figures given by Gamelin, France had 159 of the long-range and 410 of the short-range 105mm howitzers out of a total of almost 11,000 pieces of artillery. Other than the increase in 105mm pieces and the elimination of obsolete pieces, there were no major changes in French artillery between November 1918 and May 1940.[31] The only technical improvements were in the shape of the projectiles and in the powder, both of which gave the rounds slightly greater range. There was apparently little or no concern that major changes might be needed. For example, one officer noted with pride in February 1940, "Our artillery system is not essentially different from that of the last war."[32] This officer had recently presented the status of the army's armament program to the army commission of the Chamber of Deputies, and his favorable analysis of French artillery failed to note any need for improvements.

Key aspects of French artillery doctrine derived from the World War I experience also never changed, and this absence of doctrinal progress was probably more important than the lack of technological progress. The French had begun the war with a doctrine emphasizing rapid and intense fire in close support of the fighting units; they ended the war with a doctrine emphasizing massive fire under the centralized control of division and higher commanders. General Herr, who was the inspector general of artillery at the end of World War I, noted after the war that if the commander should decentralize his artillery, he would lose all control over the battle and become "disarmed." By passing control of the battle to his subordinates, the higher-level commander could not maneuver and the battle would degenerate into a series of "isolated, disjointed, sterile local actions."[33] The 1926 *Regulation on the Maneuver of the Artillery* warned,

"Finally, the systematic allocation of all artillery to subordinate elements must be avoided; it constitutes an abdication of command."[34]

The concept of centralization of artillery assets corresponded with the concept of maneuvering masses of fire. Such control was necessary for maneuver, according to the French, since it enabled the commander to concentrate his fires on the decisive point in the battle. The "decisive point," however, was one defined by larger unit commanders, and maneuver was viewed in terms of the movement of larger units, rather than smaller ones. While the French recognized the need for decentralization during an advance, the military leaders preferred to have a major portion of the artillery for the use of larger unit commanders. In an October 1922 meeting of the Superior Council of War, Pétain referred to some of this artillery as a "strategic reserve, suitable for great displacement."[35] It provided a means for the higher-level commander to exercise a major influence over the battlefield, and it was a readily available reserve that could be rapidly shifted to another area. The requirement for such a reserve meant that a major portion of the artillery was long-range, heavy artillery under the control of corps and higher commanders, the need for which had been one of the important lessons of the war. But the use of the artillery in this manner favored a more stable battlefield, rather than a highly mobile one, and it viewed mobility predominantly from its strategic, rather than its tactical, aspects. The resulting distortion of tactical and strategic mobility can be seen in the 1926 artillery regulations, which cited railway artillery as having "great" tactical value because of its ability to "occupy and leave" a position rapidly.[36]

One critic of the organization of the French artillery was Marshal Foch. In a meeting of the Superior Council of War in October 1926, he stated, "It will be necessary from the first for the divisional artillery to be the most important, then corps artillery, then the general reserves."[37] Even though most artillery was located at the division, a great degree of control was retained by the corps and army commanders. The French emphasis remained the reverse of that suggested by Foch, and after the war, General Gamelin noted that while the French had fifty-six regiments of artillery in general reserve in May-June 1940, the Germans had nowhere near that amount of artillery in reserve.[38] By misunderstanding the reluctance of the Germans to retain artillery as a reserve, he had misunderstood the thrust of German doctrine toward mobility, penetration, and decentralization, and had missed an extremely important difference between the French and German employment of artillery. The large number of artillery regiments remaining in the reserve was a clear reflection of French doctrine, since they preferred to allocate a major portion of their artillery for control by higher-level commanders and intended to fight a tightly controlled battle.

Centralization affected not only the overall allocation and control of artillery but also the ability of tactical units to receive immediate and responsive artillery fire. This effect can be seen in the relationship among the units being supported, the forward observers, and the commander of the artillery unit. According to French doctrine, forward observers did not have to accompany the units being supported. They remained to the rear, observing from a vantage point, so that they could identify centers of enemy resistance. A 1929 course at the artillery school at Metz explained that as soon as an observer collected information about a potential target to his front, he passed the information to the artillery battalion, where the commander decided if rounds would be fired. If the commander decided not to fire, or if he believed more artillery support was needed, he passed the information to his higher headquarters, where that artillery commander decided if his unit would engage the target.[39] Apparently the unit being supported had little influence over the artillery fires it received. Such methods placed the greatest emphasis on massed fires, favoring larger units rather than smaller ones.

According to French doctrine, even those requests for direct support fires which were supposed to be immediately available were not passed directly from the unit needing support to the artillery units. Requests were passed from a battalion to the commander of a regiment, and if the request affected only his units, he passed it to the artillery—probably a battalion—supporting his regiment. If it affected the maneuver of units in another regiment, he passed the request to division headquarters,[40] which could place all the artillery fire of the division on a target, if it desired. Clearly, this was an extremely slow and complex process that did little to accelerate action on the battlefield. Where the emphasis should have been on providing immediate fire, French doctrine emphasized massed fires on targets identified by higher-level commanders.

A new artillery regulation appeared in May 1936 on controlling artillery fire,[41] but the new manual concentrated on improving the rate of fire by using preplanned firing points. It did not substantially alter the complicated system of observers and fire control, in which the major problems resided. At the same time, the use of preplanned firing points was more suitable for a stable battlefield, than for a highly mobile one. In an era when vast improvements were suddenly appearing in tactical mobility, the French failed to recognize the need to revamp their fire-control system to permit greater mobility for supported units.

When one compares other nations' artillery doctrine to that of the French, it becomes apparent that the French should have been more sensitive to the apparent weaknesses of their doctrine. For example, in World War I the U.S. Army recognized some of the difficulties of applying French artillery doctrine in mobile battles. The Americans entered that war without having artillery equipment and doctrine as modern as that of the Europeans, and the American Expeditionary Force (AEF) relied greatly on the allies for trainers, methods, and manuals. Despite Gen. John J. Pershing's disdain for trench warfare and demand for open warfare and the offensive, the Americans willingly absorbed the technical methods for artillery that focused on relatively static battles. The AEF received particularly valuable assistance from the French as it trained and organized its field artillery units. When the first American units entered combat, they were primarily equipped with French artillery pieces, and they applied French artillery doctrine almost exclusively. Virtually all American artillery manuals were English translations of French manuals.

By the late spring of 1918, as the Americans began participating—with difficulty—in the more mobile operations associated with the German spring offensive, they began modifying the doctrine taken from the French and began developing their own methods. By August 1918 the Americans concentrated almost solely on open warfare, and criticism of the French methods surfaced. To make the artillery more mobile, flexible, and responsive, they proposed placing artillery well forward and making prompt movements when an attack began; concentrating artillery fire on strong points while the infantry pierced weak points; avoiding the use of rigid firing timetables except under exceptional circumstances; improving communications between the infantry and artillery; using observed fires rather than relying on unobserved fires on points on a map; and moving as rapidly as possible toward the decentralization of artillery assets.[42]

Although the Americans were, relatively speaking, novices, without the experience and expertise of the French with indirect fire artillery even at the end of the war, they had recognized the inherent rigidity of the French doctrine. The French had been superb teachers, but the impatient Americans had quickly sought their own methods, and in doing so they moved away partially from the centralized methodical battle to a more decentralized mobile battle. This recognition of the inadequacies of the rigid doctrine underlines the inadequacies of that doctrine and suggests that the French should have been more aware of its weaknesses.

French doctrine, nevertheless, continued to emphasize the centralization of artillery assets and their allocation according to the highest commander's designs. Of all the combat branches, the artillery was by far the most conservative, for it clung tightly to the methods employed in World War I. This intransigence became a major factor in the inability of the French to change their doctrine fundamentally. In that sense, French artillery was designed, as General Maurin explained, to provide the "framework"[43] for the other branches, and its failure to change ensured that the other branches remained captured within that framework.

The restrictions imposed by artillery requirements can be seen in the French doctrine for the offense. In his early 1920s course on general tactics at the War College, Col. Felix A. Lemoine described the different phases of an offensive battle. When the attack began, the infantry advanced one to two kilometers before halting in order to readjust the artillery fire. The attack again commenced, and after advancing one to two kilometers, another readjustment of fire was necessary. In order to control the advance of the infantry and to ensure artillery support, a number of intermediate objectives were established which corresponded to these advances of one to two kilometers. After a total advance of the infantry of about four to five kilometers, a displacement of the artillery and a halting of the infantry advance was required. This displacement ensured that the infantry remained under the cover of the artillery and did not go beyond its maximum range. For control purposes, the maximum advance was sometimes limited to three or four kilometers before the artillery began its displacement by increments. One rule of thumb was given by an instructor at the War College when he stated that the distance of the advance ought to be half the maximum range of the artillery supporting the attack.

The time required for the artillery to displace forward could be as much as three or four hours. This amount of time was based upon the time required to displace light artillery (the 75mm cannon), but the heavier pieces such as the 155mm gun required much more time. Col. M.N.G. Alexandre stated that displacing from a 155mm battery position required one-and-one-half to two-and-one-half hours under average conditions, but it could require as much as ten hours. Similarly, getting the battery into a new firing position usually required two hours, but it could require eight to ten hours. Thus, the interruption of supporting fire from the 155mm artillery could range anywhere from five to as much as twenty-four hours. Heavier artillery pieces required even more time.[44] Interestingly enough, these figures were based on the premise that the work of displacing was done by highly trained personnel. With less thoroughly prepared artillerymen the time required became much greater. But under the French concept, the methodical battle remained a step-by-step process that ensured maximum cooperation between the infantry and the artillery.

Another aspect of the methodical battle affected by the artillery was consideration of the proper frontage of units in the attack. Instructors at the War College explained that the dimensions of an attack front depended upon the amount of available artillery. One of the rules of thumb derived from World War I was that the depth of an attack was approximately equal to one-half the width of the base of departure. This depth preferably included the emplacement of the enemy artillery, but it was not so deep that it required major displacements of friendly artillery. The 1921 manual on the tactical employment of large units said that the attacking front had to be "at least equal to its base of departure." It argued, "If the front of the attacking troops begins to shrink appreciably, the range of artillery permits the enemy to execute concentrations of fire under the pressure of which the attack is weakened and finally is stopped."[45] The 1936 manual on the employment of large units continued to argue that the greater the initial frontage upon which an attack is made, the more considerable the results obtained from it.[46] Wide frontages, however, required great masses of artillery and prevented the concentration of an overwhelming amount of combat power along an enemy front to achieve a rapid breakthrough.

The method for computing the necessary amounts of artillery appeared in the form of an annex to the regulations of 31 October 1917 on the offensive action of large units in battle and was entitled "Annex No. III of May 10, 1918." This annex offered guidelines for the density of artillery in three general situations, including a maximum, an average, and a minimum allotment. For example, the average allotment of light artillery was one piece per eighteen meters, with six days of fire, while a heavy allotment was one piece per fourteen meters, with eight days of fire. In his 1925 artillery course at the War College, Colonel Alexandre used these simple density figures to determine artillery requirements for an attack frontage of about fifteen kilometers. According to his computations, 465 batteries of all types were required in the example he was analyzing. In 1930, Colonel de la Porte du Theil used the same method for computing the necessary density of artillery for an attack, even though he noted that the annex had expired and that current regulations did not include the density figures.[47] The use of standard densities continued until the eve of World War II. In 1936–1937 and 1937–1938, an instructor at the War College gave his students density requirements that were essentially the same as those derived from World War I.[48] In 1938–1939, a lecturer again presented the World War I density figures, but he warned the students, "It would seem that the weak allocation of 1918 may be insufficient today." He added that if one attacked with a smaller density of artillery than that of 1918, one was risking a "bloody failure."[49]

Standard densities were also used for specific types of fires. A rolling barrage, for example, that was two hundred meters wide required one battalion of artillery consisting of three batteries. Consequently, a division supported by its own artillery and the artillery of another division could attack on a front of about two thousand meters. This frontage compared favorably to the average frontage of World War I, which had ranged from eighteen to twenty-five hundred meters. In 1929–1930, at the War College, an instructor noted that even when a division was not attacking a fortified front such as that encountered in 1916–1917, a density of three to four battalions of artillery per kilometer of front was essential. With its organic five battalions of artillery, a division's maximum front would still be from twelve to fifteen hundred meters.[50] Anything beyond this forced the commander to break down his operation into different phases.

Although phases might be required because of the terrain or because of the enemy situation, the French believed that obtaining the proper density of artillery was the prime factor in determining whether to employ phasing. When the requisite densities of artillery could not be obtained, commanders would plan on using several phases within the methodical attack. The artillery could be massed for the support of one attack; after that phase ended, it could be massed in support of another attack and the completion of another phase. In his lectures at the War College in 1926, Col A.E.M. Moyrand analyzed a division attack which required four phases, with the first phase having two bounds. In another example, the students studied an attack which required three phases, with the first having two bounds, the second also having two bounds, and the third having four bounds.[51] These examples clearly reveal the extraordinary complexity of the methodical battle, but the French doctrine continued to emphasize the absolute necessity of these cumbersome and almost immobile "bases of fire." As late as 1937, a lecturer at the War College emphasized that the exercise the students had completed on the offensive maneuver of an infantry division had illustrated the necessity to maintain a "methodical rhythm" to ensure a cohesive attack and the strength of successive efforts.[52]

The technique of the methodical battle also extended to the computation of the amount of time required for the infantry to accomplish a phase or bound within the operation. For example, the rate of movement of a rolling barrage in front of attacking infantry could be carefully calculated. The planner might initially allow for an advance of a hundred meters in three minutes, and then could either decrease or accelerate this rate of advance when the attacking infantry reached the enemy trenches or raced through the enemy defenses. The concept of a timetable for an attack preceded by a rolling barrage did not quietly disappear in the interwar period, for it remained an integral part of French doctrine. Its employment was included in the 1938 infantry regulations, which clearly acknowledged that its "rigidity" made it difficult to adapt to the maneuver of infantry and tanks. Its use was most appropriate, according to the regulations, when the infantry did not have any accompanying tanks and had to make a frontal assault.[53] The use of tanks, however, did not preclude the use of timetables. A 1939 draft edition of a new manual on tanks emphasized the necessity for using timetables, which theoretically reduced the complex problem of tank-artillery liaison.[54] The timetable, according to the French, was an important part of the methodical battle, and it was an excellent method to ensure close cooperation between the artillery and the other branches.

Another result of the emphasis on the artillery and the methodical battle was that infantry units became burdened by the requirement to move heavy equipment. The French recognized this and stressed that infantry units had become less, rather than more mobile. An instructor at the War College noted that in 1914 a division consisting of four regiments would be thirteen kilometers long when it conducted a road march. By 1929–1930, a division with three regiments would be thirty-four kilometers long because of the greater number of horses and trucks required to move its heavier equipment. At the same time, if the 1929–1930 division were not entirely motorized, it could travel no faster than the walking rate of the infantry-men. From this, the instructor concluded that a 1914 division could completely march past a fixed point in about three and one-half hours, while the 1929–1930 division required at least seven hours. He noted that if the entire division were forced to move on the same route, the 1929–1930 division required ten hours to move past a fixed point, even though it had fewer infantrymen.[55] The summary notes which were provided to the students at the War College after 1935 emphasized that the existing infantry division was a product of the stabilized portion of World War I and was "much more complex and heavy" than the infantry division of 1914. Consequently, the division of the late 1930s was "less supple and less tactically and strategically mobile."[56] The movement to heavier and heavier equipment, especially artillery, had necessitated the sacrificing of mobility for greater firepower. The onerous burden of displacing massive amounts of artillery, according to the French, seriously limited the possibility of any wide-ranging or sweeping operations.

While the French created motorized divisions before 1940, their doctrine stressed that these units were different from "normal" infantry units in their strategic mobility, not in how they fought once they disembarked from their trucks. A lecturer at the War College in 1937–1938 emphasized that motorized units required protection while they displaced, and had to disembark in a protected area.[57] In that sense, the French concept of motorization was essentially the same as that practiced in World War I. The major difference was in a growing awareness of the vulnerability of motorized units to aerial bombardment. The use of motorized units did not alter the French preference for the tightly controlled battle, which maximized the contribution of artillery fire.

The French doctrine for the employment of artillery continued to emphasize the strong centralization of assets, minute planning, and the step-by-step phased battle. In contrast, the Germans moved toward decentralization and rapid, responsive fire—a doctrine which was derived from their experience in World War I but which had roots in the pre-1914 era. A lecturer at the French War College in 1925 noted that when the Germans conducted their attacks on the western front in 1918 and the war became more mobile, they had allocated much of their artillery directly to the divisions. After the rupture of the front, the organic artillery of the division followed the advancing infantry closely.[58] The Germans used accompanying artillery extensively and with great success, while the French used it only to a limited extent.[59] After the war, the French continued to place only a small premium on immediately responsive artillery, despite calls for more mobile and flexible artillery support, because of the doctrinal emphasis on the massive employment of artillery. The 1921 German field service regulations, on the other hand, stated that the infantry always needed accompanying batteries, which could even be allocated to companies.[60] Similarly, the 1933 German regulations recognized the need for immediate support of the infantry and stated that if necessary a battalion or a battery could be attached to an infantry unit.[61] The German doctrine emphasized immediate response by the artillery to infantry needs.

The French were aware of the differences between their artillery doctrine and that of the Germans. In his lectures on artillery in 1930 at the War College, Colonel de la Porte du Theil, for example, responded irritably to a 1928 article in *Militär-Wochenblatt* that criticized the French emphasis on centralized, massive artillery support. He argued that such support was also called for in German regulations. He later quoted General Maurin, the inspector general of artillery, on the preference for using sections, rather than batteries, of artillery as accompanying pieces, but he added General Maurin's qualification that this should not weaken the control of the commanding general over his artillery.[62] A lecturer at the Center of Higher Military Studies in 1937 observed that the Germans had "always" placed most of their artillery in the division. He nevertheless argued that commanders must look beyond the line of combat and place some of their artillery fire deep inside the enemy's position. According to him, centralization of artillery provided these fires and facilitated the maneuver of the division.[63]

In August 1938, an analysis of the January 1937 German regulations on artillery appeared in *Revue d'artillerie*. This analysis stressed the clear contrast between German and French doctrines. The author noted that the German regulations were almost silent on the technical characteristics and organization of artillery and on methods of employment. He noted that the Germans wanted to create a sense of initiative among their officers for resolving tactical problems according to the circumstances of the moment. He later concluded that the German regulations "make possible the immediate exploitation of events on the battlefield . . ., but they make difficult the regrouping of [artillery] means into the hands of a superior authority."[64] Thus, while recognizing the German preference for rapid centralization and immediate support, the French continued to prefer centralization and massive support. Clearly, the German doctrine was most appropriate for a mobile battle, while the French doctrine was most appropriate for the methodical battle.

The French did not rule out the possibility of a rapid forward movement that might upset a timetable, but they did not seriously address the issue of the infantry setting the pace of attack. For example, the 1938 infantry regulations stated that every possibility of seizing terrain should be exploited without delay, and added that such a seizure could come about as a result of a broad movement along an entire front or from the forward movement of only portions of the front. Despite such assertions, the authors of the 1938 regulations focused primarily upon movement by successive phases closely supported by artillery fires. The regulations explained that each successive step of the commander's planned maneuver had to be coordinated with supporting fires. In its general discussion of an attack, the regulations emphasized three major points: "the attack of the first objective"; "the consolidation and occupation of conquered terrain"; and "the attack of subsequent objectives." The attack on a second objective, however, could commence only at a time fixed in advance or by a special signal from higher headquarters. Such controls were essential if the infantry and artillery were to operate together.[65] Consequently, though the regulations suggested the possibility of rapid forward progress, they hardly envisaged a swift, continuous attack that might result in the infantry outrunning their artillery support.

Ironically, the 1938 infantry regulations placed an even greater emphasis on the methodical approach than earlier ones. In their analysis of the attack, the authors stated that regimental and battalion commanders should stipulate "momentary halts" for the units under their control after the execution of certain bounds. They added that these commanders should "regulate the resumption of movement after each of the halts in such a manner as to maintain their attack in the rhythm fixed by the General commanding the division." This qualification on maintaining the rhythm of attack had not appeared in editions or amendments as late as 1934 and indicated an even greater emphasis than before on the tightly centralized, methodical battle.[66]

A related factor appeared in the discussion of the assault on a final objective. The 1938 regulations explained that the infantry was capable of generating the moral and physical effort for sustaining an assault for only five hundred to six hundred meters. The regulations concluded, "It is difficult to have them renew it [an assault over this distance] in the course of the same day of combat."[67] The French clearly expected an attacker to sustain large losses and to become exhausted under the accurate and lethal fire of a defender.

The consideration of several factors—the complexity of coordinating the infantry and the artillery, the difficulty of maintaining a rhythm of attack established by a higher commander, and the limitations imposed by a short assault from the infantry—added further weight to the French rejection of German infiltration tactics. At the War College, in 1925–1926, Lieutenant Colonel Touchon (who was later a member of the commission that wrote the 1936 instructions and president of the commission that wrote the 1938 infantry regulations) argued:

It is by lateral fire that the infantry makes the enemy feel his advance, in taking him from the flank, the diagonal, the rear. It is by this fire that he will aid the progression of neighboring units that have been held up; it is this fire, in a word, which puts into concrete form the *infiltration* maneuver.[68]

Other authors also placed greater emphasis on fire than on maneuver in their interpretation of German infiltration tactics. They preferred to concentrate on moving to place fire, rather than moving to bypass an enemy.

Although French regulations described the use of infiltration in the attack, they did not call for driving deeply into an enemy's defenses. The January 1939 manual entitled *Regulations for Rifle Units* explained that the smallest infantry unit capable of maneuver was the rifle platoon and that the maneuvers should always be "simple." A squad would never try to maneuver by using a few of its men to provide a base of fire while the remainder moved forward. According to the manual, when a platoon encountered fire from an enemy position, it should try to outflank this resistance, rather than make a direct assault. While one squad placed fire on this point, the rest of the platoon would use favorable paths of approach toward it, move to its flanks, and then place oblique fire upon it. From the French perspective, the movement around the flanks of an enemy utilized an infiltration maneuver. The idea was not to race past the enemy resistance but to destroy the enemy and then move on toward the company objective. The same technique could be used by a company with one platoon providing fire support, while the other platoons maneuvered around the enemy. The platoons might also move by bounds, but they moved slowly and eliminated enemy resistance as they encountered it.

The 1939 regulations for rifle units left little chance for rapid movement forward. After reaching the company objective, according to the regulations, the company was supposed to halt so the commander could issue a verbal order to his platoon leaders describing how the next objective would be attacked. Regardless of the depth of the advance, the company would utilize a succession of efforts and a succession of attacks until it reached the battalion's objective.[69] Beyond a doubt, the French may have understood the importance of moving around the flanks of enemy resistance, but they had little or no understanding of how the Germans had used infiltration tactics successfully against them in 1918.

Part of the French misunderstanding of the infiltration maneuver stemmed from their seeing little chance of success in a breakthrough operation. In addition to their not believing that such tactics had been attempted by the Germans in the Great War, they doubted the potential of a swift, continuous attack that might burst completely through a deeply held defensive position. French doctrine assumed that once a defender's front was broken, he could reestablish positions to the rear which could be taken only after the employment of large and powerful forces. The defender would be able to establish subsequent defensive positions rapidly and "solder" together the broken pieces of the front. This was not simply a process of reinforcement but one of "sedimentation," in which the defenders augmented the depth of a position of resistance and reestablished the continuity and depth of the front.[70] Only after the successive enemy positions had been penetrated would the exploitation or pursuit begin. The French had been able to reconstitute their defensive front in 1918, and there was little reason to expect they would not be able to do it again in the future. The German failure in 1918, according to the French, clearly demonstrated the "inherent weaknesses" in any attempted breakthroughs.

The French also did not see any decisive action coming from a breakthrough. Colonel Lemoine, an instructor at the War College, quoted Marshal Pétain on the subject: "The breakthrough is not the *object*, but the *means* to arrive at giving battle . . . by attacking the enemy . . . on the flanks formed by the withdrawal of a part of the front." Lemoine added that the ruptures by the Germans in 1918 had created crises but had not given "decisive results." Another instructor quoted Marshal Foch to argue that a breakthrough was not aiming for penetration but instead was seeking to capture important terrain features to break up the enemy's defensive positions.[71] The concept of encirclement, or *Kesselschlacht*, apparently did not exist in French thinking. Despite their considerable analysis of the problem, the French failed to recognize that an armored force might be able to drive through an enemy's defenses before he could establish subsequent defensive positions, and that the objective of such a force might be to slice off major segments of a front.

Notwithstanding the French lack of confidence in the possibility of a breakthrough, German doctrine had an entirely different flavor and included the concept of a continuous battle. Both the 1921 and the 1933 German field-service regulations stressed the importance of the penetration, which was based upon infiltration tactics and could be developed into a complete breakthrough of enemy lines. If a breakthrough were made, the attacking troops would push forward as far as possible, leaving the widening of the shoulders of the breakthrough to the reserves.[72] The 1933 German regulations observed: "The objective of the combined arms in an attack is to bring the infantry into decisive action against the enemy, with sufficient fire power and shock action so that it is possible to drive through deeply and break down the final hostile resistance."[73] Such a doctrine assumed that continuous pressure and a deep attack would prevent the reestablishing of strong defensive positions.

The 1921 German field service regulations emphasized the need to prevent the enemy from reestablishing successive positions and the need for immediate pursuit.[74] The 1933 manual also emphasized the need to follow the enemy closely. Should the attack halt, the Germans foresaw the commitment of reserves to continue the momentum of the attack and the formation of new reserves from those units that had been passed by the forward-moving old reserves.[75] Similarly, they foresaw the commitment of reserves to reinforce success and to accelerate gains before the defender could react. They did not automatically assume the defender's mobility exceeded that of the attacker. The breakthrough, however, was only a "preparatory move," which would ultimately lead to "subsequent operations of encirclement."[76] German doctrine, in short, emphasized the advantages of one continuous battle, ultimately leading to the complete rupture of the hostile defenses and the defeat of the enemy, while French doctrine accepted the possibility of a successive series of methodical battles. The

Germans believed this continuous battle enabled them to retain the initiative and to achieve victory. And this belief existed long before German panzer forces or the blitzkrieg were created.

As for decentralization and initiative, the German approach to combat leadership contrasted sharply with the French approach. The 1933 German field-service regulations stated, "Simplicity of conduct, logically carried through, will most surely attain the objective."[77] Both the 1921 and the 1933 German regulations treated the use of phases as exceptional methods of operation rather than as the normal procedure.[78] The 1933 regulations explained that the objective of an attack should be limited only in special instances and that such an attack could win only limited success. The main purpose of an attack was to "drive through deeply." The regulation concluded, "Independence of action of the lower commanders . . . is of decisive importance at all times."[79] While the French doctrine emphasized pushing from above, the German doctrine emphasized pulling from below. The Germans recognized that while strategic or grand tactical concepts had to be formulated by higher-level commanders, the success of these concepts depended upon the lower-level commanders having the flexibility and freedom to capitalize on any momentary advantages they might gain.

The French doctrine suggested a completely different tempo and approach. The preference for short-range attacks with numerous phases and bounds, the lengthy time required to displace artillery, the use of standard densities to compute the amount of artillery needed, and the computation of timetables which indicated the rate of movement of the infantry and artillery guaranteed that the French staff officer would be overwhelmed with the amount of work demanded by such an operation. In a real sense, its complexity ensured that any concept arguing for rapid breakthroughs and long-range exploitation could easily be dismissed as fanciful thinking. The doctrine's emphasis on fire and the methodical battle could only serve to suppress innovative ideas in the French army about maneuver. Similarly, the battle of 1940 demonstrated, all too painfully, that such techniques could not be employed in the fluid environment of a highly mobile battlefield.

A clear description of the methodical battle was presented in September 1938, one year before the opening of World War II, at the Center of Higher Military Studies. This presentation, given by a general officer, graphically described an operation of an army consisting of five corps with fifteen divisions along a front of sixty kilometers. The force launched its main attack on a front of fifteen kilometers with six divisions in the first echelon, resulting in each division having about two-and-one half kilometers of front. For the remaining forty-five kilometers of front, the general officer deployed five divisions, resulting in each of these divisions having a front of nine kilometers. Four divisions remained in the second echelon, but their artillery was moved forward to provide a density of about one division's worth of artillery for each kilometer of attack frontage. The objective was selected so it was not any deeper than one-half the length of the attack frontage—about seven-and-one-half kilometers. The lecturer noted that the attack would be "traced in the arc of a circle more or less regular."[80] Unfortunately for France, this attack more closely resembled the battles of 1918 than it did those of May–June 1940. And while it reflected some use of mobility, it represented only a slight improvement over the static methods employed before 1918.

A lecturer at the War College in 1937 offered an appropriate analogy for French doctrine when he compared the methodical attack to a medieval battering ram, used to make a hole in the wall of a fortress. He noted that the analogy was appropriate because of the slowness of the operation, the complexity of the preparation, and the requirement for centralization.[81] Unfortunately, he failed to note that a modern enemy might be more mobile than a medieval castle.

The French perception of the annihilating effect of firepower had exercised a great influence on their doctrine. While exalting firepower, they saw mobility simply in terms of how to apply the firepower. At the same time, the emphasis on matériel contributed to the erection of vast "curtains" of fire, which were the building blocks for the continuous front and an additional impediment for mobility. Attacking units would not go beyond the effective range of their artillery, an idea clearly expressed in the 1936 instructions and reiterated in subsequent regulations. Because of this view of a limited battlefield, the French simply were not trained to think of a hastily assembled, distant armor attack—especially one supported by attack aircraft. Their doctrine did not stress the decisive qualities of initiative, speed, and celerity; rather, it placed emphasis on the World War I approach of carefully preparing the set-piece, closely controlled, methodical attack. While this concept may have been buttressed by eminently logical thought, it hindered the French understanding of how the nature of war had changed.

After the battle of 1940, a German general staff officer with experience in World War I observed: "On the field of battle, the individual soldier fought bravely and well in this war, but the fundamental training of the French army was faulty. It was not trained and educated in the war of movement."[82]

CHAPTER 6

Institutions and Doctrine

In seeking an explanation for the poor performance of the French military in 1940, some writers have focused on the large number of ministries in the interwar period and suggested that this turbulence weakened defense efforts. Governmental instability supposedly detracted from France's ability to construct a coherent policy and to carry it to completion.[1] While this criticism may have some validity for the conduct of foreign policy, it has less validity in the realm of military policy, since it overlooks the relative stability of the War Ministry and in the highest military positions in the interwar years.

Between 1919 and 1939, France had forty-three different ministries. From December 1932 until September 1939, she had sixteen different ministries. During the period from 1932 until 1939, however, she had only five ministers of war, and if the three-day tenure of Paul-Boncour is not counted, she had only four. Of these four ministers of war, Edouard Daladier served for fifty-two months, Gen. Joseph L. M. Maurin eleven-and-a-half, Marshal Philippe Pétain nine, and Jean Fabry seven-and-a-half. While some problems with continuity may have existed, those problems should not have been extreme. This is especially apparent when one recalls that Daladier served continuously as the minister of war from June 1936 until May 1940.

Even greater stability existed in the military positions. Marshal Pétain served as vice-president of the Superior Council of War from 1920 to 1931, General Weygand from 1931 to 1935, and General Gamelin from 1935 until the war. General Buat served as Chief of the General Staff from 1920 to 1923, General Debeney from 1923 to 1930, General Weygand from 1930 to 1931, and General Gamelin from 1931 until the war. Thus, only five military officers occupied the most important positions in the army's hierarchy from 1920 to 1939. Amongst the inadequacies in the French High Command, personnel turbulence in the key positions could not have been a serious problem.

The main problems of the High Command came from the way in which it was organized. The French did not have a smoothly functioning system in which specific individuals had precise responsibilities for analyzing issues and resolving problems. Instead of organizing a stream-lined structure with identifiable individuals in charge, they relied on com-mittees, particularly at the highest echelons, and divided the responsibility for overseeing military preparation among several general officers. Where a sense of urgency and a unity of command were needed, they had instead a bureaucratic structure, capped with committees, which functioned in a decentralized and often spasmodic fashion. The government recognized the need for a more effective High Command, but traditional republican hostility toward a strongly centralized military chain of command frustrated efforts to reform its organization. Plagued by a cumbersome organizational structure that diluted everyone's authority, the military hierarchy found it simpler to follow the less difficult course of retaining older concepts rather than adopting newer ones.

To oversee the preparation for a long total war, the French relied upon a body created before World War I. The Superior Council of National Defense (*Conseil supérieur de la défense nationale*) had been founded in 1906 to address problems primarily of a purely military nature. The experience of the Great War proved that an exclusively military preparation was no longer sufficient to prepare the nation for war, and that greater economic and industrial preparation was necessary. Consequently, the membership and concerns of the council were expanded after 1918. Composed essen-tially of the ministers in the government and the highest-ranking officers in the army, navy, and, later, the air force, this council sought to assist the gov-ernment in the mobilization and preparation of the nation for total war. In its infrequent deliberations, the council concentrated on such issues as dis-armament, the importing of fuels, the organization of the air force, and necessary financial credits. It also addressed economic and financial issues, as well as those pertaining to length of military service or size of the defense establishment.[2]

The council focused on larger issues affecting military policy and did not seek to intrude into areas that its members perceived as being rightfully dominated by military specialists. Despite its potential for great influence over national security matters, the political leadership rarely used the coun-cil to analyze or resolve important questions. Not surprisingly, the influ-ence of the military members was limited, since they could participate in the discussions but not vote. In his postwar memoirs, Gamelin complained that the council had not met for several years before the war, not even when the momentous decision to support Poland was made.[3]

Below the Superior Council of National Defense, France created a spe-cial body to coordinate the activities of the several military services. The political and military leaders recognized that the national defense council need not address issues primarily concerned with technical military preparation. Some special arrangements had to be made to provide a semblance of a unity of command beneath it. In 1932, France created the High Military Committee (*Haut comité militaire*) to engender closer contacts and assure better harmony among the three services. When created, the joint committee consisted of the president of the Council of Ministers, the vice-presidents of the superior councils of war for the three services, the three chiefs of the general staffs, and the inspector general of aerial defense. Several months after its creation, the three vice-presidents of the superior councils of war were dropped from the membership and replaced by the ministers of the three services.

During the period of its existence, from 1932 until 1936, the committee met infrequently and concentrated on issues pertaining to command in wartime and friction between the services. Despite the best of intentions, no unity of opinion or command emerged, and no equivalent of the post–World War II Joint Chiefs of Staff system in the United States emerged. The committee was unable to bridge the gap between the three services. Perhaps the most positive thing that can be said about this committee is that the services at least had an opportunity to discuss some of the issues pertaining to the operation of an effective joint command.

In 1936, the government of Léon Blum abolished the High Military Committee and replaced it with the Permanent Committee of National Defense (*Comité permanent de la défense nationale*). The new committee was presided over by the minister of national defense or the president of the Republic and consisted of the ministers, the vice-presidents of the three superior councils of war, and the three chiefs of the general staffs, as well as representatives of the Ministry of Foreign Affairs. Again, no unity of opinion or command emerged. The committee's accomplishments were also no greater than the High Military Committee's had been, for it met infrequently, having only one meeting in 1939.[4]

The French also created a committee to direct the actual conduct of a war. In the event of hostilities, the Permanent Committee of National Defense (after 1936) was supposed to be replaced by the War Committee (*Comité de guerre*), whose membership was slightly expanded but remained similar to that of the Permanent Committee. While the government would actually direct what happened in a war, it theoretically delegated its responsibilities to the War Committee. The War Committee's membership included the highest-ranking officers of the three services. Fundamental questions of wartime operations and strategy could be addressed in this forum with the political leaders present and without leaving such questions to the whims of the military leaders. Despite the great potential of this body, it too remained relatively unused, and met only twice from September 1939 to April 1940.[5]

In addition to the higher arena of national security policy, the French also failed to create a centralized system within the purely military sphere. Except for a short-lived attempt in 1932, France did not have a minister of national defense until 1936, and she did not create a chief of the general staff of national defense until 1938. As a consequence, she did not have a military leader or body specifically charged with coordinating military activities until the eve of World War II. Even then, the chief of the general staff of national defense did not have even the relatively limited powers of the ancient Generalissimo of the army: he only had powers of coordination, not of command, over matters affecting the army and air force. His powers over the navy were even more limited, for he could coordinate combined maritime operations only when instructed to do so by the minister of national defense.[6] Thus, when Gamelin became the first chief of the general staff of national defense and war, he effectively directed the activities only of the army, because he retained his previous positions as army chief of staff, vice-president of the Superior Council of War, and designated leader in the eventuality of war.

A general staff or fairly powerful headquarters above the three services never existed. After 1938, Gamelin could call together the chiefs of staff for the three services, and he could use the secretariat for the Superior Council of National Defense. Yet he had no distinct staff group charged with analyzing and coordinating the details of national security policy. Also, he had no power to enforce any of his decisions. In sum, no semblance of a unity of command or even of staff work existed. The reliance on committees and decisions by consensus, which ruled the highest echelons of national security policy, extended through the relationships among the three services.

Despite this apparent disunity, the primary focus of French defense policy remained on the army. This is most evident from Daladier, as the minister of war, being named as the first minister of national defense and war, and from Gamelin, as the leading army general, being named as the first chief of the general staff of national defense and war. In comparison to the army, the air force and especially the navy played a less important role. Except for the air force, whose role was not yet as apparent or as entrenched in bureaucratic and political favor, no one could doubt the immediate danger of German land forces, and no one could forget the dominant role of the army in the Great War. Consequently, the army's desires usually prevailed.

Even though general agreement and support existed for the army's preeminent position in the military establishment, the army did not escape the tendency toward the fragmentation and diffusion of power. The question of a relatively powerful and strongly hierarchical army high command had long been controversial in France. Before World War I the political authorities simply refused for years to place a single general in charge of their military forces. To this end, they placed one general in charge of the General Staff and designated another as the wartime commander of French forces and vice-president of the Superior Council of War. They also limited the powers of the two generals over subordinate military commanders. As a consequence, no one actually commanded French forces in peacetime. The political leaders refused to risk the possibility of the proverbial "man on horseback" acquiring complete control over the military and overthrowing the republican government.

In 1911 and 1912, as the threat of a war became greater, the government took measures enabling Marshal Joffre to become the designated leader in the eventuality of war and the chief of the General Staff. As such, he unified the two major military components of the High Command and gained more control over the French army than any general officer since Napoleon.[7] Despite these greater powers, Joffre did not have unlimited control in peacetime over the army bureaucracy. He did not command the army, and many chiefs of bureaucratic departments in the High Command answered directly to the minister of war rather than to him. After the war began and after Joffre assumed command over the army, his powers expanded enormously and spread into almost all aspects of French society. Three years of bloody trench warfare, however, ultimately ended the almost unchecked power of the military. The "Tiger," Georges Clemenceau, assumed power, and his slogan became "War is too important to be left to the generals." This blunt but brilliant politician represented the zenith of civilian power over the military in the Third Republic.

After the war, the military hierarchy sought a new command structure that would limit the authority of the war minister and concentrate more authority in the hands of a single military leader. This proposal was never even given to Clemenceau for consideration. General Mordacq, the "Tiger's" military assistant, later stated that he did not "dare" give such a proposal to the minister.[8] Although the plan may have seemed logical enough from the standpoint of military efficiency, the civilian leadership distrusted the intentions of the professional military. In the absence of an alternative that was acceptable to both military and political authorities, the pre–1911 hierarchy was reestablished, along with its problems of ministerial instability and diffusion of power. There was to be no repetition of the prewar acquisition of authority by Marshal Joffre, which some believed had resulted in the disastrous offensive doctrine. Neither was there to be a repeat performance of the accumulation of vast power over the military that Clemenceau had managed to acquire during World War I.

When the French resurrected the peacetime hierarchy of the army, the major parts of the High Command of the French army once again became the triad of the minister of war, the Superior Council of War, and the chief of the General Staff. By law, the war minister was the most powerful and influential of the three. In practice, however, he exerted his powers in the broader areas of policy and monetary credits and did not interfere in the day-to-day administration of the army. The tendency of the minister to defer to the technical expertise of the army's military leaders and bureaucrats ensured that he had less influence in the interwar period over the technical aspects of strategy, tactics, organization, and equipment than did the chief of the General Staff or the Superior Council of War. He usually exerted his influence in the fashion of communicating and establishing political limitations, monetary constraints, and manning levels within which doctrine and strategy had to be established.[9] Of France's war ministers from 1932 to 1940, Daladier undoubtedly had the greatest reluctance to become involved with technical questions, especially from April 1938 to March 1940, when he also was burdened by the responsibilities of the president of the Council of Ministers. By focusing upon broader issues, he followed the lead of the Chamber of Deputies and Senate army commissions, which also tended to defer to the military experts.[10] In 1937, Paul Reynaud complained about the unwillingness of the government to play a stronger role in directing the affairs of the High Command,[11] but no war minister in the interwar period managed to dominate the army.

A possible opportunity for a single general officer to have stronger powers throughout the army's High Command did exist immediately following the Great War. After accepting the position of vice-president of the war council in 1920, Pétain was also offered the position of chief of the General Staff. When it became apparent that Pétain might refuse the second position, Marshal Foch sent General Weygand to plead with him to accept the position and thus unify the army's hierarchy. But Pétain refused. His explosive response to Weygand's request was, "Chief of the General Staff! I cannot see myself going every evening for the signature of the minister."[12] The two key positions of the chief of the General Staff and vice-president of the Superior War Council remained separate until 1935. Weygand later confessed that agreeing to such a division of authority was the "greatest mistake" of his life.[13] While Weygand might not have had enough influence at the time to prevent such a division, his comment underlines the importance of Pétain's decision.

The unwillingness of the political leaders to have a single general dominating the army appeared soon after the end of the war. Two days after publication on 23 January 1920 of a decree that reestablished the Superior Council of War, notice of an erratum appeared; the decree had mistakenly talked of the "Inspector General of the Army," instead of the "Vice-President of the Superior Council of War." The title "Inspector General of the Army" was deleted and replaced with "Vice-President" of the Council,[14] a position whose primary responsibilities had been hammered out before 1914. While this error may have been an honest one, it clearly indicated that the government did not originally intend to create a military position whose occupant was specifically identified as the military leader of the peacetime army. The vice-president of the council, nevertheless, remained the Generalissimo, or designated leader, of the French army in wartime, and he was given greater powers than the pre-World War I occupant of the position. The 23 January 1920 decree placed the General Staff of the army under the Generalissimo's "high authority," and designated the chief of the General Staff as his assistant. This theoretically gave the designated commander more authority over the army's general staff than he had before 1911–1912, but less than he had when Joffre had simultaneously been chief of the General Staff, vice-president of the council, and Generalissimo.

Despite the uproar in 1920, a decree on 18 January 1922 legally established the position of inspector general of the army. This decree gave the officer occupying the position the right to inspect, but not to command, all arms and services of the army. Marshal Pétain was shortly thereafter named to the position. As inspector general, Pétain could legally supervise and inspect the army's preparation for war, but these powers were not a major expansion of the de facto prerogatives of the vice-president of the Superior Council of War. The occupant of that position had been able to exercise such authority—with the minister of war's approval—since the early 1890s. The new power given by the decree, and the most controversial, was the requirement that the chief of the General Staff "submit for the examination of the Inspector General of the Army all questions concerning organization, training, and mobilization." Such correspondence required the endorsement of the inspector general before it was passed to the war minister.[15]

A roar of disapproval emerged from the Chamber of Deputies, where several politicians perceived a lessening of the powers of the minister. One deputy asserted, "I regret . . . that the Minister of War may have the air of being the parliamentary undersecretary of the Inspector General of the Army."[16] André Lefèvre, who had been war minister from 21 January to 16 December 1920, objected to the inspector general seeing materials before they went to the minister.[17] He considered this a threat to the powers of the civilian minister.

In spite of the political discontent, Pétain managed to retain the position of inspector general, along with being Generalissimo and vice-president of the war council. However, the complete subordination of the chief of the General Staff to him, and the serious undermining of the powers of the minister as a result of this authority, never occurred. The decree was not withdrawn, but material was frequently sent to the minister by the General Staff without Pétain or his successor, General Weygand, having seen it. Other military agencies also continued to have direct access to the minister, as they had had before World War I. Similarly, discussions in the Superior Council of War sometimes occurred in the 1920s on subjects in which General Debeney, the chief of staff, was obviously better informed than Marshal Pétain. As General A.M.E. Laure noted in his study of Pétain, a close relationship existed between the Marshal and Generals Buat and Debeney, who had been his wartime chiefs of staff.[18] These personal relationships were extremely important to the smooth functioning of the High Command and were probably more important than the formal but imprecise relationships established by the decrees of 23 January 1920 and 22 January 1922. Placing the chief of the General Staff under the inspector general's "high authority" and requiring certain General Staff correspondence for the minister to be reviewed by him was far from the rigid subordination of the chief of the General Staff to the inspector general.

Neither Pétain nor Weygand acquired complete control of the military hierarchy. Only Gamelin managed in 1935 to unify the positions of chief of the General Staff and vice-president of the war council. The decree enabling him to occupy both positions, however, effectively (but not officially) eliminated the title of inspector general of the army. The minister's report for the decree summarized the difficulties with the system which existed between 1920 and 1935.

> The Chief of the General Staff was found to depend on two authorities: that of the Vice-President of the Superior Council of War and that of the minister. . . . The minister, for his part, had to face two different authorities, each in actual fact responsible to him.[19]

Although the government eliminated some of this complexity after 1935, Gamelin was essentially one individual occupying two separate positions. He was not referred to as *the* inspector general, and he definitely did not have wide-ranging command authority. At the Riom trial, the Vichy government noted that Gamelin was the Generalissimo of the French army and consequently held him responsible for many of its matériel and operational shortcomings. On his copy of the charges, Gamelin scribbled, "The title is one thing. The power is another."[20]

The fragmentation of the military hierarchy, nevertheless, did not provide a smooth civil-military relationship. Despite their consultative role, members of the Superior Council of War saw themselves as defenders of military programs frequently attacked by unknowing or misinformed politicians. Similarly, political leaders tended to view members of that council—to use the words of Paul Painlevé—as "simple military technicians." The difficulty lay in establishing a precise line between military questions and political questions, or in reconciling the requirements of military efficiency with the demands of political imperatives. In September 1925, a presidential decree permitted members of the government to participate in the Superior Council's discussion in order to "enlighten" them on the political repercussions of their suggested solutions to problems.[21] Distinguishing between military and political advice, however, remained extremely difficult, particularly in the realms of economic and personnel resources.

The clearest example of this difficulty was the controversy surrounding the number of active divisions and the length of service for conscripted soldiers. Following World War I, the Superior Council of War stated a preference for two-year service, and agreed to reductions in service only if certain conditions such as a prescribed number of career soldiers were met. It finally agreed to eighteen months of service, but added the qualification that further reductions would place the national defense in "peril."[22] For more than five years, the council steadfastly opposed, but reluctantly approved, decisions by the government for reductions in the term of service. The most explosive meetings of the entire interwar period occurred in April 1925, when the council presented a letter to the political leadership that was extremely critical of one-year service. The council unanimously affirmed, "[T]he very existence of the army will be gravely compromised and the security of the country cannot be assured."[23] In November 1926, Foch noted that the government had not taken into account the advice given by the council on 10 April 1925, and Weygand observed that France was following public opinion in its move toward one-year service, rather than following the advice of the council.[24] Despite the council's reservations, service of eighteen months was established in April 1923 and service of one year in April 1928.

During this entire period, the army suffered as it was caught between the insistent demands of the Superior Council and the dwindling resources provided by the government. In several meetings of the council, Pétain noted the "lamentable state" of the army and its "essentially provisional" organization. His observations were seconded by General Guillaumat in a March 1926 meeting.[25] Perhaps the most incisive observation, however, came in January 1924, when General Debeney (in his first meeting as chief of the General Staff) observed that the army had been plagued by instability since the Superior Council had refused to accept eighteen months of service.[26] His comments suggested that the council had prolonged the instability and thus weakened the army. In May 1933, General Weygand stated that in his report as inspector general of the army in May 1932, for the first time since one-year service had been instituted, he had found French units manned with "sufficient, well-behaved, and well-trained soldiers."[27] The 1935 annual report of the inspector general of the infantry, General Dufieux, also stressed the improvements in training and preparedness of the French army. Dufieux believed the army had first achieved its highest possible level of readiness with one-year service in 1933.[28]

By 1932–1933, one-year service was fully established and the disruptive effects of its adoption had ended. The army had completed the implementation of the 1927–1928 laws. Halting the opposition to the shorter term of service finally ended the instability that had plagued the army for almost a decade, and permitted the army to turn its attention to more purely technical questions. The adamant opposition of the Superior Council to a reduction in service and in the size of the army had served only to delay the inevitable. The High Command had not failed to implement French laws; rather, it had futilely devoted much of its energy to criticizing and objecting to laws it considered potentially disruptive or destructive.

Strained civil-military relations did not end in the late 1920s. Successive crises were brought on by a move toward disarmament from 1930 to 1935 and by the reduction in the number of effectives during the "lean years," which was caused by the low birth rate during World War I. The crises exacerbated already angry tempers within the two critical institutions. General Weygand paid one minister of war the highest compliment: "Mr. Maginot thinks like a patriot, like a soldier one might even say. . . ." His opinion of other war ministers was much less favorable, and he complained in his memoirs that the "era of difficulties" began with the arrival of Paul-Boncour in June 1932.[29]

General Weygand openly complained of the poor utilization of the war council by the successive war ministries of Marshal Pétain and General Maurin. In the last days before his compulsory retirement from the war council because of age, he charged that the council had not been consulted on actions to take against "dangerous insufficiencies."[30] Conflict and mutual distrust continued after Weygand. In his postwar apologia, Gamelin claimed that when he was appointed the vice-president of the Superior Council of War and also the chief of the General Staff, General Maurin, who was the war minister, told him, "For you, training and the preparation for operations; for me, personnel, matériel [and] administration, while taking your advice."[31]

During the parliamentary investigation on the fall of France, General Weygand identified this conflict between the political leadership and the military as a key to understanding France's rapid collapse. He testified, "This [mutual distrust] is properly insane . . . [and] is at the base of our defeat. It is necessary that between our military leaders . . . and those who have direct charge over our interests there exist a complete understanding."[32] The sense of understanding Weygand was seeking, however, was for a stronger military participation in the decision-making process that affected the military establishment, and for a concomitant smaller political participation in that same process. The sense of understanding the minister of war was seeking was for the military to accept the civilian leadership and its programs and to get on with the necessary preparation for the eventuality of war. As perhaps should be expected, the refusal of the political leadership to create a unified and hierarchical command did not make the military completely obedient to or respectful toward the civilians, nor did it end the divisive arguments between the two groups. The strains in civil-military relations decreased only after the return of two years' service in 1935, the beginning of rearmament and greater financial expenditures in late 1935, and the appointment of the politically reliable Gamelin as chief of the General Staff and vice-president of the war council. In reality, questions of civilian control were subsumed by fears of a rearming Germany.

Returning to the issue of doctrinal reform, the "absurdity"[33] of France's having fragmented the army hierarchy was the absence of a clear delineation of responsibility and authority for the army. The complex variety of competing and often parochial institutions within the High Command ensured that efforts to modernize French forces were neither as efficient nor as effective as they might have been. For complicated questions (such as the incorporation of new doctrine and technology into the army), the bureaucratic structure beneath the minister of war, chief of the General Staff, and vice-president of the Superior Council of War was influenced in varying degrees and sometimes confusing fashions by the three major components of the army's high command. Similarly, the complexity and inefficiency of the military hierarchy also ensured that no single idea, individual, or institution dominated the formulation of military policy or doctrine. This was particularly true for those questions which required the concurrence of the navy or air force, whose high commands were organized like that of the army. In exchange for complete assurance of military obedience, France opted for a less effective military hierarchy.

Throughout the interwar period, the subordinate elements of the High Command operated in an environment of confusing and sometimes conflicting authority. The French General Staff was not a simple hierarchical system of staff specialists. Of all the agencies within the General Staff, the departments (such as the Department of Infantry, Department of Artillery, etc.) prospered the most in this environment and operated with a surprising degree of independence from 1920 to 1935. The departments were responsible to the minister of war, and their functions and powers compare closely with those of the notorious bureaus and bureau system that were partially reformed and modernized by Elihu Root in the U.S. Army at the beginning of the twentieth century. In addition to their responsibilities for personnel, matériel, training, and organizational problems within their branch or service, they performed most of the administrative work pertaining to doctrinal issues. They also provided budgetary information through the General Staff to the controller general, who actually prepared the budget. As a reflection of their autonomy, they referred to the general staff of the army as the "11th department."[34] Since the departments were numbered by seniority, with infantry, cavalry, and artillery one, two, and three respectively, the implication was that the General Staff was the most junior and least influential of the departments.

The departments had long been a thorn in the army hierarchy's side. Before World War I, Joffre attempted to end their autonomy by making them responsible to the General Staff but was unable to accomplish this. General Mordacq, Clemenceau's military assistant, complained of the "anarchy" within the central administration of the army during the war. After the reestablishment of the pre–1911 command structure in the early 1920s, this perceptive, politically aware general argued that the directors of the departments were no longer under the direct control of the minister and were dependent upon no one.[35] None of the reforms in the interwar years effectively ended this muddled independence which continued the "anarchy" of the prewar and Great War years.

The French government essentially reestablished the pre–1914 system in 1920. No major changes were made in the February 1909 decrees that established the departments within the central administration of the Ministry of War. The minister of war continued to appoint the various directors of the departments and to delegate to them the authority to make "immediate executive decisions." More importantly, he also delegated to them the authority of his signature. Consequently, the directors had the power of the minister's signature to buttress their wide-ranging demands. Given the complexity of the problems and the fact that there were more than ten departments, the various directors tended to consider themselves as the "defenders"[36] of the interests of their branch or service. They also tended to identify those interests according to their own perceptions. In terms of an overall program, the results could only be fragmented efforts and conflicting views.

Part of this autonomy ended in 1935. The decree of 18 January attempted not only to unify the positions of vice-president of the Superior Council of War and chief of the General Staff, but also to extend the authority of the General Staff over the departments.[37] Robert Jacomet, who had served as the controller general of the army, explained, "The General Staff of the army was thus happily placed for the first time outside and above the departments."[38] The authority of the virtually autonomous departments, however, was not completely ended, since they were only placed under the General Staff, not subordinated completely and obedient to it. While such a subordination might have led the General Staff to become an operating agency rather than a coordinating one with a detached, nonpartisan view, the problem was that no single agency actually unified the efforts of the fragmented High Command. A decree in July 1938, for example, still listed the departments as part of the central administration of the Ministry of War. After the war, Gamelin insisted that they had remained under the minister.[39] No steps were taken to ensure the end of the parochial views and efforts of the departments, and they maintained their responsibility for their own branch or service.

The inspector generals of the various branches and services theoretically had greater power than the departments, particularly after they were permitted in May 1926 to be members of the Superior Council.[40] The inspectors were furnished copies of all studies and reports affecting their branch or service, and they presided at commissions studying equipment for their area. While they did not command, their powers to study and to inspect units or exercises, and to report to the minister of war or the vice-president of the Superior Council of War gave them a great deal of authority over their branch or service.

Some inspectors, such as General Dufieux, had an important influence over questions of doctrine or technology. As inspector general of the infantry in the 1930s, he played a key role in the exercises and studies concerned with mechanized formations. When complaints or criticisms were made about the doctrine or weapons of his branch, he was responsible for explaining deficiencies—sometimes directly to the minister of war. The reports of the inspectors in the Superior Council were also important, for these frequently became the basis for discussions or the rendering of advice by the council. Within those discussions, the pronouncements of the inspectors on their branches were rarely challenged and often had great influence in the discussion of their interrelationship with other branches, such as in the discussions on the placement of artillery in cavalry and armored formations. The personalities and convictions of the inspectors were crucially important. For example, the dynamic character and firm convictions of General Weygand in the council's discussions of the motorization of cavalry divisions were essential in gaining its favorable decisions for that branch. In contrast, the assertion by General Giraud, the inspector general of tanks, that "all tanks, even those of 70 tons, are infantry tanks" did not help change the views of the council on the potential of the tank.[41] In short, the pronouncements, reports, and studies of the inspectors frequently exercised a great influence over questions of doctrine, organization, and equipment for their branch or service, but the inspectors lacked the command authority to make immediate changes in any area.

The relationship of the departments with the inspector generals of their branch varied with the individuals acting as inspectors or departmental heads. The departments, for example, provided a great deal of information to the inspector generals and, by virtue of the delegated authority of the minister of war, appointed the inspectors as presidents of commissions. At the same time, the comments by departmental heads on inspections made by the inspector generals were sometimes cavalier at best. Several of the inspectors, however, such as Generals Charles M. Condé and Dufieux, effectively influenced the departments. Their capabilities and reputations enabled them to overcome temporarily the autonomy of the departments. The greater influence of the inspector became especially apparent when the director of a branch was a colonel and the inspector a general officer. The usual splitting of responsibilities between the inspectors and the departments, nevertheless, ensured the survival of parochialism and intransigence.

The final body which participated in the formulation of doctrine was the general staff of the army, especially its third bureau, which handled operations and training. Its focus was on the overall preparation and preparedness of the army, and it served to unify partially some of the disparate tendencies within the various echelons of the army. For example, when a specially appointed committee wrote a regulation for a branch, the General Staff read a draft edition to ensure that it agreed with the doctrine established by the army and did not violate any concepts contained within the instructions for larger units. If portions of a draft regulation violated accepted doctrine, the third bureau could order the draft be changed so it would agree with other regulations. While the General Staff may have assisted in writing several doctrinal pamphlets on tanks in the mid-1930s, most work peculiar to particular branches was handled by that branch. The General Staff maintained close liaison with study groups and commissions, and sometimes forwarded summaries or reports to the minister of war about such projects. Despite these administrative responsibilities, the General Staff did not control such projects or provide firm direction to them.

The Superior Council of War became the most important element for providing some unity to the disparate tendencies within the High Command. Given the parochial concerns of the departments, the limited powers of the inspectors of the various branches and services, and the lack of authority and responsibility of the General Staff, decisions by the Superior Council of War had a special authority, even though that body could legally only give advice. Interestingly enough, the united voices of the inspector generals in the council often had greater impact than did their individual voices. The council's recommendations influenced the formulation of army doctrine, and on issues that were clearly of a technical military nature, the council's "advice" could assume the authority of a directive to the army.

Despite this aura of authority, the diverse institutions of the French army did not always obey the Superior Council of War or listen to its advice. The Superior Council had a comparatively greater influence over the organization of the frontiers than over doctrinal and technological matters. Since it had no other military institutions with which it had to contend for directing the frontier strategy, its analysis and recommendations were not hampered by decentralization or passive disobedience. The relative ease with which the council influenced the frontier defenses, however, was not the case with most other questions confronting it.

During the period from 1920 until 1939, the council met eighty-six times in an official status to address issues ranging from the solution of training problems to the proper organization of units, the selection and design of weapons, and the approval of general doctrinal concepts. The council discussed the proper organization of the infantry, cavalry, and armored divisions. It discussed and approved the selection of the automatic rifle, the 25mm and 47mm antitank guns, the 75mm antiaircraft guns, and the 105mm "long-range" artillery piece. It also discussed and approved the armored reconnaissance vehicle, the infantry tracked vehicle, and the D- and B-type tanks. Additionally, it exercised a very strong influence over the proper employment of cavalry and tank formations, discussing both in detail. Since it also discussed the proper organization of the artillery, as well as the three-tank versus the five-tank platoon, its concerns were not solely with larger units.

The council's concerns extended into all areas of military policy. Though the Superior Council did not recommend higher ranking officers for promotion, twenty-three of the meetings dealt solely with questions concerning the retention or placement of general officers, or with the declassification or transfer of military property. A major portion of its meetings concerned the discussion of mobilization and concentration plans, as well as the entire problem of defending the frontiers. One subject of discussion was the condition of the army, especially in terms of the status of its equipment and the training of its personnel. The council devoted many hours to long discussions about general concepts related to the proper organization and employment of the army. As has been seen, its role in the placement of fortifications along the frontiers was decisive.

Although the council approved most military projects it discussed, it was by no means a "rubber stamp" in terms of approving every project submitted for its discussion. For example, a project in 1932 on communications between the infantry and artillery had strict conditions placed upon it concerning the emplacement of the communications equipment within the units.[42] At the same time, members of the council did not always agree among themselves. In a March 1926 meeting on the tank program, one general officer questioned the need to expend money on tanks that would only end up being "pieces in a museum."[43] Having the vice-president of the council and the chief of the General Staff in favor of a project also did not result in automatic approval. As mentioned earlier, when the council discussed in June 1932 the best method for defending the French frontier along the Belgian border, even though the government insisted upon frontier fortifications, it decided by a vote of seven to six that the best method was to penetrate into Belgium and organize a position there. Both Weygand and Gamelin voted for organizing a system of permanent fortifications on French territory. The council's discussions and recommendations were thus not foregone conclusions. Members often expressed sharply different opinions. But the council rarely disapproved a measure supported by the inspector general of the branch or service which it affected.

Other than the absence of the authority to enforce its decisions, the major weakness of the Superior Council of War was its inability to control its agenda. The council could be called into session only by the minister of war or the president of the Third Republic. When it met, it discussed previously arranged questions and either rejected, accepted, or accepted with modifications or conditions the questions presented to it. The council sometimes added questions or topics of its own, but these generally related to the subject being discussed. For example, when the council discussed the proposed law on cadres and effectives in an October 1926 meeting, it became involved in a discussion of training problems within the infantry company. Its solution was to recommend that the number of lieutenants in the company be increased.[44] Members were usually furnished the topics of discussion before the official meeting. Preparatory sessions of the council enabled the members better to inform themselves on the question and often to present a more unified front to the minister of war and the president of the Republic. In an April 1925 meeting on the proposed recruiting law, for example, President Doumergue opened the meeting by asking the results of the preparatory meeting of military members of the council.[45] If a topic were too complex or required additional study, the council often referred it to a special committee. In a December 1925 meeting, for example, the council decided to have a technical study done on the best types of fortifications and armament for the defense of the frontiers.[46] The flexibility derived from this ability to add questions, have preparatory meetings, and refer questions to special committees enabled the council partially to overcome its inability to control its agenda.

Nevertheless, neither the Superior Council of War, the chief of the General Staff, nor the minister of war maintained an iron control over the army. While needed unity should have been provided by the minister of war, no civilian minister effectively challenged the technical expertise of the military hierarchy. Daladier, for example, argued after the defeat that he had little or no authority on technical matters of doctrine, organization, and equipment.[47] He was content to bow to the military experts within the High Command on such questions and asserted his authority primarily on matters of personnel and resources. Yet only the minister's authority could effectively unify the divergent tendencies of the numerous departments, inspectorates, and General Staff bureaus. Once the minister assented to the expertise of the "simple military technicians," he agreed, in effect, to a decentralized and fragmented High Command. The granting of the power of his signature to the departments ensured that they could effectively evade the authority of the General Staff and of the vice-president of the Superior Council of War. The High Command had been organized so the authority of the minister of war could unify the disparate elements, but once the minister acknowledged his own technical incompetence, an efficient and effective High Command was difficult, if not impossible, to construct.

In the final analysis, the French High Command lacked a clear chain of authority and responsibility that could provide the army a firm sense of direction for developing its doctrine and designing its weapons. While overcentralization may stifle initiative, the fragmented organization of the French High Command also stifled creative solutions to doctrinal problems. Additionally, the need for a common doctrine sometimes became an obstacle to creating an improved doctrine. Since the doctrine and equipment for each branch or service had to be compatible with that for all other branches or services, an individual branch could not make a major change without the acquiescence of the other branches. Only the influence and advice of the Superior Council of War, buttressed by the authority of the vice-president of the council and the chief of the General Staff, served to unify the various elements and overcome parochial objections partially. It was in this environment of confusing authority and vague powers that French doctrine evolved. And such an environment favored the development of a doctrine relying on the strength of the defense, methodical battle, and firepower—time-proven and widely supported precepts for which a consensus of support was always guaranteed.

The example of the efforts involved in drafting the *Regulation on Tank Units* in 1938–1939 illustrates the complexity of the problem. The commission that drafted the regulation was appointed by the director of infantry and included selected officers from military schools, armored units, and the General Staff. Consultative members were also appointed to ensure compliance with other regulations and doctrinal concepts, and to provide technical assistance in specific areas. When the draft of the regulation was completed, the commission submitted it to a variety of officers and institutions for comments and suggestions.

The institutions that examined the draft regulation included the third bureau of the General Staff, which made a number of specific suggestions, including major revisions of the draft introduction to be signed by the minister of war. The commission received proposed revisions from most of the departments and all of the consultative members. The Department of Artillery criticized the methods envisaged for the employment of artillery, and the commission incorporated some of its suggestions into its proposed changes. The artillery consultative member of the commission also criticized the regulation's artillery concepts, but he broadened his remarks to include areas that were not directly related to the artillery. The consultative member who was charged with ensuring compliance with concepts in the 1936 instructions on the tactical employment of large units also addressed a number of issues not directly related to the instructions.[48]

General Georges made comments on behalf of the Superior Council of War. Several letters from him included critical comments,[49] and many, but not all, of his suggestions were incorporated. A sharper and more critical letter from Georges soon appeared, demanding that the other changes be incorporated and explaining the doctrinal misperceptions of the commission.[50] Several days later, a letter from General Gamelin appeared which supported Georges's objection and underscored the need to adopt his ideas. Gamelin stated, "I am formally opposed to the advent of the regulation on tanks if it does not take these observations into account."[51] As if his own authority were not enough, he observed that the Superior Council of War had recently addressed one of the issues in question and had agreed with Georges.

Production of a new regulation thus became a very involved and detailed process. A commission had to consider the strident and often conflicting demands of the various individuals and offices within the High Command. Interestingly enough, the minister of war apparently provided no comments and received a completed project only after it had passed through the appropriate channels. In the case of the 1939 regulation on tank units, publication finally occurred in the spring of 1940.[52] The confusion and parochialism existing within the military elements of the High Command had delayed the appearance of a badly needed regulation.

The problem of the effect of new technology on doctrine also cannot be disentangled from the problem of institutions. France lacked an effective system for the incorporation of new technology into its military arsenal. Part of the reason for an absence of a unity of effort in the incorporation of new weapons into France's military system revolved around the confusion of authority in the High Command. The poorly drawn lines dividing the minister of war, the Superior Council of War, and the General Staff spilled over into the arena of doctrine and technology. Even though members of the military hierarchy almost unanimously agreed that technical progress was essential for tactical success,"[53] France's approach to new technology in the decade following World War I can only be described as confusing.

Before World War I, the French army had possessed a relatively simple organization for the development of new equipment. The artillery was responsible for matériel developments in armaments, while the engineers were responsible for practically everything else.[54] Although the experience of World War I demonstrated that this system was inadequate for the demands of modern war, the army did not make extensive changes in it after the war. The one major change was the creation of technical sections for the infantry, tanks, and cavalry, which were responsible for monitoring matériel developments for these branches. With the exception of the tank section, each was assigned to its respective department. Responsibility for tank developments was split between the infantry and artillery until the tank technical section was moved from the Department of Artillery to the Department of Infantry in May 1920.[55] Although it was extremely interested in tank developments, the Department of Cavalry did not create a tank section. Instead, it attempted to ensure that its technical section always included an officer who was knowledgeable and interested in tank development.[56]

No effective centralized system for the consideration of new technology existed within the French army until General Weygand became vice-president of the Superior Council of War in the early 1930s. In his memoirs, Weygand notes that during his tenure as chief of the General Staff, he became convinced that neither the vice-president of the Superior Council of War nor the chief of the General Staff were able to control, as their functions required, the direction and overall quality of weaponry developments. He attributed this failure to the absence of an organization or officer of the General Staff specifically charged with the adoption, testing, and placing of war goods into production.[57] Where there should have been a clear sense of direction, confusion reigned.

To end this confusion, Weygand created two new organizations: the Consultative Council on Armament, and the Technical Cabinet. The purpose of the Consultative Council was to provide the overall goals for the armaments program. It guaranteed some degree of coordination in the development of new armaments and also ensured that the military hierarchy was properly informed on these developments. Its membership included the vice-president of the Superior Council of War, the chief of the General Staff, the departmental heads and inspector generals of the several branches, the director of fabrications, the secretary general of the War Ministry, and the chief of the Technical Cabinet.[58] The Technical Cabinet was designed as a focal point for the collection of information on the research, testing, and manufacturing of new weapons. According to General Weygand, it permitted him to give general directions and to order necessary changes that could hasten research activities and give higher priorities to the most important research.[59] The Technical Cabinet also acted as a permanent secretary for the Consultative Council and provided liaison between the council and the technical sections of the various branches. Despite this impressive membership, neither the Technical Cabinet nor the Consultative Council could actually establish objectives for the development of new weaponry. Such responsibility effectively remained with the departments of the individual branches.

General Dassault, the first chief of the Technical Cabinet, testified before the parliamentary investigating committee after the war about the effectiveness of this new system. He praised the ending of the "state of anarchy" that had reigned until the new system was established and argued that new technology could now "follow a line of development leading without too many digressions to the desired objective."[60] The great stumbling block, however, remained the problem of establishing the "desired objective."

On 29 April 1933 Daladier, the minister of war, created the Department of the Fabrication of Armaments. In addition to acquiring the broad matériel responsibilities of the Department of Artillery, which retained some responsibility for automotive developments, the new department executed armament plans conceived by the other departments. When prototypes were built, it tested and modified them as necessary, although it could not decide whether the vehicle or weapon would be accepted, since field testing of equipment and units remained the responsibility of the individual departments.[61] Thus, the new Department of the Fabrication of Armaments served as a conduit for orders and an organization for conducting initial tests, but it did not control the elaboration or development of weapons. In essence, the Department of the Fabrication of Armaments operated on the same levels as the other departments and was never superior to them.

In January 1934, the Technical Cabinet created by Weygand was abolished and replaced by the Section of Armament and Technical Studies, which became part of the General Staff.[62] The new section performed essentially the same function the Technical Cabinet had performed, but now it reported to a deputy chief of the General Staff. In July 1935, a law confirmed the existence of the Department of Fabrications and Armaments and formalized the existence of the bureaucratic structure for the consideration of matériel development. It simultaneously created a corps of engineers for the manufacture and testing of armaments.[63]

By 1935, the semblance of a hierarchical system for matériel developments, headed by the Consultative Council on Armament, existed. The Section of Armament and Technical Studies in the General Staff performed the detailed staff work associated with the armaments program. It provided essential information to the Consultative Council, and it coordinated the activities of the various departments and acquired the necessary budgetary credits. Accomplishing the latter task required the armament section to coordinate with the chief of the General Staff, the secretary general of the War Ministry, the war minister, and finally the Finance Ministry—all of which, of course, was no easy task. The departments of the various branches and the Department of Fabrications and Armament theoretically operated—relatively speaking—beneath the Consultative Council and the armament section. The Department of Fabrications and Armament executed the armament plans conceived by the other departments and conducted some initial testing, but the individual departments retained responsibility for initial equipment requests and field testing. If there were disagreement between the departments, the General Staff supposedly arranged or imposed a compromise.

A centralized, hierarchical system, nonetheless, did not actually exist. After the war, the first director of fabrications and armaments explained that the several changes did not actually increase the General Staff's involvement in matériel development, since that organization had never done anything other than request information.[64] Similarly, the officer who had been the chief of the armament and technical studies section in 1939 complained that the deputy chief of the General Staff charged with following technical developments did not have enough time to follow such questions in detail.[65]

Significant problems continued to revolve around the question of who was to control the direction of technological advances. The law of July 1935 stated that the Department of Fabrications was to conduct "all research, studies, and tests, following the instructions received from the General Staff."[66] But the General Staff never exercised this responsibility effectively. The essential characteristics of the system remained those of decentralization and inefficiency, because the responsibility for developing and accepting new technology remained with the departments of the individual branches. The cumbersome system was confusing even to those who worked with it. After the war, General Gamelin acknowledged before the parliamentary investigating committee that the entire process was complex and difficult to understand.[67]

Weygand and Daladier's reforms in the mid-1930s, therefore, had not created a system for propelling new technological achievements forward. They had ended some of the confusion and some of the redundancy, but they had not created a system whereby the responsibility for development and management of matériel lay with a specific agency within the High Command rather than the bickering and relatively independent branches or services. Clearly, army needs were subordinated to branch needs, an obvious perversion of priorities.

France even had difficulty with those weapons of war for which there was little disagreement concerning their purpose and method of employment. The example of the antitank mine illustrates this. After the fall of France, General Gamelin admitted that France suffered from a "flagrant inferiority"[68] with regard to this valuable tool of war. In fact, France had 80,000 mines on hand on mobilization, but only 40,000 of these had fuses. Only 400,000 to 500,000 had been manufactured when Germany attacked.[69] The question then becomes why France did not have more mines, and who had failed to order them. The postwar parliamentary investigating committee sought an answer to this question. After questioning a number of officers and civilians who had worked in the various armament sections of the General Staff and War Ministry, General Martignon, the ex-director of the Fabrications of Armament Department under the minister of war, gave an answer. He explained that sufficient mines were simply not requested early enough.[70] Even this simple task had become muddled in France's complex command structure. One could even say that the example of the antitank mines demonstrates that France's bureaucratic system promoted inefficiency, rather than efficiency.

The de facto retention of responsibility for technological developments by the departments completed the process of fragmentation and decentralization of the High Command. When the responsibility for technological developments was coupled with their dominance over doctrinal issues, the departments tended to pursue individual branch needs without regard for army needs. Only the authority of the Superior Council of War, the vice-president of the council, and the chief of the General Staff transcended the parochialism of the departments. Yet even their authority was diluted by the absence of a clear chain of command, the confusion over authority between the civilian and the military hierarchy, the inability of the Superior Council to control its agenda completely, and the lack of authority by the council to enforce its recommendations or advice.

When the French constructed their bureaucratic system for the High Command in peacetime, their basic assumption had been that the power of the minister of war could unify the disparate elements of the military hierarchy. But when the minister bowed to the technical authority of the military leaders and delegated the authority of his signature to the directors of the individual branches and services, a unity of effort and direction was no longer possible. Where firmness and a sense of direction were essential, France had confusion and mistrust. In such an environment, retention of old doctrine was easier and more likely than the formulation and dissemination of a radically innovative doctrine.

The cumbersome procedures in the military hierarchy did not disappear when the war started. Although the army was already awkwardly organized, the army's High Command was reorganized in January 1940 in such a fashion that it suffered from even greater inefficiencies. At the beginning of the war, Gamelin functioned as the commander in chief of the northeast front and had General Georges as his deputy. The general headquarters operated under Georges's control and was located at La Ferté-sous-Jouarre, about forty miles east of Paris. General Gamelin placed his personal headquarters and a small staff at the Chateau de Vincennes on the outskirts of Paris and at least once a week traveled to La Ferté to be briefed by Georges. Toward the end of December 1939, he informed Georges that he had decided to separate his headquarters from that of Georges and to make him the commander of the northeastern front. This relieved Gamelin of the pressures of directly commanding the northeastern forces and left him free to coordinate the operations of all theaters. General Doumenc, one of the early exponents of the tank, assumed the responsibilities of the *major général,* or chief of staff, to Gamelin.

Although Gamelin kept his personal headquarters at Vincennes, his new headquarters was located at Montry, midway between Vincennes and La Ferté, and included selected elements from each of the General Staff's bureaus. Among others, it included officers from the operations bureau concerned with activities outside the northeastern front; personnel specialists concerned with the broadest possible issues, such as the formation of new units; and intelligence specialists concerned with matters other than German forces. While the office for railroad transportation remained with Georges's headquarters, Gamelin had Doumenc retain responsibility for its operation. Despite the effort to make a clean split between the two headquarters, neither Gamelin nor Georges had a complete staff. Doumenc found himself working at Montry in the morning and at La Ferté in the afternoon. Staff members were constantly on the road to confer with their counterparts on the other staff and often found themselves duplicating each other's work. The ensuing confusion could only have detracted from the army's efforts.[71]

After the war, Georges testified that he had complained repeatedly about the command and staff relationships. Gamelin supposedly refused to consider these protests and insisted he required a large staff to control the activities of all theaters of operations.[72] With a responsibility embracing the entire war effort, Gamelin believed he had to look beyond the narrow confines of the northeastern front. He unfortunately failed to recognize how completely the danger of the German threat outweighed all other considerations.

The matter was made worse by Gamelin's isolation at the Chateau de Vincennes. He had no radio or telegraph communications and relied on telephone and messenger for information. Gen. Joseph Vuillemin, the air chief of staff, found he could communicate more rapidly and effectively with the headquarters of Montry and La Ferté than with Gamelin.[73] Clearly, the entire arrangement smacked of the World War I experience when higher-level commanders had had time to consider their actions carefully and to direct them with leisure from afar. This approach was not abandoned until 20 May 1940, when General Gamelin was relieved and replaced by General Weygand. France's new leader swiftly assumed personal command over the battle, improved communications from his headquarters, and provided energetic and enthusiastic leadership to the army.

Notwithstanding the tragic specter before France, it was too late. She had prepared for and gone to war with a cumbersome military hierarchy ill-suited to innovative and flexible responses in peace or war. In the face of an all-out lightning war, she learned all too painfully that her military hierarchy lacked a unity of effort and a level of efficiency essential to modern warfare. What was not so apparent then but is obvious now is that those same deficiencies interfered with her efforts to formulate a more modern doctrine. Whether in peace or in war, France's military institutions were more capable of dealing with the technological, doctrinal, and command problems of 1914 than those of 1940.

CHAPTER 7

The Development of the Tank

Throughout the interwar period, the French firmly believed that the tank was one of the most important weapons introduced during World War I, but they also believed that the most important function of the tank was to assist the infantry. Faced with an overwhelming increase in firepower, many French officers considered the armor-protected tank a natural vehicle for assisting the infantry in its difficult tasks on the battlefield. The failure to perceive a more independent mission for the tank is partially rooted in the French experience in World War I and in the numerous vehicles left over from that war. It is more deeply rooted in the army's reluctance to allow the tank to overturn its doctrine. Even though the tank promised more mobile and wide-ranging operations, its employment was carefully enclosed within and constrained by the doctrine of the methodical battle, which precluded mobile operations. Only the light mechanized division of the cavalry escaped the deadening influence of that doctrine.

When World War I ended, in November 1918, France had approximately 4,000 tanks. This included 3,187 Renault FT-17, 400 Schneider, 400 St. Chamond, and 100 British Mark V tanks. The first tanks employed by the French were the massive 14.6-ton Schneider and 25.3-ton St. Chamond tanks, which were ordered in the spring of 1916. On 16 April 1917 at the Chemin des Dames, 132 of the Schneiders became the first French tanks to enter combat, but they contributed little to Gen. Robert Nivelle's disastrous offensive. Their first combat action was under less than successful circumstances. While the larger tanks were considered massive breakthrough vehicles, the French soon began producing thousands of the smaller and cheaper 6.5-ton FT-17s, which were more suited to accompany the infantry. This trend reflected the French acceptance of the idea that a large number of smaller machines had a better chance of success and survival than the heavier and more expensive tanks. Following the armistice, France produced about 400 more of the FT- 17 tanks. By March 1922, she had 3,572 of the light tanks.[1] The tanks left over from World War I remained the major part of the French armored force through the mid-1930s.

One cannot overestimate the influence of the equipment remaining from World War I. Specifically, with more than 3,500 FT-17 tanks still in the French inventory after 1918, and with units and depots overflowing with them, many French soldiers never had any experience with armored vehicles other than the fragile FT-17 until the early 1930s. The lightly armored, two-man tank weighed 6.5 tons, had a maximum range of 25 to 30 miles, and was only capable of a speed of 4.8 miles per hour under ideal conditions. On cross-country movement the tank was reduced to a speed somewhere between one and two-and-a-half miles per hour. For traveling long distances, it had to be hauled by train or truck. Because of its slowness and light armored protection, the FT-17 tank would normally advance with or slightly precede the infantry. To let the tank audaciously advance far ahead of the infantry was obviously a mistake and would risk its being destroyed without actually helping the infantry in the attack. The presence of such tanks thus did little to convince many officers and soldiers of the potential of armored operations.

Several regulations on the employment of tanks appeared soon after the war ended. The doctrine contained in these manuals codified wartime practices. The 1920 manual entitled *Provisional Instructions on the Employment of Tanks as Infantry Weapons* clearly expressed the prevailing French perception of tanks immediately following the war. It stated, "Tanks are not able to conquer or occupy terrain by themselves alone. They are only a strong aid placed at the disposition of the infantry." The manual also emphasized that tanks should always be employed in mass, in depth, and on a large front.[2] The 1920 infantry regulations repeated this view of the tank and its role and argued that tanks could not fight by themselves and were "designed to facilitate the forward movement of the infantry in crossing passive obstacles or active resistance. . . ."[3] The 1921 instructions on the tactical employment of large units also emphasized that the tank was "designed to augment the offensive power of the infantry. . . ."[4]

Both the 1920 manual on the employment of tanks as infantry weapons and the 1921 instructions on the tactical employment of large units envisaged only two types of tanks: the light and the heavy. The 1921 instructions explained that the light tanks had the "role" of "accompanying the infantry and of fighting in intimate liaison with it," while the heavy tanks were "designed to smash a way for the infantry and light tanks by using their mass and their fire to break down the defenses of strongly held centers of resistance."[5] Thus the two types of tanks and the doctrine for their employment corresponded closely to the tanks and the doctrine employed in World War I.

Though the lessons of the war seemed apparent to the French military hierarchy, it conducted a series of special studies after the war to ensure that France proceeded in the right direction with the new weaponry. The first study was completed in February 1919, the second in March 1919. Neither was a detailed or wide-ranging analysis, and both followed the outline of the methods derived from the war. The preference of the High Command for the light tank was evident when the March study proposed an extremely small tank, manned by a single individual. Work on this tank, however, was never begun.[6]

The French completed their first in-depth peacetime study of the tank program in July 1919. In contrast to the two major types of vehicles used in World War I (the heavy and the light tank), this study called for three major types of tanks: the accompanying, battle, and rupture tanks. These tanks corresponded respectively to light, medium, and heavy tanks. The study also called for a variety of other tanks specifically designed for such tasks as communications, liaison, observation, and artillery observation. While the accompanying tanks would carry only machine guns, the battle and rupture tanks would carry cannon and machine guns. The accompanying, or light, tanks performed the task of moving with and assisting the infantry in its battle against the enemy infantry and their weapons, especially the machine gun. The rupture, or heavy, tank performed the task of smashing enemy defenses; it could be used against heavily defended positions, in the battle against machine guns, and for protection of the other tanks against anti-tank weapons or enemy tanks. The battle, or medium, tank also assisted the infantry by aiding its maneuver, rather than overcoming enemy defenses.[7] While France possessed light and heavy tanks, she had none of the medium tanks, whose role was rather imprecise in French thinking but whose evolution was to be the key in the emergence of new ideas on the employment of armored forces.

The inclusion of the battle tank in the 1919 program clearly came as a result of the influence of Gen. Jean-B. Estienne, who has every right to be known as the "father" of French armor. In addition to being the first in the French army to conceive the idea of the tank, he dominated the creation of the French tank force from 1915 to 1918 and organized the first French tank units.[8] Following the war, he remained head of the tank corps until it was subordinated to the infantry in May 1920. When the army created a new position of inspector of tanks in February 1921, Estienne assumed the new position and remained there until his mandatory retirement in 1927. In this position, Estienne's bureaucratic powers were extremely limited, since he was technically an assistant to the inspector general of infantry.

When the army moved the tank technical section from the Department of the Artillery, which had responsibility for most matériel developments, to that of the infantry, Estienne also had little control over the tank elements within the Department of Infantry.

Despite these limitations, Estienne had a greater influence over French armored forces in the years immediately following the war than any other tank enthusiast. In a lecture given in February 1920, he said, "The appearance on the battlefield of the tracked, mechanical vehicle is an event whose importance equals that of the invention of gunpowder."[9] He went on to describe a new armored force of 100,000 men and 4,000 tanks, able to move 80 kilometers in a night. As the years passed, he became increasingly vocal and passionate about the need for an independent tank force and for the development of a battle, or medium, tank.

In January 1921, General Estienne became a member of the commission under General Buat, chief of the General Staff, that was charged with concocting a new tank program for the French army. Despite Estienne's limited bureaucratic powers, the creation of this commission provided him and his supporters a unique opportunity to exert great influence over the destiny of the French tank. During the two meetings of the commission, Estienne's pronouncements and observations dominated the deliberations, and the commission's conclusions were an evident reflection of his beliefs. In many ways, the deliberations of the 1921 commission represent the zenith of the movement toward producing an independent tank force. The commission was dominated by tank enthusiasts and included not only Estienne but other officers whose names would become intimately associated with the development of French armor.[10]

The 1921 commission concluded that France needed only two types of tanks: a battle and a heavy, or rupture, tank. In suggesting the elimination of the light-tank development program, the commission evidently wanted the battle tank to fill the roles previously filled by the light and medium tanks. Arguing for the infantry and artillery to adapt their methods to the capabilities of the tank, the enthusiasts foresaw the battle tank as the focal point of the army's attention, not the infantry's. The new tank would be a fast tank, and the infantry, according to Estienne, would have to follow in trucks or in trailers towed by the tanks. The new battle tank would have the ability to move a hundred kilometers in a night, weigh a maximum of thirteen tons, have 25mm of armor, have a radius of action of eight to ten hours, and be armed with a machine gun and a 75mm or a 47mm cannon. As for the rupture tank, it permitted the attack of organized enemy positions.[11] The commission did not fix the technical characteristics of the rupture tank, for it awaited the production of the new heavy 2C tank. Development of this tank had begun during World War I, and when completed, it weighed seventy tons, had 30mm of armor, and carried a 75mm cannon and four machine guns. Such weapon systems, the enthusiasts believed, could transform the nature of war.

The 1921 commission did manage to redirect France's tank-building effort from the light tank to the medium tank. Although development of a 9-ton light tank had begun after the war, this was soon abandoned in favor of doing nothing more than improving the Renault FT-17 tank, which remained an important part of France's tank force because of its great numbers. From 1921 to 1924, the French army concentrated on the development of a relatively simple yet forward-thinking program based upon the battle and rupture tanks. To facilitate and accelerate development of the new battle tank, General Estienne was placed in charge of its development. Progress came slowly, but by 1924 a "specimen" of the new battle tank, which eventually emerged as the B-1 tank, was ready. Unfortunately, it weighed twenty-one, rather than the projected thirteen, tons. This unexpected weight, as well as the complexity and expense of the prototype, meant that the tank could not be constructed in the large numbers desired by the High Command.

That the 1921 commission had not convinced everyone of the need for a light tank to accompany the infantry soon became apparent; it had only succeeded in temporarily slowing the light tank's development while accelerating that of the medium tank. In the early 1920s, numerous articles appeared in military journals about the role of the tank. While some argued for the tank to play an accompanying role, others argued for the tank to play a more independent role. The public debate indicated that many French officers believed that two types of tanks could not fulfill the entire range of essential functions on the battlefield, and that several specialized armored vehicles were preferable to an all-purpose battle tank. Many officers wanted a light tank that could operate very closely with the infantry and that would replace the already aging FT-17. By the end of 1924 the army began to reconsider its priorities.

To consider a change in philosophy, the High Command created another commission to analyze the tank program. Presided over by General Giraud, the inspector general of tanks, the new commission completed its work in October 1925. Its report recommended the development of three types of tanks: light, battle, and heavy. According to the report, the light and heavy tanks performed those tasks previously envisaged for them: accompanying the infantry and rupturing enemy defenses, respectively.

The report also supported the need for a battle tank which could fulfill the mission of the light tank if necessary, but which had other functions. The report explained:

> The action of the light tanks and the battle tanks should be combined on the battlefield: the first being numerous and having the accompaniment of the infantry as their mission; the second, the element especially charged with protecting the first against the enemy antitank weapons and tanks and [with] attacking the protected machine guns of the defense.

According to the report, the improvement of antitank means and the appearance of enemy tanks required a "more rapid and a more strongly armed tank," but if there had been any hope for an independent mission for the tank, it did not appear in the 1925 report. The study noted, "The essential mission of the tank is the accompaniment of the infantry. . . ."[12] The 1925 report was thus a defeat for the battle-tank enthusiasts, since it reinvigorated the light-tank program and linked the battle tank to the infantry battle. It also established the standard French approach to the tank that was to endure through 1939. No single all-purpose tank could fulfill the specialized and different requirements of the accompanying and battle tank roles.

Such changes in philosophy or priority required the intervention of the High Command, and in March 1926, the Superior Council of War considered the tank program. The meeting began with the deputy chief of the General Staff reading the October 1925 study done by General Giraud's commission. When completed, he explained that the question before the council that day was to determine whether the army should develop three different types of tanks. An involved discussion followed in which each participant supported the view, as Foch explained, that "the tank is an indispensable arm of the infantry." After the inspector general of tanks noted that every tank, regardless of weight, was an infantry tank, Pétain concluded, "The tank is enfeoffed to the infantry." The council then unanimously adopted the proposition that the army needed a light tank weighing less than thirteen tons and that another tank weighing approximately twenty tons, obviously Estienne's battle tank, was also needed. When the president of the Republic asked whether a rupture tank should be developed, the council agreed with Pétain when he said, "It exists." The seventy-ton 2C tank evidently fulfilled this need. The final question pertained to whether three prototypes of the battle tank developed by General Estienne should be produced, and the council agreed that three were needed. In

April 1926, the minister of war, Paul Painlevé, approved the tank program that had received the Superior Council's seal of approval.[13] The French military was fully committed to the production of three types of tanks.

Though the battle tank enthusiasts had been bloodied, they had not been beaten. Work continued on the battle tank after three prototypes were received by the army. Following some technical difficulties with the engine, the first battle tank, which had been designated the B-1 tank, was delivered to the Commission for Tank Tests at Bourges on 7 May 1930, more than four years after its development had been approved. Meanwhile, work had also commenced on the light tank. The infantry initially concentrated on an improved version of the FT-17 tank but then experimented with an entirely new tank, the Renault "NC," in 1926.[14] By 1929, development of a new light tank, the D-1, had begun. Both the B-1 and D-1 tanks experienced continual technical problems. Before either had completed its tests, the tank technical section in the Department of Infantry noted that even though they met the conditions of the 1926 program, the armor of the B-1 was probably too light and the engine of the D-1 too weak.[15] These two technical difficulties became major obstacles in the subsequent development of the light and medium tanks. Calls for heavier armor plating to provide better protection from antitank weapons invariably increased the weight of the tank and caused the engine to be too weak for the heavier vehicle.

Two new regulations on tank units appeared in 1929, but neither offered new ideas on the employment of armored forces or reflected the thoughts of the 1921 commission under Estienne. The manual entitled *Regulation on Light Tank Units* was an "improved" version of the 1920 manual with a similar title. It was also considered an annex to the 1928 infantry regulations. The preface suggested the entire tone of the manual when it said that "the action of light tanks should only be conceived within the framework of infantry combat."[16] The second regulation, *Instructions on the Employment of Combat Tanks*, stated that its purpose was to explain the general "rules" governing the employment of tanks. The "rules" were clearly limited, for the regulation included the statement, "Combat tanks are accompanying weapons of the infantry. . . . In combat, committed tank units are an integral part of the infantry dispositions."[17] This assertion was also included in the first paragraph of the volume pertaining to combat in the regulation on light tank units.[18] The French explicitly stated their perception of the proper way to employ tanks in the 1929 regulation on combat tanks:

> Tanks are only supplementary means of action placed temporarily at the disposition of the infantry. They considerably reinforce the action of the infantry, but they do not replace them.[19]

While the manual emphasized that tanks were best employed in mass, the concept of *chars de manoeuvre ensemble*, or tanks for a mass maneuver, had not yet appeared.

The same manual on the employment of combat tanks also explained that there were three different types of tanks: light, medium, and heavy. The light tank was the Renault FT-17, and its major purpose was clearly that of accompanying the infantry. The heavy tank was the 2C tank which could be used against strongly organized enemy positions, against enemy automatic weapons outside the radius of action of the light and medium tanks, and for the protection of light and medium tanks against enemy antitank weapons and tanks. According to the manual, the medium tank was the Mark V tank, a British-made veteran of the Great War. Its purpose was also one of attacking fortified positions. Because its armor protection was less than that of the 2C, it could only be employed in times of limited visibility with strong fire support. While the 2C tank was the only "new" tank mentioned in the manual, its entry into the French arsenal had caused the Mark V tanks left over from World War I to be relegated to the position of medium tanks, even though the French never had more than ten of the 2C tanks.

If there were any notions of new methods derived from the introduction of the B-1 battle tanks, they did not appear in the 1929 regulations. The preface to the regulation on light-tank units underlined the two major changes in the regulations. The first concerned supply and maintenance, which were designed to make the tank units more self-sufficient and more easily partitioned among the infantry units. The second was necessary because of the adoption of one-year service and concerned the simplification of training in order to make it as "intensive" and as effective as possible.[20] Otherwise, the information contained in the 1929 regulations was essentially a codification of the methods employed in World War I. Very little had changed in French doctrine in the ensuing ten years.

In 1930, the French made changes in the tank program which were eventually to eliminate the requirement for a heavy tank and bring about new attempts to improve the light tank. When the Superior Council of War met in June 1930 to approve a study on motorization completed by the General Staff, one of the most important points was the elimination of the heavy tank. This study suggested, and the council approved, having only light and medium tanks.[21] Although the heavy-tank program was not officially eliminated until June 1934, and the final surviving six 2C tanks were destroyed by a German bomber at a railway siding in May 1940, the council's recommendation to eliminate the heavy tank accorded with the recognition of the vulnerability of the large machines and the complexity and difficulty of keeping them in operation. At the same time, an underlying assumption appeared to be a belief that the emerging models of the medium tank could fulfill the function traditionally assigned to the heavy tank. This tendency had been demonstrated in the 1929 tank regulations, which made little distinction between the functions of the medium and the heavy tanks. In future years, the doctrine for the employment of the medium tank came more and more to resemble the earlier doctrine for the employment of the heavy tank. By the late '30s, the medium tank was even referred to as the "heavy" tank.

In 1930, the French intensified their efforts to improve the light D-1 tank. A note from Captain Deygas of the tank technical section suggested that a light tank with stronger armament and more rapid speed could be obtained by improving the D-1 tank. While Deygas referred to the new vehicle as a light tank, which would be named the D-2 tank, his suggestion did not make clear whether it would accompany the infantry or act in a different fashion. Determining whether the tank would be classified as light or medium was an important decision, since the light tank fulfilled the accompanying function, while the medium tank fulfilled a different function not yet clearly defined in French doctrine. To confuse matters further, Deygas also suggested building a D-3 tank, which would have much lighter armor and a stronger motor and be much faster than the D-1.[22] The French, however, concentrated their resources on the development of the D-2.

Between 1925 and 1935, the introduction of improved antitank weapons made the major problem in tank development the question of armor protection. The 1925 study on the tank program had noted the need to increase the thickness of the armor plating on the new battle tank from 25mm to 30mm, and subsequent suggestions by the director of infantry, as the lethality of the antitank weapons became more apparent, emphasized the need to increase the armor plating thickness to 40 or 45mm.[23] While infantrymen tended to suggest greater armor protection at the expense of speed to ward off antitank rounds, tank enthusiasts preferred the addition of some armor protection without decreasing vehicular speed. The trend toward heavier armor was energetically resisted by the inspector general of tanks, General Bezu, who argued, "The armor plating should be the maximum possible compatible with the three other parameters of the tank (weapons, speed, and weight), determined according to the purpose for which the tank is constructed." He also argued that providing additional armor plating should not diminish the speed of the tank and cited the difficulties with the new D-1 tank, whose maximum speed of twelve kilometers per hour made it unusable with fast mechanized formations.[24] The issue of balancing armor protection against speed was a crucial one. The choice revolved around whether the tank should be a heavily armored machine which simply bowled its way through and crushed its opponents, or whether it should be armored enough to protect it from most infantry weapons, but light enough to use its mobility to strike at weak points and drive deeply into enemy lines.

The inspector general of tanks did not have the power to halt the accelerating trend toward increasing the armor protection of French tanks. The director of the Department of Infantry, who had greater influence over the technical design of the tanks, concluded that the "struggle of the shell against the armor plating" would result in the progressive increase in the tank's weight. According to the men who had the true power over the tank program, the increasing accuracy and capability of antitank weapons required the addition of greater armor protection for the tank despite the "insurmountable difficulties" in matériel and mobility.[25] Faced with the greater firepower of the defense, the High Command moved to provide greater armor protection for the tank.

If a greater premium were to be placed on maneuver, evidence of its importance was essential. The most likely source of this evidence was the several field tests conducted by the French army in the early 1930s. In November 1931, Colonel Touchon, who had made his reputation as an instructor at the War College, had become the commandant of the School of Application for Infantry and Tanks, and would become the primary author of the 1938 infantry regulations, suggested the formation of a special unit to experiment with "modern" methods of combat. The suggested tests were conducted in September 1932 at the Camp de Mailly and included three companies of D- 1 tanks (forty-five tanks) and the three existing B-1 tanks.

The test results were far from being a vote of confidence in the tank. The commander of the mechanized detachment rendered the only favorable report on the exercises. The report of Colonel Touchon, who was the chief "umpire" of the exercises, questioned the potential of mechanized units. He noted that they could attack or maneuver against a weakened enemy without all his weapons, but that they would be "doomed to failure" against an enemy with minefields emplaced and artillery not seriously weakened by counter-battery fire. Colonel Touchon also examined the possibility of forming an armored group consisting of two battalions of D-1 tanks and one battalion of B-1 tanks. He concluded that while such an organization might have a greater capability for maneuver, it too lacked the ability to attack a strongly defended enemy position.[26] General Dufieux, the inspector general of infantry, repeated many of the observations of Touchon, especially those critical of the ability of mechanized forces to complete a rupture of enemy positions. He concluded that the time was not right to form special tank units, and that the armored forces could make their greatest contribution in close liaison with the infantry, artillery, and aviation. According to General Weygand, this negative report on the September 1932 exercises virtually halted the movement toward independent armored forces.[27]

The French army conducted additional tests in 1933, but these tests also resulted in critical questions concerning the potential of armored forces. The tests were conducted at Coëtquidan by Col. Julien F. R. Martin, who had conducted tests earlier in 1930 with Renault FT-17 tanks. Perhaps the most surprising aspect of the tests was the rather severe views of Martin, who was later to become the inspector general of tanks. Martin argued that the crew members of the new tanks could not see well enough for the tanks to operate alone. Consequently, the occupation of conquered terrain remained the task of the infantry. As for their acting as a source of immediate support for the infantry, he explained, "The action of the tanks can substitute for the direct support and close protection demanded heretofore of the artillery." Even more remarkably, he argued that armored units tended to move too quickly, thereby losing part of "their offensive capability and [becoming] vulnerable to counterattacks." According to Martin, the solution to the problems of the tanks' vulnerability and their tendency to race forward too quickly lay in successive objectives. If these objectives were placed about fifteen hundred meters apart, the infantry and artillery could provide protective fires, and the tanks' movement could be more closely controlled.[28] Martin's report irrevocably linked the tank to the methodical battle. The notion of successive objectives about fifteen hundred meters apart under closely coordinated artillery fires soon became an essential part of French armored doctrine.

As for the difficulties of controlling the new tanks, the problem of limited vision in the B-1 tank had already been noted in other tests. Soon after the reception of the first B-1 tank, one of the testing commissions emphasized that in the rain or in rough terrain, the vehicle advanced "very slowly and almost blindly."[29] When a commission under the Department of Infantry tested the new tank, it also noted problems of controlling the vehicle. While it concluded that many advantages could be obtained from the B-1 tank when it was used to "reinforce" the action of accompanying tanks, the commission expressed reservations about the ability of the tank in more independent actions. It strongly emphasized the difficulty of controlling the vehicle in an exploitation because of vision, orientation, and communication problems. At the same time, the commission stressed the vulnerability of the B-1 tank to enemy tanks and antitank weapons. The commission concluded that even though the B-1 was "a very good all-terrain vehicle," it was "actually an imperfect combat weapon."[30] Such problems undoubtedly influenced the decision in 1934 to produce an improved version of the B-1, which was designated the B-1 bis.

In the early 1930s, the High Command made other studies of the tank that asked fundamental questions about its role. In June 1932, General Maurin presented the results of a special study to the Superior Council of War addressing the proper design of a tank to be used in a defensive role. Maurin discussed three major alternatives, the first being what he called the "tank solution," or the use of the B-1 tank. The second, an armored self-propelled cannon that resembled the tank destroyers of World War II, would have a 75mm cannon mounted on the chassis of a D-1 or D-2 tank. The modified turret containing the 75mm cannon could be quickly removed and replaced with the standard turret of the D-1 or D-2 tank. Extra turrets would be built for this purpose and would supposedly enable the new vehicle to be converted quickly into an offensive weapon system. The final solution suggested by General Maurin was a towed turret, mounted on four wheels and carrying a 75mm cannon. The movable "turrets" could be towed into defensive positions by tractors and moved to other positions once the battle was over. According to Maurin, the best solution was placing a modified turret on the D-1 or D-2 chassis. The reporter who transcribed the minutes of the Superior Council meeting noted General Weygand's astonishment at Maurin's preference, and the discussion quickly turned to another subject.[31] Maurin's suggestion, however, closely corresponded to the prevailing perception of how a future battle had to be fought. First, the enemy's attacks had to be halted by using such weapons as Maurin's armored self-propelled cannon with replaceable turrets. Next, a counterattack would eject the enemy from his hasty defensive positions and eventually deal the final blow. Weygand's astonishment at Maurin's preference illustrates his own recognition that such a schema might not be as simple or effective as it seemed.

Though no more than three B-1 tanks were ever available during this period, the several field tests and analyses of the armored forces in the early 1930s played a decisive role in the modernization of the French army. In fact, these field tests probably played a far more important role in the long term improvement of the army than did other occurrences such as the several disarmament conferences from 1932 to 1934. While discussions preceding and following these conferences occurred in a time of French economic crisis and may have irritated some military leaders, they resulted primarily in a temporary reduction in funds. They may also have slowed down the development of a new "B—B" tank, which would have weighed 35 tons and thus would have exceeded the previously accepted thirty-ton limit on tanks.[32] Any negative effects, however, were only temporary. In contrast, the reassessment of the tank program from 1932 to 1934 had a great effect on the modernization of the army. At the expense of the medium-tank program, it led to an intensification of the effort to build a better light tank suitable for accompanying the infantry.

In a January 1933 meeting of the Consultative Council on Armament, the inspector general of artillery observed that the D-1 and B-1 tanks were unsuited to accompany the infantry. His major objection was that these two tanks were too fast for the infantry. The 1932 tests had demonstrated that when the infantry defensive positions had been overrun by the attacking rapid tanks, the infantry had been able to continue their operations only after rejoining their own accompanying tanks. Also, the appearance of more powerful antitank weapons clearly made the Renault FT-17 obsolete. In the view of the Consultative Council, the combination of these considerations supposedly demonstrated the need for a new light tank.

The initial analysis by the Consultative Council on the need for the light tank discussed two alternatives for the French tank program, with an annual expenditure of 50–60 million francs a year, totaling about 550 million francs over ten years. The first course of action considered the purchase of about one hundred fifty B-1 and improved B-1 tanks and about two hundred fifty D-2 tanks, totaling about four hundred tanks. The second course of action considered the purchase of about one hundred B-1 and improved B-1 tanks, two hundred D-2 tanks, and five hundred light tanks, totaling eight hundred tanks. The total cost of both programs was supposedly the same.[33] The advantages of eight hundred tanks versus four hundred tanks were obvious to those favoring a newer tank to accompany the infantry: the potential number of light tanks would be decreased. The study strongly suggested that greater combat potential and more tanks could be obtained by channeling more money into the purchase of light tanks designed to accompany the infantry. Although the redirection of the tank program would come at the expense of the medium tank, supporters of the accompanying tank believed the need for that tank was greater than that for a medium tank.

The Consultative Council on Armament soon chose the alternative with the greater number of tanks. On 30 June 1933 it suggested a new program for light tanks to the minister of war, and shortly thereafter the minister approved the production of a light tank.[34] In September 1933 and March 1934, the High Command placed orders for prototypes of the future R-35, H-35, and F.C.M.-36 tanks.

General Estienne scathingly criticized these actions. As a veteran of the subterranean wars in the French headquarters, he recognized the profound effect the proposed program would have on his attempts to create a large, mobile armor force. After mandatory retirement for age in 1927, Estienne had been attached to the tank technical section of the Department of Infantry as a civilian but with the pay and privileges of a general officer, and had retained some influence over the development of the medium or battle tank. In October 1933, General Estienne expressed his reservations about the new program to Gen. André Corap, a division commander who had been a member of the 1921 commission for creating a French tank program. A résumé of Estienne's observations was apparently circulated among key military officials shortly thereafter.[35] A month later, Estienne expressed his views again, this time by a more carefully written note. His major point in both instances was that all the credits for the development of armored vehicles should be concentrated for the creation of a single tank rather than a variety of tanks. In this sense, he was returning to the ideals originally expressed in the 1921 program, when the light tank had been omitted and only the medium and heavy tanks included. He explained:

> Let there be, in the actual conditions of weapons and armament, two armies, A and B, equal from the point of view of the value of their men and the market value of their matériel; they have each spent 500 million to have, for A, 500 tanks weighing 30 tons, and for B, 1,000 tanks weighing 15 tons. . . . The triumph of army A cannot be doubted, because it is able to attack with its tanks while the adversary can only try to defend with his.[36]

Unfortunately, Estienne's remarks fell on deaf ears. The call for an effective and modern light tank to accompany the infantry had persisted for almost fifteen years and received wide support from the officer corps. According to the supporters of this concept, the D-1 tank was too fast for the infantry, and by comparison, the D-2 tank being developed was even faster. At the same time, the battle or medium tank, which had emerged as the B-1 tank, had been officially accepted as an eventual replacement for the light tank only for the short period following publication of the 1921 commission's conclusions. By 1933, the call for a light tank, even if it came at the expense of the battle tank, could no longer be repressed or mollified with the D-model tanks.

In March 1934, the Superior Council of War discussed the direction of the French tank program, and Gen. G. M. Velpry, the inspector general of tanks, provided a full study of the tank program to its members. Gamelin began the meeting by noting that the army had only three B-1 tanks, but seven others were being built. There were one hundred sixty D-1 tanks, grouped into three battalions, with twenty-five of the tanks being unassigned. While it required two years to build the B-1 tank in three different factories, it took fourteen to fifteen months to build the D-1 tank. After mentioning the anticipated production of fifty D-2 tanks within a short while,[37] Gamelin observed that the B-1 was a complicated machine, could never be produced in mass numbers, and was two-and-one-half times more expensive than the D-2. General Dufieux noted that while the B-1 was an excellent tank, the D-2 was "inferior to the B-1 in armor plating, speed, and maneuverability." While the D-1 and D-2 had originally been conceived as light tanks, the report of the inspector general of tanks categorized them as medium tanks which could perform the same function as the B-1 tank or act as an accompanying tank.[38] After Weygand noted that the D-2 did not solve the problem of accompanying the infantry, the council's discussion indicated that while the B-1 might be suitable as a medium tank, the D-1 and D-2 were not appropriate for fulfilling the need for light tanks and were not as effective as the B-1 in fulfilling the need for a medium tank. The council eventually concluded that the D-model tanks should be adopted only as "transition" tanks. It also approved the B-model tanks.

The Superior Council members agreed on the need for developing a new light tank, especially since the D-model tanks were no longer considered accompanying tanks. General Debeney explained, "The infantry will not move if they do not have the support of tanks." The inspector general of tanks' report acknowledged that prototypes for a new light tank had already been produced by the Hotchkiss manufacturing firm and Puteaux arsenal, following the minister of war's approval of a new light-tank program in June 1933. After further discussion on the role to be played by the light tank, the council unanimously approved the adoption of an accompanying tank, and asked that the choice of prototypes for the beginning of mass manufacture be completed by the end of 1934.[39] While the council had not initiated the renewed development of the light tank, it obviously supported such a program. Moreover, its approval provided the seal of acceptance to what was to become a firm redirection of priorities in the tank program. By June 1936, the General Staff decided that three-quarters of the tanks should be light and one-quarter medium or heavy.[40]

Doubts about the resurgence of the light-tank program undoubtedly remained. Copies of General Estienne's stringent criticism continued to circulate, and in January 1936, General Martin, who conducted the 1933 tests of armored forces and who was soon to be the inspector general of tanks, addressed the issue in a lecture at the Center of Higher Military Studies. While he did not suggest that France had all the answers to the questions about the best employment of the tank, Martin strongly supported the direction the French tank program began to take in 1933. After reading Estienne's note of November 1933 to the audience, he discussed the maneuvers of 1933, in which he had participated and from which no data supporting the need for an independent or autonomous armored force had been acquired. Martin's conclusion was clear: "[T]he tank 'to do everything' does not exist." He argued that the accompanying tank was essential for the infantry, since it could provide much more accurate and responsive fire than the artillery. Similarly, the proper method of controlling the tanks was through the use of successive 1,200- to 1,500-meter bounds. While operating under the protection of infantry and artillery fires, the tanks could provide support that was more rapid and more "intelligent" than that provided by the artillery.

As for those calling for the employment of tanks in an "autonomous" fashion, Martin referred his listeners to the tank proponents in Great Britain. To suggest the excesses of those enthusiasts and to warn his listeners of the dangers of such excesses, Martin said, "England is the school of mechanization *à outrance*." The implicit labelling of Estienne and other tank enthusiasts as extremists demonstrated Martin's obvious preference for a balanced tank program containing both medium and light tanks. Between the two extremes of all light or all medium tanks, Martin evidently preferred the center position. In that sense, his presentation before the Center of Higher Military Studies represented a reiteration of the views he had expressed in his report on the 1933 tests at Coëtquidan.[41]

Questions about the wisdom of the French tank program did not cease. In March 1936, General Velpry, the inspector general of tanks who had been Estienne's right-hand man, expressed his concern to the chief of the General Staff about the proposed increase in numbers of light tanks at the expense of the medium tanks. Though he had supported the March 1934 recommendation by the Superior Council of War to redirect the tank program, he explained that while an increase in the number of light tanks would diminish the difference in numbers of tanks between France and her potential enemies, it did not provide an "element of technical superiority." According to Velpry, only the battle tank could provide this. He explained that the advancement inherent in the battle tank was comparable to that made in the artillery when the model 1897 75mm cannon was introduced.[42] His comments apparently had little effect.

As for the construction of the new light tank, the initial technical characteristics provided by the Consultative Council on Armament in June 1933 required the new tank to weigh a maximum of six tons, have a speed of eight to ten kilometers per hour, have armor plating of 25mm thickness, and be armed with one machine gun and a small-caliber cannon. Problems were soon encountered, however, with the armor plating. Following demon-

strations of the new 25mm antitank cannon's effectiveness, the Consultative
Council decided to increase the thickness of the armor plating to 30mm,
which necessarily increased the maximum weight to nine tons. After receiving prototypes from several firms, the army conducted tests in 1934 under
the control of General Dufieux and selected the Renault prototype over the
others. Although the Hotchkiss prototype was much faster than the Renault
and cost about half as much, the High Command preferred the ruggedness
and reliability of the Renault tank. In January 1935, however, the Consultative Council announced that this prototype was unacceptable, predominantly for reasons of insufficient armor plating and exposed tracks. After
requesting other prototypes from other firms and following additional tests,
the Consultative Council announced its preference for an improved
Renault prototype.[43] The first R-35 tanks, which were less expensive than
the D-2, began arriving within the first few months of 1936, and the final
version of the tank weighed 10.3 tons fully equipped, had armor plating of
40mm thickness, and was armed with a short-barrel, low-velocity 37mm cannon and a machine gun. It also had a two-man crew, which conserved manpower but kept the tank commander so busy that elaborate maneuvers were
virtually impossible. With a limited top speed of twenty kilometers per hour,
a much slower normal operating speed of ten to twelve kilometers per hour,
and problems of command and control, the R-35 was precluded from any
function other than that of infantry support.[44]

The first manual reflecting the growing emphasis on accompanying
the infantry was the *Provisional Notice on the Employment of D Tanks in Liaison
with the Infantry*. The manual was initially approved in July 1934, and
included a preface signed by Marshal Pétain as minister of war. The preface
carefully noted that the D-tank could be employed as an accompanying
vehicle or within a mechanized unit. Conditions were especially appropriate for using mechanized units at the beginning of a campaign when the
enemy was not fully equipped, his units spread across broad fronts, and his
troops not yet battle-hardened. In April 1935, a circular from the General
Staff specified that mechanized units were best employed when the enemy
was "weak, surprised, or disorganized." Otherwise, the D-tank was normally
employed in "intimate liaison" with the infantry. According to General Martin, this concept for employment of the D-tank came from the 1933 tests at
Coëtquidan.[45]

The new doctrine was the first clear articulation of the concept of *chars
de manoeuvre ensemble*. The tanks for mass maneuver were not constituted
into units larger than a battalion. Apparently, a variable number of tank battalions would be grouped into larger units according to the needs of a specific mission. Specially designated armor commanders would then assume

command of these battalion groups. As for the actual employment of the D-model tanks, they would normally be employed ahead of the infantry and their accompanying tanks in order to destroy the stronger defenses of the enemy. After they overran an enemy position, the following infantry and their tanks would then move forward to destroy the enemy resistance completely. They could also be committed against an enemy flank in an oblique fashion, or they could thrust more deeply into the enemy's rear.

The *chars de manoeuvre ensemble*, therefore, were little more than a leading wave of tanks that prepared the way for the infantry, which was the decisive arm, or that enabled an infantry unit to move. Such doctrine relegated the medium tank to a role very similar to that previously assigned to the heavy tank. Without the permanent formation of larger units, without permanent headquarters, without a philosophy of independent, autonomous maneuver, there was little chance that these battalion groups could accomplish an audacious offensive stroke. Although the concept of mass maneuver tanks remained a major component of French doctrine, it represented a regression in expectations for the medium tank, whose mass maneuver represented a different type of infantry support rather than a new method of restoring mobility to the battlefield.

Other regulations reflected France's acceptance of the "principle" of mass employment of the battle tanks ahead of the infantry. The 1936 instructions on the tactical employment of large units summarized the possible missions for the tank. The first mission listed by the instructions was to accompany the infantry and to "operate in close liaison" with it. The tank was especially useful for attacking automatic weapons that might slow down the infantry's progress. The second mission was to "advance well ahead of the infantry and accompanying tanks, toward their successive objectives." Such a mission was intended for the mass-maneuver tanks, and the manual later explained that the tanks for mass maneuvers were retained under the control of the large unit commander and committed into battle when they could assist the maneuver of the large unit, rather than simply that of the infantry. The third mission listed in the 1936 instructions was to "attack armored formations of the enemy." This had long been a function of the medium or battle tank, and so it remained. The fourth mission was "penetrating deeply" into the enemy's positions as soon as his defenses were in disarray. The objective was to reach the most distant weapons and command groups. Finally, the instructions added that tanks could form the framework of "mechanized detachments" for an exploitation or could be an "element of maneuver" for the commander of a large unit.[46]

In early 1937, the army conducted further studies on the tank, this time in field tests at Sissone in April 1937. The participating forces included one company of B-1 tanks, one company of D-2 tanks, and one battalion (three companies) of R-35 tanks. The major result of the test was the "proving" of the concept of tanks of mass maneuver. The report noted that when such tanks were protected by strong artillery fire, and when they operated through a series of successive efforts, they could assist the infantry and the accompanying tanks in their forward movement and in their deep conquest and occupation of the terrain. The report also emphasized the need for artillery support. With more powerful antitank weapons, artillery fire had to be employed against such weapons. Such support, however, could only be provided through the use of successive objectives and thereby limited the rate of advance of the tanks, which had to operate under an umbrella of artillery protection. These conclusions ensured that the methodical battle would not be overturned by the tank; rather, the tank had become an integral part of that step-by-step, carefully controlled battle.

Other important conclusions came out of the tests, one of which was that the R-35 was suitable only as an accompanying tank. At the same time, the B-1 and D-2 tanks were clearly identified as "tanks for mass maneuver." If only accompanying tanks were employed in a battle, a proper density was about forty tanks per kilometer, but if both accompanying and mass maneuver tanks were employed, about sixty to seventy tanks per kilometer were essential. The proper ratio of mass maneuver to accompanying tanks was 1 to 2.[47] The formal summary of the several reports concluded, "The principle of the massive employment of tanks is confirmed."[48] There was no call for the formation of an armored division. The general officer in charge of the tests, apparently content with only moderate change, concluded that it was necessary to run exercises in the "domain" of the armored brigade.

By 1937, the subject of artillery support for tanks became crucially important, even though officers had intensely debated the subject for more than a decade. Although the 1929 manual on the employment of tanks in combat had emphasized that the tank could be protected from enemy fire by having it work in "intimate cooperation" with the other arms,[49] such cooperation became increasingly important in French doctrine throughout the 1930s as antitank weapons became more and more threatening to the tank. In the field tests of 1932, Colonel Touchon strongly emphasized the need for close cooperation between the artillery and the tanks. His observations were reinforced by the comments of General Dufieux.[50] In the 1933 field tests at Coëtquidan, Colonel Martin reiterated the importance of artillery support and the difficulty of coordinating it with the tanks.[51] After seeing some tank maneuvers in the fall of 1936, the director of infantry observed that using the better-protected medium tanks in a mass maneuver in front of the accompanying tanks increased the chances of rapidly "submerging" the enemy antitank weapons. He emphasized, however, that the "principle" mission of the artillery was to "assure" the protection of the tanks.[52] Similarly, the commander of the 1937 field tests at Sissone also emphasized the need for "powerful and methodical" artillery fire to protect the tanks' actions. Consequently, the number of artillery tubes that were needed to support an attack by tanks would not diminish, even though the actual number of rounds fired would decrease because of the faster rhythm of the attack. Or, as the commander of the exercises concluded, "No economy of artillery, but a shorter, more violent, and denser action."[53]

Throughout the series of field tests in the 1930s, observers had often emphasized the difficulty of achieving close coordination between the tanks and the artillery. In October 1937, a special commission, presided over by General Georges, addressed the question of the means and nature of artillery fire for armored units. According to this commission, timetables were especially useful. If successive objectives were selected about twelve to fifteen hundred meters apart, artillery units could provide fire support according to a preplanned schedule. While the scheduled fires would not be absolutely inflexible, their establishment would simplify the problem of establishing and maintaining liaison between the artillery and the tanks. When General Condé, the inspector general of artillery, stated at a commission meeting that such timetables would not constrain the maneuver of the tanks and that the artillery could execute them easily, General Dufieux agreed. Lt. Col. Jean Perré stated that the major problem was one of communications, and suggested that an artillery liaison officer be placed in each tank battalion. The commission agreed, but stipulated that these liaison officers should not be sent to an echelon below the battalion. Discussion on this point ended when the commission approved the use of timetables.

The question of artillery organization also appeared at the commission's meeting. General Georges asked why a specific artillery battalion could not provide direct artillery support to a specific tank battalion. General Condé's response aptly summarized the basic issues. He explained that the need to facilitate maneuver of a unit through the use of artillery support favored the use of direct support artillery. That is, a specific artillery battalion would have to support a specific tank battalion or group of battalions. Condé explained that if this were done, almost all of a division's artillery would be allocated to support specific maneuver units. He concluded, "But all the artillery must participate in the support of the tanks for the mass maneuver." If the tanks for a mass maneuver were to succeed, they had to have mass artillery support, not simply the support of one artillery battalion. To decentralize the artillery, according to Condé, was to misuse the artillery. The commission agreed, and by doing so, ensured that the tanks remained tied to the massive employment of the artillery.[54]

As usual, the French considered the decentralization of artillery an abdication of command by higher commanders. The centralization of the artillery remained a key to the methodical battle, and solutions favoring rapid maneuver rather than massive firepower were unacceptable. The French believed the speed of the attack was conditioned by the ability of the artillery to provide support, and this important assumption remained a crucial factor in subsequent attempts to create large armored formations. Such formations could move no faster than their artillery, which would remain under centralized control at as high a level as possible.

In December 1937, a new manual entitled *Provisional Notice on the Employment of Modern Tanks* appeared. The manual only considered "existing" units, so it did not address the question of large mechanized or armored units. Yet it is a good summary of tank doctrine in 1936–1937. The manual stated that tanks could not occupy terrain, and that if they stopped on the field of battle, they risked being destroyed. At the same time, the tanks could not engage targets beyond a range of four hundred to five hundred meters because of vision problems. Consequently, the tanks had to cooperate closely with the artillery and infantry. As for employment, tanks should be employed by surprise in great numbers, on large fronts, and in deep attacks which "envisaged at least the destruction of the artillery dispositions." The manual included the requirement that tanks move by successive bounds, protected by the fire of the artillery and infantry, and also explained the purpose of the mass maneuver tanks. While the ability of the tank to support the infantry reduced the requirement for artillery fire support, the major reduction in the consumption of artillery ammunition came as a result of the increase in the "rhythm of the attack."[55] In sum, the manual repeated many of the ideas emphasized in French doctrine during the previous several years.

By 1937–1938, France believed that the tank would play an important role in any future war, but she had not abandoned her perception of the tank as a vehicle to assist the maneuver of the infantry. General Dufieux's final comments on the tank program before his retirement as inspector general of the infantry demonstrate the prevailing perception of the tank. He explained:

My profound conviction is that these machines are destined in a future conflict to play a decisive role; that which the infantry was not able to do without tanks in the last war, it will be even less able to realize in future operations. The tank . . . must be the arm of preference in a nation poor in personnel.

He then added, "But for usefully and surely playing this role, the tank must be strongly protected." As for the problem of balancing protection against speed, Dufieux explained, "War is a question of force where the advantage . . . rests with the most powerful machine and not . . . with the most rapid machine."[56] By 1937, France's doctrine and the design of her tanks reflected Dufieux's preference for heavily protected tanks working in intimate liaison with the infantry. The doctrine emphasized the great fire-power and the massive protection of the tank, not its ability to restore mobility to the battlefield. The doctrine was not a carbon copy of the methods of 1917, but, as General Velpry noted in 1937, the major difference in the French view was the acceleration in the rhythm of the battle.[57]

The failure to recognize the true potential of armored mobility continued through 1939. Many of the doctrinal concepts from previous manuals were repeated in a 1939 draft edition of the *Regulation on Units of Combat Tanks, 2nd Part: Combat,* which concentrated on the infantry's accompanying tanks. A draft introduction from the minister of national defense and war initially included a phrase from the 1936 instructions about the anti-tank weapon confronting the tanks as the machine gun had confronted the infantryman during World War I. The commission charged with writing the manual, however, deleted the phrase and asserted that with the introduction of improved antitank weapons, the tank could attack only with the "protection and support" of the artillery and in "intimate liaison" with the infantry. As for possible missions for the tank, the draft manual repeated those listed in the 1936 instructions and said that tanks could impart "a more rapid speed to operations."[58]

When the draft regulation discussed the tanks for a mass maneuver, the method for using successive bounds of approximately fifteen hundred meters again appeared. The only criticism of this concept came from General Loizeau, who was a consultative member of the commission and who represented the General Staff. Loizeau argued that a typical distance of fifteen hundred meters should not be given, since the actual distance would vary greatly according to terrain, enemy dispositions, strength of the base of fire, etc. He nevertheless did not argue against the use of successive bounds.[59] The manual also envisaged the tanks being employed in a "zone of action," but General Georges criticized this term, since he believed it indicated "a zone limited only laterally in which the unit maneuvers."[60] Georges apparently preferred more explicit wording that emphasized the successive objectives and their limiting effect on the tanks' maneuvers.

The 1939 draft manual placed a greater emphasis on artillery than any of the previous manuals for tanks and offered the novel approach—for the French—of the artillery adapting its methods to the tanks. Reflecting a common theme in the 1930s, it argued that the "great quantity" of antitank weapons on the battlefield required even more support from the artillery. Similarly, the breaching of minefields, which would be more numerous, also required additional artillery support. The draft regulation, nevertheless, recognized the need for the artillery to organize itself around the "disposition" of the tank units. Compared to previous thinking, this was a major change which sought an alteration of the methodical approach. But Georges objected. His solution was to make as few changes in the artillery's organization as possible. He believed that special artillery support battalions should support particular tank units only in the most exceptional cases, such as when a tank unit had a zone of operation that overlapped the firing zones of several artillery battalions. In that case, changing the responsibility for supporting the tank unit as it passed through several zones was too complex and required too much prior planning. Otherwise, Georges preferred the system established in the 1938 infantry regulations, which provided for centralized artillery support.[61] Simply put, Georges preferred the methodical approach.

Despite the attempted change in artillery doctrine, the 1939 draft manual did not represent an attempt to overthrow French doctrine completely. The regulation also included the use of timetables, which were an essential part of the artillery's method of providing fire support to the tanks moving from one successive objective to another. The authors of the manual had sought unsuccessfully to modify only a small portion of the methodical approach.

As for the density of the tanks, the regulation stated that twenty tanks per kilometer was the minimum essential number for the employment of tanks of mass maneuver. It explained that a division attack required two or three battalions of accompanying tanks and one or two battalions of tanks for mass maneuver. The inclusion of such numbers demonstrated the High Command's acceptance of the need for tanks if an infantry attack were to succeed. But Georges objected to the inclusion of such figures. He argued, obviously correctly, that tanks could not be allocated the same way artillery was allocated. By that he meant that the allocation of the tanks could not be determined by a rigid formula that indicated proper densities. He believed that tanks should only be employed in important areas, not throughout the front of an attack.[62] Georges, however, was not arguing that an overwhelming mass of tanks could or should be concentrated along a narrow portion of a front, in pursuit of a penetration, nor did the manual make this argument.

Other important concepts appeared in the draft regulation. In the portion discussing organization, the manual addressed the issue of armored operations by units larger than a battalion. Above the battalion level, the manual explained, there were only previously designated commanders and staffs for "groups of tank battalions." At the army level, there was a general officer designated as the commander of tanks in that army, and he was assisted by a staff. Within the corps and the division, no specific commander of tanks was designated. At those levels, the most senior commander of a "group of battalions" would assume command of any ad hoc combination of multiple groups of battalions.[63] Such an organizational structure reflected the French intention to use a major portion of their tanks in battalion-sized organizations, rather than larger ones. The doctrine also reflected the assumption that if larger groupings were necessary, time would be available to create them. Such assumptions were, of course, based on perceptions of mobility that proved to be dramatically wrong in 1940.

By stressing the need for aviation to work closely with the tanks, the manual reflected an awareness of this important new weapon. Aircraft were considered especially useful for employment against antitank weapons.[64] While the incorporation of such ideas did indicate some forward thinking, the overall value of the manual was, however, limited. It encompassed only measured or careful change when more radical change or reform may have been possible or even necessary. The 1939 manual continued to view the tank as an infantry support weapon, even though that support might be provided at the larger, rather than the smaller unit level.

The manuals appearing between 1934 and 1939 solidified the concepts of infantry-support tanks, mass-maneuver tanks, and the methodical battle, and these concepts became firm fixtures within French armored doctrine. The doctrine for employing infantry-support tanks included essentially the same methods employed in World War I, and the major tanks employed in this fashion, the R-35 and H-35, were improved versions of the FT-17 tank. While the concept of mass maneuver tanks evolved from the doctrine for employing the World War I rupture or heavy tanks, it envisaged much closer cooperation between the artillery and the tanks than existed in the Great War. Only the artillery could protect the tank against the lethal fire of the antitank weapon, which would be much improved and in greater numbers than on the World War I battlefield. Achieving the requisite cooperation between the tanks and the artillery, however, could only be accomplished through prescribing successive objectives, artillery timetables, and central- ized control—or, in other words, the methodical battle. The French doc- trine for the employment of the tank clearly restricted its maneuver and linked it to the tightly centralized battle.

In the two decades between 1919 and 1939, French perceptions of the various roles for the tank and the priorities placed on these roles changed slightly, but its overall focus never changed markedly. The experience and equipment of World War I favored the allocation of the tank into light and heavy roles. Yet General Estienne and his followers managed from 1921 to 1924 to add the medium or battle tank to the tank program and, momentarily, to decrease the emphasis on the infantry tank. Following the reassessment in 1925, France accepted the need for a light, medium, and heavy tank, but most officers agreed that the infantry tank was the most important. The 1932–1934 reassessment led France to eliminate the heavy-tank program, decrease the emphasis on the medium tank, and increase the emphasis on the light tank. In making this choice, the High Command decided to continue the tank as an adjunct of the infantry, rather than to begin the creation of an autonomous independent force, and it began the production of hundreds of light tanks during a period of economic crisis. In essence, the military hierarchy chose to modernize the army incrementally and to increase the importance of the accompanying tank. Rather than creating something vastly different, the military leaders subordinated the tank to an outmoded doctrine concentrating on the benefits of armor protection and scarcely conceiving of the true value of this new weapon.

The differences between French and German views of the tank were identified by a German officer in an article published in *Militär-Wochenblatt* in 1937. The main differences he saw between the two approaches concerned the objective of the tank attack. The field-service regulations, *Truppenführung*, explained the concept of a German attack: "Tanks and infantry which work together usually will be assigned the same objective, if possible the hostile artillery."[65] To get to the enemy's artillery, the German regulations prescribed a deep penetration by the tanks and a continuous thrust from the main line of resistance through the enemy's defenses, about four to five kilometers. The French sought to reach the enemy's artillery, but they planned on getting there by moving with successive bounds. The leading wave of the tanks for a mass maneuver would move to the first objective and await the arrival of the infantry and the accompanying tanks. After the infantry reached the first objective, the tanks for a mass maneuver would push forward again and be followed by the infantry and the accompanying tanks. The German officer described this as "seven minutes of attack and seventy minutes of waiting for the arrival of the infantry."[66]

The second difference identified by the officer concerned cooperation with the artillery; he believed that the French placed "twice as much importance" on the various arms cooperating together than did the Germans.[67] The French thought an infantry attack could be decisive only if carried out with tank support and if supported by artillery. In the name of combined arms, they preferred to subordinate each arm to the others and rejected the possibility of the tank acting relatively independently. The French wanted the tank to be bound tightly to the infantry and to be restrained by the tether of artillery support. Their emphasis on combined arms on the battlefield overruled any possibility of the tank performing a function other than supporting the infantry. Though the Germans agreed on the necessity of having the arms cooperate, they did not stress the combining of the arms to the same extent as the French and at the expense of more mobile operations. Their more flexible doctrine recognized the importance of exploiting all the strengths of the tank.

Another important difference identified by the German officer concerned the requirement for close liaison with the infantry. The 1933 *Truppenführung* stated: "When closely tied to the infantry, the tanks are deprived of their inherent speed and may be sacrificed to hostile fires."[68] The regulations also explained: "The infantry must utilize the [shock] effect produced by the attacking tanks to advance rapidly."[69] The French, on the other hand, downplayed the importance of the tank's speed and insisted on the tank staying close to the infantry. They sought to compensate for the consequent greater vulnerability of the tank by increasing the thickness of its armor plating. Preferring that the tanks provide immediate support to the infantry, they did not want them to rush forward and leave the infantry exposed. The Germans anticipated the possibility of the tanks setting the pace of the attack; the French remained focused upon the rate of advance of the infantry and artillery.

Ironically, the German officer identified the main differences between the two doctrines to convince his readers that the Germans had overestimated the potential of the tank. He sincerely believed his army might learn some important points about the employment of tanks from the French, who, as he pointed out, had had more experience in war and peace with the tank.[70] Despite their relative inexperience with the tanks, however, the Germans had progressed beyond the French in their understanding of the role and potential of the new weapon.

CHAPTER 8

The Creation of Large Armored Units

A few French army officers had long recognized the possibilities in grouping tanks into division-sized units. On 15 February 1920, for example, General Estienne, at the Conservatoire National des Arts et Métiers, discussed the strategic advantages of a large, independent armored force.[1] In July 1927, before the Center of Higher Military Studies, Col. André Doumenc described the tactical advantages of a large armored force. In 1928, Doumenc submitted to the General Staff a project for the organization of an armored division, similar to that which would later be realized by the Germans.[2] While he was a member in 1930 of the tank technical section of the Department of Infantry, Lt. Col. Marie J.P. Keller wrote a special study on the need for a mechanized division that could "rupture" enemy defenses.[3] When Lt. Col. Charles de Gaulle published his book in 1934 on a professional armored corps, his special army included three thousand tanks and six armored divisions.[4] The official effort to create division-sized tank units, however, did not actually begin until the late 1930s, and the French did not form their first armored divisions until January 1940. Although the first light mechanized division was formed officially in 1935, its function, as will be discussed below, clearly differed from that of the later armored divisions.

Throughout the debates and discussions on forming large tank units, the military hierarchy believed it could not form the first armored divisions until sufficient medium tanks were available to equip an entire division. Since France had only a small number of medium tanks for almost the entire interwar period, the High Command saw no compelling reason to create large armored units, even though production of the B-model tank remained painfully slow. By January 1936, the army had only seven B-1 tanks, and this number slowly increased to seventeen in March 1936, thirty in February 1937, and thirty-five in September 1937. Following the decision to produce an improved version of the B-1, production of the B-1 tank ceased and that of the B-1 bis began. In May 1937, the French army had four

B-1 bis tanks, and this slowly increased to seventeen in September 1937, thirty-five in January 1938, forty-seven in July 1938, and seventy-one in January 1939. The first model of the B-1 ter, another improved version of the B-1, arrived in April 1938, but only a few models were ever manufactured. By the beginning of 1939, there were only 107 B-model and fifty D-2 tanks. In comparison, France had 790 R-35, one hundred H-35, and eighty-nine F.C.M.-36 tanks.[5] Beyond a doubt, the High Command could have formed—if it had wanted—armored divisions with the infantry tanks. The army's leaders, however, were reluctant to strip tanks from the infantry, whose needs remained most important in their eyes, to form an unproved and untested armored division.

Despite the sincere desire of the tank enthusiasts for a larger number of the B-model tank, its extreme complexity made it unsuited for mass production and resulted in its being produced very slowly. During the period between March 1936 and March 1937, for example, the French produced 13 B-1 medium tanks and 422 R-35 light tanks. Among other problems, the steering system for the B-1 was very exacting and delicate. Since the 75mm cannon was mounted in the hull, it could only be traversed by turning the entire tank. This required a very sophisticated steering mechanism. Also, the demand for better protection against antitank weapons led to a decision to increase the thickness of the armor plating in the B-1. In contrast to the 1921 plan for the medium tank to weigh a maximum of thirteen tons and the armor plating to be 25mm thick, the B-1 bis had armor plating of 60mm and weighed thirty-three tons. When the Consultative Council on Armaments agreed in January 1935 to increase the armor plating of the new model of the B-1 to 60mm, it added the stipulation that the increase in armor plating should not decrease the mobility of the tank. In fact, weight increases reduced the cruising radius from more than nine hours, to about five hours and fifteen minutes.[6] The decrease in cruising range and agility was the practical result of the proponents of protection winning the debate against those of mobility. Throughout its development, constant modifications and slow production plagued attempts to field more B-model tanks.

The French High Command recognized the production difficulties with the B-model tank. In October 1930, the inspector general of tanks conducted studies on establishing specifications of a new tank that would use much of the technical experience from the B-1. If produced, this tank would have been designated the B-2. In 1932, two other prototypes, designated the B-3 and the B-B, were discussed. Even though the minister of war ordered prototypes of the B-2, B-3, and B-B tanks, none were ever produced. In late 1935 or early 1936, the inspector general of tanks began a study on a new thirty-five-ton tank, whose specifications resembled those of the B-2. In the same period, the Department of Infantry ordered a proto-type of a new twenty-ton tank, which in no case would go beyond a total weight of thirty-five tons. The same request proposed that the new tank be called the G-1. The suggestion for a massive forty-five-ton tank also reap-peared during this period, but was squashed when the director of infantry branded it as being "without real utility."[7]

Unfortunately for France, the army had begun in the early 1930s to reconsider the B-1 tank during the period when discussions at the confer-ence on disarmament at Geneva indicated a possible limitation of twenty-five tons on the weight of tanks. This delayed the anticipated studies, since the improved B-model tanks might have weighed as much as thirty-five tons.[8] Then, reductions in the 1934 budget slowed the development of a new medium tank. Finally, the massive resurrection of the light-tank pro-gram undoubtedly came at the expense of the medium tank. While the precise effect of these factors cannot be determined, the High Command's reassessment of the tank program from 1932 to 1934 and its redirection thereafter adversely affected the long-term development of the French tank and undoubtedly had a greater effect than the disarmament talks or the budgetary restrictions. Instead of producing a better medium tank, it pro-duced hundreds of infantry support tanks. Had the High Commission aggressively pursued the development of a new tank in the early to mid-1930s, a better tank than the B-1 might have been produced, but by the middle of 1938, it was too late to begin development and production of a new medium tank. The crises of 1938 underlined the need to have large amounts of modern equipment as soon as possible, and France's previous experience indicated that the development process might take several years. Her insistence on having sufficient medium tanks before she formed her first armored division, however, gave her little choice but to await pro-duction of sufficient B-model tanks. She refused to untie herself from the anchor of the "perfect" weapon.

The center of the discussion on forming and organizing large armored forces was the Superior Council of War, which was very deliberate in its con-sideration of armored divisions. General Gamelin stated in an April 1936 meeting, "The problem of constituting . . . large [tank] units has been stud-ied in France since 1932; the development of the antitank weapon has caused the renouncing of this conception." While the 1932 field tests had seriously delayed the creation of large tank units, subsequent tests had also not furnished evidence to support the creation of such units. Gamelin repeated other important findings from those tests when he explained that a tank attack could succeed against a soundly constructed defensive system only if it were supported by a "strong" artillery, which would be used against enemy antitank weapons. He added that the German armored divisions seemed incapable of completing a rupture of strong defenses, and seemed most appropriate to attack weakly held defenses or to conduct an exploitation. Throughout the discussion, members of the council seemed to view large tank units as large groups of mass maneuver tanks, which performed essentially the same function as the mass maneuver tanks but at a higher organizational level. While the council did recommend in April 1936 forming France's second light mechanized division, which was a mechanized cavalry division, none of its members argued for a more energetic program of testing or forming an armored division.[9] As far as they were concerned, the ad hoc combination of battalions of mass-maneuver tanks was sufficient.

In late 1936, France slowly began to accelerate the creation of large armored units as she began to improve and modernize her force. The government had already reestablished two years' service in the army in March 1935, and had also slightly increased defense expenditures in 1935, but the real rearmament of France began in late 1936, following the remilitarization of the Rhineland in March, the outbreak of the Spanish Civil War in July, and the German extension in August of military service to two years. With an increasingly threatening international environment, the government increased the defense budget from 11.48 billion francs in 1934 to 12.657 in 1935, 14.848 in 1936, 21.235 in 1937, 28.976 in 1938, and 93.687 in 1939.[10] Although these increases lagged behind those of Germany, which was spending more than double these amounts in terms of percentage of the gross national product,[11] France began what she believed to be a massive rearmament and modernization program. After all, Germany had to reconstitute her equipment almost completely, while France had a large quantity of equipment on hand in which massive sums had already been invested. As part of the armament program of September 1936, France proposed to create, among other things, fifty battalions of light tanks and twelve battalions of "heavy" tanks, evidently B-model tanks. The latter twelve battalions would equip two armored divisions of six battalions each.[12]

The High Command also began more energetically in 1936 to investigate the possibility of large armored formations. In October, Gamelin "invited" the members of the council to study the question of forming an armored division. In November 1936, Daladier, the minister of national defense, ordered the study of the possible future employment of armored divisions.[13] But the High Command made no move to create such a division immediately. At the Riom trial, Daladier insisted that the military hierarchy could have formed an armored division in 1936 if "they" had wanted.[14] His comment illustrated his belief that such decisions were clearly in the realm of a technical, military question and beyond the proper authority of the civilian minister of war. The military leaders, however, would not rush into an unproved concept, and they would not create an armored division until there were sufficient B-model tanks in France's inventory.

On 15 December 1937, the Superior Council discussed in detail the organization of an armored division. Gamelin began the discussion by explaining that the type B and D tanks were tanks for a mass maneuver and referred to these tanks as "heavy" tanks. While he accepted the need to organize armored brigades in peacetime, he noted the difficult question of whether it was necessary to organize the brigades into divisions. Gamelin argued that it was easier to split up a division into brigades than it was to form a division from brigades, a fact that supported the need to form an armored division. He concluded by noting that a large tank unit could be used in a "powerful" counterattack, but that it could also play an important role in the exploitation of a breakthrough, as well as in a flanking maneuver. General Dufieux offered a word of caution. He explained that France would not have enough B-1 tanks to form six tank battalions until the beginning of 1939. He believed it was dangerous to group all the heavy tanks in one division. Gamelin insisted, nonetheless, that the existing "heavy" tanks be organized into a brigade so that special studies on the employment of the armored division could be conducted. The final decision of the council was to constitute a special group under the inspector general of tanks to study the proper composition of the armored division.[15]

In February 1938, the minister of national defense ordered the constitution of the special study group recommended by the Superior Council of War. General Martin, the inspector general of tanks, was placed in charge of the study. His selection as director of the study group ensured that the ideas he initially expounded after the 1933 Coëtquidan maneuvers and reiterated in his January 1936 presentation at the Center of Higher Military Studies would remain an integral part of French doctrine. Tragically, when France needed a man of great vision and imagination, she received instead an officer who was content to apply the ideas and methods of the past.[16] The study included the creation of a large armored unit in 1938 for the first time in France. The unit was supposed to include one battalion of B-1 tanks, one battalion of B-1 bis tanks, one battalion of D-2 tanks, and two battalions of infantry. It would also include one battalion of 75mm and one battalion of 105mm artillery. Extensive field tests were scheduled for March 1938 and October 1938, but they were interrupted first by the annexation of Austria by Germany and then by the Munich crisis.[17] Such tests could not be conducted in a time of international tension. Thus the major results from the special study remained almost purely theoretical. No armored division came from the study group's effort.

General Martin cannot be accused of completely lacking any perception of the future possibilities of armored warfare, since his final report did contain a proposed organization for an armored division. He suggested it include two "demi-brigades," which were units smaller than the normal brigade and which included no regiments. The division consisted of four tank and two infantry battalions, half of which would be assigned to each demi-brigade. Two 105mm artillery battalions, with the shorter-range howitzer, provided organic fire support. The special study group also wrote a draft edition of a manual on the employment of armored divisions, but the provisional manual followed the directions of Gamelin by limiting its focus to the "general case of operations conducted against an enemy imperfectly installed on terrain and disposing of reduced means."[18] The study group produced five copies of the draft notice in October 1938 and sent copies to Gamelin and Georges. The concepts in the draft were highly reminiscent of those employed with the tanks for mass maneuver. If the several crises in 1938 had not interrupted the planned tests, more progressive concepts might have emerged. With the unimaginative Martin as the study-group leader, however, such a development was not likely.

With the international situation becoming more threatening in 1938, the Superior Council of War discussed the capabilities of the tank more intensely in December 1938. After beginning the discussion by noting how the partial mobilization of September 1938 prevented annual maneuvers and field trials, Gamelin said that numerous studies had been made and the potential of the tank was clear. He then referred to armored divisions as "rare and precious" units, and stated that one armored division had to be created in 1939, with three ultimately being created. Gen. L. A. Colson noted, however, that due to matériel limitations, the first two armored divisions could not be formed before the beginning of 1941. In the midst of the discussions, Gamelin explained his perception of how the large armored units should be employed. He said their best use was in an action "on the decisive point in the battle," and explained that an armored division could achieve a "result which could not be attained in the past." While Gamelin obviously accepted the possibility of large tank units playing a crucial role in future battles, he nevertheless believed it was "impossible to constitute in actual fact in times of peace, this large unit with all the means for which it may have need in all the phases and forms of its action." In peacetime, the armored divisions should have only "strictly indispensable elements," and, according to Gamelin, any other solution was "premature." Except for Gen. Pierre Héring, the other members of the council agreed. Héring insisted that the armored division should be organized in a fashion where it could operate in a more autonomous manner; this required additional artillery, communications, supply, air defense, and maintenance support.

While the differences in organization might seem nothing more than a debate over resources, they revolved around entirely different notions of how an armored division should be employed and of how a future war might be fought. From Héring's viewpoint, greater combat and support capability could enable a tank division to operate in an independent and much more fruitful fashion. He insisted the armored division should not be "obliged to advance in successive jumps according to the classic process of slow attacks based on the movement of infantry and artillery."[19] From Gamelin and the other council members' viewpoint, the armored divisions operated in the same manner as other tanks for a mass maneuver. While a division was much larger than the other mass-maneuver organizations, which were battalions or ad hoc groups of battalions, their concept envisaged it being employed in a step-by-step and carefully controlled fashion within the methodical battle. Though Gamelin proved himself a stronger proponent for armored forces than some of the other members of the council, he failed to recognize the capability of the armored division to restore maneuver to the battlefield. He still considered the tank units to be most valuable for their ability to add considerable firepower to an attacking force and for their potential for crushing any opponent in their path, and he believed a tank division provided more firepower and mass than any other organization.

Despite the shortage of medium tanks, the military hierarchy had no intention to form the first armored division with tanks other than medium tanks. At the Riom trial, Col. Jean Perré stated that Gamelin anticipated formation of the first armored division in October 1940. Only then would sufficient "heavy" tanks be available.[20] Due to matériel limitations and in accordance with the recommendations of General Martin's study group, however, the new division would contain only four tank battalions, rather than the six originally included in the 1936 rearmament program. By continuing to link the formation of the first armored division to the presence of sufficient B-model tanks for equipping the entire division, the High Command delayed the formation of the first armored division at a time the French army badly needed such units for experimentation and training. Only the German demonstration in Poland of the use of armored divisions finally overcame the reluctance of the High Command to form an armored division without the perfectly designed and heavily armored medium tanks, which were now being called "heavy" tanks. The rapid collapse of Poland provided a sense of urgency to the creation of armored divisions that had not previously existed.

When the first two armored divisions were formed in January 1940, each had a demi-brigade of light tanks, another of heavy tanks, and a final one of motorized infantry consisting of only one or two battalions. Each demi-brigade of tanks had two battalions. One demi-brigade had in each battalion forty-five H-39 tanks, an improved version of the H-35 tank with greater speed and a more powerful 37mm cannon. The other two battalions had thirty-three B-model tanks, giving each division a total of 156 tanks.[21] Meanwhile, France continued to wait for more B-model tanks; the High Command would not divert infantry-support tanks to the formation of additional armored divisions, and production of the B-model tanks remained agonizingly slow. Additionally, the hastily formed divisions suffered from a lack of equipment, such as tank retrievers, road transporters, and antitank guns.

The Provisional Notice on the Use of Units of the Armored Division, which had been written by General Martin and his study group, was published in February 1939. The ideas contained within the manual were a direct extension of the ideas appearing in the 1932 and 1933 field tests and developed or modified in subsequent years. The manual concentrated on the employment of the armored division to assist the maneuver of a larger unit, which was obviously an infantry unit. It also discussed the actual employment of the division as if it were simply a much larger grouping of mass-maneuver tanks. The French still intended to employ the large tank units to increase the offensive power and assist the maneuver of the infantry, which remained *the* decisive arm.

The manual also included a concept for successive objectives, but the bounds were increased to three to four kilometers because of the great size of the division. The tanks would be "habitually" organized into two echelons with two or three battalions in the first echelon and one or two battalions in the second echelon. While the first echelon fought its way to the next objective, the second echelon protected its flanks or reduced centers of enemy resistance bypassed by the first echelon.

The manual did make a number of improvements in the employment of the artillery. For example, the manual noted that the tanks would not necessarily halt their attack to permit the displacement of the artillery. The manual also noted that the commander centralized the artillery when it was necessary, but had to decentralize the artillery to ensure a rapid exploitation. To give greater flexibility to artillery coverage, the manual proposed having ground observers in armored vehicles following the attacking tanks. If possible, the observer placed himself on the crest of a hill overlooking the attack and directed the supporting artillery fire from there until the attacking tanks reached the next crest. If the terrain were woody or visibility limited, the observer followed the tanks closely. But with the limited artillery (two battalions) in the proposed tank division, most fire support came from the corps or army being assisted by the tank division. Thus, while there were some improvements in the division artillery's responsiveness, most fire support remained centralized and actually outside the control of the division commander.[22]

In short, the 1939 manual on the employment of the tank division made that large unit perform within the constraints of the methodical battle. The successive objectives, the tight control, the employment of echelons or waves of tanks, and the dependence on artillery support provided by other units ensured that the division operated in essentially the same fashion as a battalion of mass maneuver tanks. If there were a difference, it was mainly in scale. The frontage and firepower of the division were much greater, and the anticipated depth of the attack was deeper. Similarly, the division's major purpose was to assist the maneuver of an infantry corps or army, rather than of a regiment or division, but General Martin and his study did not foresee the creation of a mobile battlefield. Where a new doctrine was possible, the French were content to make incremental changes in the methods which had slowly evolved through the 1930s.

In contrast with the careful employment envisaged for the armored division, the French army considered the light mechanized division of the cavalry eminently suited for more mobile operations. Although the organization of the division changed during the 1930s, by May-June 1940 the first and second light mechanized divisions had a reconnaissance regiment equipped with forty-five Panhard armored cars and a brigade consisting of a regiment of truck-borne infantrymen and a squadron of sixty light reconnaissance tanks. They also had a combat brigade consisting of two regiments with each regiment having eighty-seven SOMUA S-35 or eighty-seven H-35 or H-39 tanks.[23] Though earlier concepts were not as forward thinking, the light mechanized divisions by 1939–1940 were designed to fulfill the traditional roles of cavalry units on the battlefield and also to be able to accomplish, with appropriate reinforcement, missions usually assigned to infantry or armored divisions. Ironically, the wartime doctrine for the employment of the mechanized cavalry units, except for the emphasis on cavalry-type operations, closely resembled the eventual doctrine of most Western powers for the employment of mechanized units during the battles of World War II. The important problem becomes one of determining why the doctrine for the employment of the light mechanized division was so much farther advanced than the doctrine for the employment of the armored division by 1939–1940.

Efforts for the mechanization and motorization of the cavalry began in the late 1920s—often to the disgust of the cavalrymen, who remained attached to their horses—but they did not accelerate rapidly until after 1930. When a new regulation on the cavalry appeared in 1930, it emphasized the evolving nature of cavalry tactics but reflected very little that was fundamentally new. Following organizational and weaponry changes, the manual explained, the cavalry was particularly suited for "rapid engagement on extended fronts," for "abrupt and violent" action by fire, and for the conduct of the exploitation. The cavalry division could also be employed on security or reconnaissance missions, and as a "highly mobile reserve of fire." While the division could be employed in the offensive, it was best suited for employment in weakly defended intervals, on exposed flanks, or against unprepared defenders. The regulation emphasized that an attack by a cavalry division was different from that by an infantry division, for a cavalry division attack was based on "the exploitation of the effect of surprise," while an infantry attack was based on a "succession of efforts." Defensive combat, however, was like that of the infantry division; it was based on the "establishment of barrages of continuous fire." As for the effect of firepower, the regulation strongly emphasized that fire and movement were "intimately bound together." There was no inordinate emphasis placed on firepower, since the cavalry had depended on mobility as one of its distinct characteristics for centuries.

Although the 1930 regulations concentrated on the horse cavalry, it also mentioned the employment of tracked vehicles, trucks, and motorcycles. It did not anticipate, however, the appearance of large, mechanized cavalry units.[24] Nonetheless, the 1930 regulations provided a foundation on which future mechanized doctrine and units could be built. Through its emphasis on mobility, the rapid use of firepower, surprise, and immediate exploitation, the cavalry doctrine provided a natural framework for mechanization efforts. This contrasts sharply with infantry and artillery doctrine, which emphasized mobility and flexibility much less.

While General Weygand was chief of the General Staff, from January 1930 until February 1931, and vice-president of the Superior Council of War, from February 1931 until January 1935, the French army made major advances in the mechanization of its cavalry formations. Weygand's role in the modernization of French cavalry was of crucial importance. In 1933, he followed the suggestion of Gen. J.A.L.R. Flavigny, the director of the Department of Cavalry, to create the light mechanized division, and in June 1934 he began studies on the development of a cavalry tank.[25] This tank was eventually to be the SOMUA S-35 tank, probably the best tank on the battlefield in May–June 1940 because of its great mobility, superior weapons, and excellent armor protection. The new tank weighed 19.5 tons, had a maximum speed of forty-five kilometers per hour, had a maximum armor plating thickness of 55mm, and was armed with a 47mm cannon and a machine gun. Unlike the B-model tank, it never suffered complex development problems. In 1935, the cavalry ordered a hundred of the S-35s before the tank completed required army testing.[26] In contrast to the delayed formation of large units of B-model tanks, the cavalry formed the light mechanized division before the arrival of the first S-35 tanks. The eagerness of the cavalry enthusiasts to form large mechanized units differed sharply from that of the infantry officers who were charged with developing tank units.

With the appearance of the light mechanized division and the possibility of stronger tanks, a new cavalry regulation, entitled *Provisional Notice on the Employment of Mechanized and Motorized Units of the Cavalry*, appeared in 1935. The new regulation did not replace the 1930 regulation, but it closely defined the missions of the light mechanized division, including the conduct of security and reconnaissance operations, the exploitation of a breach of enemy lines, and the sealing of a breach in friendly lines by occupying a defensive position or by counterattacking. Although the division could be employed in the offensive, it was most suited, according to the regulation, for movements to contact and for operations after a front had been ruptured by other units. When the regulations described how an attack should be conducted with the light mechanized division, it emphasized that such an attack should be closely supported by the artillery and infantry and should not be conducted against an enemy in a strongly held position.[27] In 1935, General Flavigny, commander of the first light mechanized division, explained that the division was best suited for offensive operations on an enemy's flank or in the exploitation of a breakthrough.[28]

Even though the mechanized cavalry divisions could be used in an offensive or defensive manner, French doctrine in the mid-1930s still placed a greater stress on traditional cavalry missions of reconnaissance and security. At the War College, in 1935–1936, an instructor noted that the mechanized division could accomplish the same sort of missions for a large motorized unit that a nonmechanized cavalry unit could accomplish for the "normal" large units.[29] The doctrine for employing the light mechanized division thus did not differ greatly from the doctrine for employing other cavalry divisions. The major difference was the recognition that the capacity of the mechanized unit for movement over long distances was greater than that for the horse-cavalry units. The 1936 instructions on the tactical employment of large units succinctly summarized the capabilities of the light mechanized division:

> Equipped for the distant search of intelligence, capable of assuring its own security, it is able to fulfill, with necessary reinforcements, all the missions assigned to large units of cavalry; it is able in particular to assure the reconnaissance and the security indispensable to large motorized units.[30]

In the late 1930s, the French continued to study the proper employment of the light mechanized division, and by 1939 they placed greater emphasis than before on the offensive capability of the division. The change was not an immediate one. In 1938, several lectures on the new division were presented at the War College and the Center of Higher Military Studies. The major theme of these lectures was the capability of the mechanized cavalry division to perform traditional cavalry missions. One lecturer especially emphasized the much greater mobility of the mechanized division over the horse-equipped division. While the lecturers did not foresee the division conducting a static, position defense, they did emphasize the offensive capability of the mechanized unit. They qualified this assertion, however, by adding that the division should be employed before the enemy strongly reinforced his defenses.[31] In 1938, General Flavigny emphasized the offensive capability of the light mechanized division. He pointed out that the division was equipped with the SOMUA S-35 tank, which was better than the D-model tank, and that it was also equipped with the H-35, the equal of the R-35 tank. The presence of these two tanks enabled the division to conduct frontal attacks, as well as attacks on an enemy's flanks. Flavigny emphasized that such missions should be given to the mechanized cavalry divisions only in "exceptional" circumstances. Since many of the subordinate units with the division were not suited for the offensive, the best mission for the mechanized division was one in which all elements could participate—obviously the traditional cavalry missions of reconnaissance, security, and exploitation.[32]

When he returned to the Center of Higher Military Studies in 1939, Flavigny placed even greater emphasis on the offensive potential of the light mechanized division. As in the past, however, he stressed that the division should not be used for attacking fortified regions or strongly organized defenses. When he discussed the actual conduct of an attack, he stressed the need for artillery fire to be employed in successive bombardments, separated by approximately fifteen hundred meters, and argued that as many as one hundred armored vehicles could concentrate along a one-kilometer front.[33] Though the successive objectives smacked of the methodical battle, Flavigny accepted a possible concentration of armored vehicles that was significantly greater than the fifty to seventy anticipated by many of his fellow officers. His presentation in 1939 also demonstrated the growing recognition by the cavalry of the greater offensive and defensive capability of the light mechanized division.

A new regulation for the cavalry appeared in 1939 and replaced the 1930 cavalry regulations and the 1935 provisional notice on the employment of motorized and mechanized units of the cavalry. The new regulation was undoubtedly the most forward-thinking regulation on mechanized cavalry or armor operations written by the French army during the interwar period. The regulation stated, "The cavalry finds its employment in all the phases of the battle. . . ." Missions for which the cavalry was particularly appropriate were reconnaissance, security, and exploitation, as well as "intervention in the battle, which requires rapid displacement, through all types of terrain and over large spaces. . . ."

As for the light mechanized divisions, these units, according to the regulation, could conduct an offensive either against an enemy flank or in a frontal attack. Flank attacks were preferred, but if a frontal attack was necessary, it could be conducted against an enemy who had not had the time to prepare his defenses, or against an enemy who did not possess all his defensive weaponry or units. After other elements made a penetration in an organized position, the mechanized division could conduct the final steps of the breakthrough, which would permit its rapid passage to the exploitation. When tanks more powerful than the S-35 (evidently the B-model tanks) reinforced the division, it could participate even more completely in the offensive by "penetrating rapidly and deeply into the enemy disposition." As for the defense, the light mechanized division could reconstitute a front after an enemy breakthrough by occupation of a subsequent defensive position; it could also counterattack an enemy penetration. The regulation explained, "A light mechanized division is especially suited to fulfill such a mission." If necessary, it could also occupy a static defense in the same fashion as an infantry division, but such employment was "exceptional" and required major reinforcements. Thus, while the light mechanized division was best suited for the traditional cavalry missions of reconnaissance, security, and exploitation, it could also accomplish missions such as a breakthrough that heretofore had been considered beyond its capability. In every sense, the 1939 regulation anticipated a more mobile and wide-ranging battle than that anticipated by any other regulation. It was also more modern in the sense of recognizing the great potential of mechanized formations.

The 1939 cavalry regulations also recognized the requirement for complex command and control systems on a highly mobile battlefield. This can be seen in its discussion of the artillery. The regulation emphasized the need for the artillery to make rapid displacements and to provide fire support in the rapidly changing situations of cavalry combat. The regulation further noted, "The will to follow the fight closely and in sight, [and] the spirit of initiative of the subordinate leaders, are indispensable for obtaining all the possible output from this arm." Although the regulation emphasized successive bounds and the progressive displacement of fire, it carefully noted the need to move quickly to prevent the enemy from reestablishing his defensive positions. Given the highly mobile nature of the battle envisaged, close cooperation was considered essential for success on the battlefield. The regulation stressed the need to establish liaison by making frequent contacts between the commanders, moving artillery observers forward, and employing liaison teams.[34] Thus, the organizations and methods of the artillery were adapted to the cavalry's style of operations, rather than adapting the cavalry's methods to the artillery's organization. The speed of the attack depended upon the speed of the mechanized formations, rather than on the speed of the infantry or the rate of displacement of the artillery.

The military hierarchy was greatly pleased with the light mechanized division. A note in November 1939 from the director of the cavalry to the General Staff described the division as an "extremely elaborate" and "ultra-modern" combat unit.[35]In a March 1939 meeting of the Superior Council of War, Gamelin described the mechanized division as having "become armored divisions which have, in addition, flexibility." In another meeting, in July 1939, he praised the divisions as "a fortunate solution, more fortunate than the Panzer division."[36]

The concept for employment of the light mechanized division, nevertheless, was clearly different from that of the soon-to-be formed French armored divisions. While the armored division was considered an organization highly suited for the massive employment of tanks within the methodical battle, the light mechanized division was designed to fulfill the traditional cavalry missions, as well as many of the missions that might be assigned an infantry or armored division, within a much more mobile and fluid battle. Hence, the armored division doctrine agreed much more with the overall French doctrine than did the mechanized cavalry doctrine. The French army accepted this difference, because the light mechanized divisions were designed to fight in front of or to the flank of units engaged in a methodical battle, not to be engaged with them. Throughout the evolution of the mechanized cavalry doctrine, this anomalous situation favored its development. Without suffering from the constraints of the philosophy of the methodical battle, the cavalry enthusiasts remained relatively free to obtain the maximum potential from the new organization.

When one compares the evolution of the doctrine of the armored units with that of the mechanized cavalry units, several other reasons appear to explain the more advanced nature of the cavalry doctrine. From the beginning, the traditional missions of the cavalry accorded more completely with the future missions of armored units. Instead of being dominated by the infantry and artillery concepts of firepower, centralization, and the methodical battle, the cavalry emphasized mobility, the rapid use of firepower, surprise, and immediate exploitation. Such concepts enabled the tank to fulfill its potential more completely.

At the same time, the cavalry units were extremely fortunate to have the dynamic influence of General Weygand to further their development. Weygand had long been a supporter of mechanization of the cavalry. When he became chief of the General Staff and then vice-president of the Superior Council of War, he was in a position to assist the cavalry in its efforts to create the light mechanized division. In contrast, the armor enthusiasts never had a supporter of the same power and influence as Weygand, who was vice-president of the Superior Council when the negative reports from the September 1932 tests at Mailly were rendered, and who did little to help the armor enthusiasts escape from the grasp of the infantry.

Even though General Estienne was clearly the "father" of the French tank, he never possessed influence beyond the narrow confines of the tank community. Despite his achievement, his power was limited even there. Throughout most of the interwar period, the inspector general of tanks was subordinate to the inspector general of infantry and never possessed the same degree of power. Similarly, the tank technical section was a sub-element of the Department of Infantry, whose influence it never escaped. Perhaps more importantly, the cavalry escaped the deadening influence of someone like General Martin, who as the inspector general of tanks failed to grasp the potential of the new weapon. In sum, the development of armored doctrine and vehicles clearly occurred under the thumb of the infantry, while that of the cavalry occurred in a much more autonomous and independent fashion. The French developed their armored doctrine within the infantry ideal, rather than developing something completely new and different.

The development of cavalry doctrine for larger unit operations was also favored by a longer period of experimentation. Following the creation of the first light mechanized division in the mid-1930s, doctrine for mechanized cavalry initially did not differ much from that for nonmechanized cavalry. Yet, as the years passed and as the cavalrymen gained more experience, the greater potential of the mechanized cavalry formations slowly became apparent. The cavalrymen reaped tremendous benefits from their willingness to form the light mechanized divisions before every piece of equipment had been produced. In contrast, France attempted relatively few field tests with large tank formations and did not actually form the first armored divisions until four months after the war began. And the High Command steadfastly clung to its demand for sufficient medium tanks to be on hand before the divisions were formed. In comparison to cavalry doctrine, armored doctrine was thus much more theoretical, and armored leaders had much less experience commanding and employing their units. While the tank units received severe criticisms during the several field tests for their inability to overrun a strongly defended enemy position, the cavalry never suffered from these criticisms. The cavalry conducted such a mission only under exceptional circumstances. Such missions were considered for the cavalry only after the light mechanized division had been formed. The technical design of its tanks also favored the cavalry. Having witnessed the tediously slow development of the B-model tank, the cavalry selected a simpler and, in fact, much more capable vehicle that could be mass produced. In that sense, it learned from the mistakes of the tank enthusiasts.

Another factor favoring the development of the cavalry tank concerned the mission of the light mechanized division. From the High Command's viewpoint, the operation for which the division was particularly suited was providing a strong covering force in an area such as Belgium. If the French army moved into Belgium at the beginning of a war, the light mechanized division could move forward rapidly and conduct a very strong mobile defense against a sudden incursion of enemy armored vehicles. The division could also cover the movement and deployment of the motorized divisions. On the other hand, the armored division was primarily associated with the offense and with assisting the offensive maneuver of larger infantry units. If it were necessary to employ tanks in the defense, units smaller than a division, in the French view, were more appropriate than larger ones. Consequently, the mechanized cavalry divisions coincided more nearly with the perceived needs of France than did the armored divisions and were formed much earlier. Gamelin reflected this belief in the July 1939 meeting of the Superior Council of War when he described the light mechanized division as a more "fortunate" solution than the panzer division.

France's movement toward mechanization was thus characterized more by its fragmentation and diversity than by its uniformity or clarity of purpose. The French concluded that an all-purpose battle tank could not be created, since the characteristics of the ideal tank could never be combined in one tank. A high-speed, heavily armored, low-cost vehicle was technically impossible to create. A tank to accompany the infantry was developed through infantry channels, a medium tank was developed through the energetic efforts of General Estienne and his disciples, and a cavalry tank was developed, naturally, by the cavalry. Each development channel sought to produce a tank with characteristics designed to maximize its potential utilization with that particular branch, whether to accompany the infantry, act as a main battle tank, or perform in a cavalry role. And each channel produced a variety of test vehicles and prototypes which consumed enormous quantities of precious resources and intellectual energies. None of these channels ever seriously doubted that the tank was an important addition to the battlefield. The significant debate concerned how the tank was to be used on the battlefield, and the differing concepts existing among the several institutions about employment prevented the emergence of a single, dominant idea on the role of armor. For that reason, the debate over the function of the individual tank was an inseparable part of the debate over the formation of large armored units.

The debate over the proper function of the tank also subordinated the technology of the tank to the already existing doctrine. In the normal fashion of the French High Command, each branch decided what it wanted the tank to do and then energetically pursued the construction of a tank designed and equipped to accomplish this end. In the case of the infantry tank, the French designed a tank specifically limited by the doctrinal constraints of the infantry and artillery intensive methodical battle. In the case of the medium tank, the armor enthusiasts became captured by the attractiveness of the "perfect" tank, which, unfortunately, was almost beyond the capability of French industry to produce and definitely beyond its capability to produce in the same mass numbers as the light infantry tank. In the case of the cavalry tank, the French designed a highly mobile and capable tank that doctrinally but not technologically was ill-prepared for anything other than the traditional cavalry mission. Throughout the debate, there was never a willingness to compromise and combine limited and precious resources into a single effort for creating a tank relying on the most modern technology and a highly flexible doctrine. France thus dissipated her efforts, for she had decided early in the 1920s that the "tank to do everything" did not exist.

In fairness, one must admit that concentrating all her efforts in one area might not have changed France's fortunes. When one seeks change in a bureaucratic system, one does not open closed minds or move projects forward simply by creating a more centralized and disciplined system; creative ideas or forward thinking do not necessarily prosper in such a system. For France, a more highly centralized effort may have resulted in an even greater dominance of the methodical battle ideal and a further dilution of the medium tank and cavalry tank programs. Since only an extremely small portion of the army's hierarchy recognized the potential of mobile warfare or approached questions of technology and doctrine from that perspective, no real possibility of a completely different approach actually existed. In that sense, the failure was both conceptual *and* institutional. To suggest otherwise is to give credit where credit is not due.

When the battle of France was fought in May-June 1940, the allocation of French tanks reflected the army's doctrine. According to the figures given by Lt. Col. Charles de Cossé-Brissac, the French army had twenty-five battalions of accompanying tanks on the northern and northeastern frontiers on 10 May 1940. This was a total of 1,125 tanks. The three light mechanized divisions had a total of 582 tanks, and the five cavalry divisions had a total of 110 tanks. There were also three armored divisions with a total of 624 tanks, with more than half of these being H-39 instead of B-model tanks.[37]

Although these figures do not include the fourth armored and fourth light mechanized divisions, which were formed after 10 May, almost half the French tanks were employed in an infantry support role. Less than 25 percent were employed in the French armored divisions, two of which were formed in January and one in April 1940. When these inexperienced divisions entered combat, they were inadequately prepared for the mobile warfare the Germans forced upon them. Their late formation and lack of preparation was a direct consequence of the French army's inability to understand the extra dimension mobile armor added to the battlefield.

CHAPTER 9

Conclusion

At the Riom trial, from February through April 1942, a parade of general officers attempted to defend French doctrine and to criticize weaknesses in armament, training, and morale. According to their testimony, the underlying reasons for the French defeat lay outside the realm of most military authorities, and thus their criticisms sought to shift the blame to the political leaders and to General Gamelin. For example, General Keller angrily defended the doctrine for the employment of tanks after Daladier read a letter dated July 1940 from Keller about French tank officers who were accused of indiscipline if they went beyond doctrinal constraints and charged ahead of the infantry. Keller argued that the defeat was not a question of doctrine but one of employment. He noted that if the defensive front at Sedan had not been rapidly penetrated, if the army had been able to withstand attacks by German aviation or had had an effective means to protect itself against such attack, or if the morale of the army had not been "entirely damaged" by a general depression of France's morale, "the tanks would not have been employed as they were."[1] Other officers repeated the same sort of theme. General Touchon argued that the methods employed by the Germans in 1940 were "absolutely" the same as those in French regulations, and concluded, "The doctrine is thus certainly sound."[2]

In the privacy of headquarters buildings, however, where criticisms could be shielded from the public, some members of the defeated High Command had acknowledged their shortcomings more readily than they would at the Riom trial. In late 1940, the General Staff, and soon thereafter the minister of war, asked the inspector generals of the various arms to provide analyses of the lessons to be drawn from the ill-fated campaign. In responding to this request, the inspector general of the infantry, General Gerodias, explained in early 1941 that the enemy's aviation had been the principal enemy of the infantry, and that a second had been tanks operating in close cooperation with the aircraft. He observed that while the antitank weapons had been capable of defeating the enemy vehicles, they had lacked sufficient mobility. After mentioning other difficulties, he concluded by emphasizing the need for improved communications, the decentralization of command, the allocation of combat support weapons to subordinate echelons, and the development of a "maneuver spirit" among infantry leaders through a flexibility in command and an exposure of infantrymen to unexpected situations in combat.[3] Some of the problems identified by General Gerodias had been addressed by General Huntziger as war minister in a general order published on 25 November 1940. Huntziger said that the French army had relied too much on textbook solutions before the war, and that future training exercises should emphasize having commanders solve unanticipated problems, make decisions, and issue concise orders rapidly.[4] Although such observations indicate that some military leaders did have reservations about the adequacy of the 1940 doctrine, most ignored or denied the most flagrant deficiencies of that doctrine in the glare of publicity surrounding the Riom trial, as they attempted to argue that the army could not follow its doctrine because of the intrusion of other factors or that the doctrine was similar to that of the Germans.

Despite the fervor of those defending the doctrine, their assertations could not obscure the basic fact: the French could not completely apply their doctrine in 1940 because its major components were simply inapplicable to a more modern and mobile battlefield. The inordinate emphasis on firepower prevented the French from understanding how improvements in tactical mobility, coupled with tactical methods originating from the German infiltration tactics of World War I, could overturn many accepted and combat-tested methods. The notion of a carefully controlled and tightly centralized battle belonged to another era, and the sense of chaos, lack of control, and futility which emerged from the French participation in the 1940 campaign demonstrated the inability of the French to force their method of fighting onto the Germans. The methodical battle was appropriate only if the enemy fought in a similar fashion, but the concept of the blitzkrieg was as different from the methodical battle as an envelopment is from a frontal assault. With its strong emphasis on mobility, individual initiative, continuous battle, and rapid decentralization of control, the German doctrine was starkly different from that of the French. To the list of "ifs" given by General Keller at the trial, one should add, "If only French doctrine had been more modern."

When one considers the weaknesses of this doctrine, one must acknowledge that the French were not preparing from 1919 to 1939 to refight World War I. The doctrine did change, and that of the second decade in the interwar period was different from that of the first decade. From 1919 to approximately 1929, relatively few changes occurred, since most manuals published during this period did little more than codify, explain, or slightly modify wartime practice. The major difference from wartime practice was that the doctrine placed a greater emphasis on a somewhat more mobile, rather than a purely static, battlefield. During the 1920s, the French established the basis of the methodical battle, and military thinkers began their ill-fated focus on the methods used to halt the Germans in the spring and early summer of 1918 and to deal them the final blow in the summer and fall of that same year. Perhaps the most important new concept appearing in this decade was General Estienne's battle tank.

In the late 1920s and throughout the 1930s, a variety of new concepts and new methods appeared. Some of these were a product of the 1927–1928 laws, as the military sought to simplify many of its procedures for the soldiers serving for only a short term. Important studies on motorization were made in the early 1930s, as were studies on the employment of antitank weapons. With the appearance of the concept for mass-maneuver tanks, armored doctrine also changed. In the same period, the cavalry concentrated on the problems of motorization and mechanization, and by 1935, it was easily the most modern of any of the French branches.

If one were to graph the French faith in and emphasis on the offensive, the high point would be before 1930 and the low point would be afterward. Even though the 1936 instructions on the tactical employment of large units placed greater emphasis on the offense than did the 1921 instructions, the French believed the power of the defense had increased over that of the offense because of improvements in firepower. At the same time, the withdrawal from the Rhineland, the growing strength of the German army, the awareness of the inadequate training of a recently mobilized French soldier, and the recognition of the complexity and difficulty of mobilization encouraged the military hierarchy to prefer the defense initially. War plans of the French army reflected this change: the plans of the 1920s strongly emphasized the offense, while those for 1929 and the 1930s envisaged an initial defense. Throughout the interwar years, military leaders considered the defense a means to weaken a stronger enemy and the offense as the means to deal him the final blow, but the perception of the sequential relationship between defense and offense became even more powerful as the 1930s passed.

The phenomenon of the first decade of the interwar period in sharp contrast with the second decade also applies to the army as a whole. While it is common to speak of the "interwar army," it is clear that the problems faced and the solutions found from 1919 to approximately 1929 varied greatly from those for 1929 to 1939. Some of the factors leading to a decline after 1919 in the army's readiness came from a sort of "natural" atrophy following the war; some also came from an unwillingness of the military leaders to accept a markedly reduced role in national affairs. During and after the World War I demobilization, the army concentrated on the transition from a mass wartime army to a much smaller peacetime one, and as the struggle over the short term of service continued through the late 1920s, the army was gradually and continually weakened. Most reservists were excused from reserve training sessions because of their wartime service, and the army's equipment suffered increasingly from the problems of age as the years passed. The low point in the army's condition was probably reached in 1929. The upturn came between 1928 and 1930, with the application of the 1927–1928 laws, the withdrawal from the Rhineland, and the beginning of the construction of the Maginot Line. By 1933, the army's condition had improved as one-year service was completely implemented, and the army, under General Weygand's leadership, devoted more attention to problems of training, equipment, and doctrine. After the reinstitution of two-year service in 1935, the increased emphasis on reserve training, and the availability of new equipment, the army's condition had probably improved to the degree suggested by General Héring, who at least partially understood the value of tanks and who commanded the "Army of Paris" in the last desperate days of 1940. In 1942, he explained, "In the years 1936, 1937, [and] 1938, I clearly saw the renaissance of the army. . . ."[5] There was a clear sense of better preparedness in the army and an increasing certainty that the best methods had been found. The French army may not have been anxious for the bloody war it anticipated, but it did not lack confidence in its tactics, organization, and equipment.

In *Strange Defeat*, Marc Bloch described how amazed he had been in 1918 when he saw a demonstration showing two infantry companies: one equipped, organized, and drilled as those of 1914, the other as those of 1918.[6] If one were to compare the French army of 1918 with that of the late 1930s, the contrast would have been just as startling. New armored vehicles and units had been introduced, the light mechanized division created, many of the infantry divisions motorized, and thousands of airplanes incorporated into the air force structure. But while equipment and organizational changes had modified the appearance of the army of the 1930s, the apparent difference was misleading, for French doctrine in a relative sense had regressed rather than progressed. Although it was modern in the sense that it was far from being a copy of World War I doctrine and concentrated upon the use of new weapons such as the tank, airplane, antitank gun, and improved artillery, it was not modern in the sense of devising the best method for employing those weapons. Similarly, French doctrine was not so modern as it might have been, since the older doctrine and notions of the methodical battle and firepower dominated the methods for employing the new weaponry. It is the partial change or the failure to change completely which is the most important characteristic in the evolution of French doctrine.

Despite the changes in the 1936 instructions, the addition of new armaments, and the improved condition of the army, much remained the same, and some of the changes were not for the better. It was after 1930 that the emphasis on the defensive and the methodical battle reached its zenith, that mechanization got firmly off track, and that French doctrine remained affixed to some of the methods of the past. The first armored divisions were not created until after World War II began, and the majority of the French tanks were employed as battalions in support of the infantry. By 1939, French artillery matériel and doctrine had changed only slightly from that of 1919. The artillery was organized to provide massive fire support for large units rather than immediate fire for smaller units, and control over the artillery remained strongly centralized. The movement and displacement of artillery dominated the rhythm of combat and greatly influenced the methodical aspects of French doctrine. The failure of the artillery to move toward greater decentralization and flexibility slowed the improvements occurring in other branches. As the 1930s passed, French doctrine became progressively more rigid, and after 1935, the stress on the strength of the defense, firepower, and the methodical battle became greater than ever before. Such methods may have been appropriate for the period from 1919 to 1929, but they rapidly became obsolete thereafter.

The failure to change sufficiently is rooted in the political, institutional, historical, and strategic relationships that induced the French to mold and adapt the new weaponry to the prevailing doctrine. The army viewed technological developments from the perspective of already accepted concepts and did not perceive new ideas or weapons overturning or forcing a fundamental transformation or revision of accepted doctrine. The enervated and enfeebled High Command, whose lack of sufficient innovation partially stemmed from its having to rely on decision by consensus, found it easier to compromise than to construct something fundamentally new. Although those charged with developing new weapons and doctrine analyzed many new ideas in a fairly sophisticated and quasi-scientific manner, most new concepts and weapons appearing after 1930 were simply grafted onto the older methods or assimilated into existing organizations. The coalescence of new technology and old doctrine ensured that French doctrine did not gain the maximum advantages from the new weapons, even though some modifications in organization, equipment, and doctrine occurred, and that the new weapons of war were effectively tied to the older methods of war. Tragically for France, the great reduction in German army equipment after World War I enabled that country to consider the new technology in a more objective fashion and to change more readily without the constraint of a huge investment in older weaponry. Although the German process of doctrinal modernization was by no means simple or guaranteed to succeed, the French process was complicated by the abundance of existing equipment that limited but did not halt its creation of something fundamentally new.

The failure of the French to change sufficiently did not occur because of woefully inadequate financial support. The extent of the financial support can best be seen on a comparative basis. Between 1918 and 1935, France spent a greater percentage of her gross national product on national defense needs than any other great power. Except for 1936, Great Britain never spent as large a percentage in peacetime as did France. Between 1936 and 1940, Germany spent a greater percentage, but she devoted a significant portion of her expenditures to the purchase of equipment, much of which France had already purchased. By 1938, military funding in France was 2.6 times as much, in real terms, as it had been in 1913.[7] Even though the military obviously could have used more money, particularly in pay for personnel, it did not suffer egregiously from a lack of funds.

More importantly, while one can argue that additional monetary resources may have enabled the French army to modernize more completely, little evidence suggests that more money would have resulted in fundamental changes in several important sectors. For example, greater expenditures would not necessarily have resulted in greater confidence in the training of the reserves, in the earlier creation of modern armored units, in the acceptance of decentralized and mobile concepts, or in an improved or dramatically different doctrine. Additionally, had the money spent on the frontier fortifications not been used for that purpose, there is little to suggest, first, that the government would have spent the same sums on modernizing the army, or, second, that the extra money would have resulted in a better prepared force than the one fielded in May-June 1940. Similarly, a study in the archives of the *Service historique de l'armée de terre* notes that during the period from 1920 to 1934, the French army spent 116 million francs on the development and production of the tank, while 92 million francs were spent on light reconnaissance cars and light armored vehicles.[8] Only 56 percent of the money spent on the development of armored vehicles from 1920 to 1934 was spent on the development of the tank. Despite these restricted funds, the French still managed to field an appreciable number of tanks on the northeastern front; they had 2,285 of their own tanks, without counting those of the allies, while the Germans had 2,574 tanks in their ten panzer divisions. Beyond the technical differences in the armored vehicles themselves, the main difference was not in the number of tanks but in how they were organized and employed.

The key question about the French experience is not how much money was spent but how the money was spent. Although monetary resources may have been constrained from 1932 until 1935, for example, the army began or accelerated development of a variety of weapons during this period, such as the D-tank, S-35 tank, B-1 bis tank, 25mm antitank gun, 47mm antitank gun, and 105mm long-range howitzer. During the period of greatest economic constraints in the early 1930s, the army formed the first light mechanized division and initiated production of the R-35 and H-35 tanks. Production of these tanks signaled an expansion of the light-tank program and the clear victory of the perception of the tank as an infantry support weapon rather than as an independent arm. Yet this change also occurred in a time of limited resources. Thus, while more money may have resulted in somewhat greater numbers, for example, of tanks, artillery pieces, or antitank guns, more money would not necessarily have resulted in those weapons being employed or designed differently or in France being defended successfully in May–June 1940. Or, in another case, even if more money had been available, there may not have been an increase in the ridiculously small number of antitank mines; the small number available resulted more from the lethargy and fragmentation of the army's hierarchy than from inadequate funding. For the same reasons, having additional funds also would have had little or no effect upon France's basic strategy. Only some fundamental changes in thinking could have altered the main outline of the 1940 solution.

In analyzing the reasons for the military catastrophe and the army's failure to modernize completely, one cannot simply cite the existence of the Maginot Line, or refer to a Maginot "mentality." Given the vulnerability of the natural resources, population, and industrial centers along the northeastern frontier, the military hierarchy had little choice but to provide some sort of protection for those vital areas, and fortifications were a logical and appropriate means of protection. Since France could devote greater attention to unprotected areas without having to fear an attack anywhere on her frontiers, the Maginot Line did not directly result in a weakening of the French army, and, in fact, it simplified the task of the military. When the battle was fought, the failure to anticipate the rapid movement of large forces so quickly through Luxembourg and the Ardennes was rooted in the incorrect perception of that area as an obstacle and a misunderstanding of the mobility available from the new weaponry, not in a failure of the Maginot Line. For more than two decades, the military leaders expected the Germans to make their main attack through Belgium and became even more convinced in their views after the erection of the frontier fortifications in the northeast. Amidst their firm convictions that the

Germans would not do otherwise, they failed to allow room for the unexpected, and once the French lost the initiative to the Germans they could not regain it. The mistake was not the building of the Maginot Line; the mistake was creating an army that could not reply to the unexpected or respond to the limited threat. Where flexibility was needed, France and her military were content with an inflexible concept of war and a rigid, step-by-step doctrine.

After the war, Daladier insisted that the causes of the defeat were "profoundly military."[9] Since he was one of the ministers of war who effectively fragmented the powers of the High Command by delegating the authority of his signature to the departments, it is ironic, if not pathetic, that he would apparently attempt to shift the preponderance of blame onto uniformed members of the military. The substance of his assertion, nevertheless, is correct if one takes it to mean that military reasons can readily explain the military failure of 1940. Yet such reasons suffice only as long as one includes in the explanation those who were not "simple" military technicians, and acknowledges the military impact of the nation in arms, an inefficient and parochial High Command, and the problems of the frontiers. One must also acknowledge the effect on military doctrine of one-year service and a national preference for the defense.

Within the realm of military explanations, the political leaders of France cannot escape some of the blame for the improper preparation of the army. Their contributions to the failure were not in providing too few resources or in making military concerns too low a priority on the nation's agenda. In fact, most firmly believed in making available the resources of the entire nation to the military in the event of war. Despite this support, they contributed to the failure through the creation of an army that bore little resemblance to those of other eras. Their insistence on a short term of service, their denial of the need for larger numbers of officers and non-commissioned officers on active duty, and their refusal to increase the size of the forces compelled the military to seek simpler solutions and to rely on the correction of flagrant inadequacies only upon mobilization for war. The rough and unwieldy instrument they provided the military leaders severely constrained the practical alternatives for the development and fielding of a modern force.

The political leaders should also bear much of the burden of the responsibility for the inadequate organization of France's military hierarchy. Their refusal to construct a strong and effective High Command with great powers over clearly defined areas of responsibility weakened and diluted any efforts for reform and contributed greatly to the reliance on traditional methods. Without centralization and with strong reliance on decisions reached by committees, bureaucratic compromise or conflict became the main concern of those working to improve military readiness. The great influence exerted by General Debeney in the 1920s and the emergence of General Gamelin, the quintessential staff officer and bureaucrat, as the most important military leader in the late 1930s speak volumes on the extent to which the High Command had degenerated and to which the military system relied on staff specialists. Had France's military leaders been less concerned with bureaucratic details and more concerned with the major issues of policy, strategy, and doctrine, she undoubtedly would have fared better in 1940.

The political leaders also failed to recognize the constraining effect military policy could have on foreign policy, especially during a crisis such as the remilitarization of the Rhineland. As a group, they should have understood more clearly the effects of their decisions about duration of service and mobilization procedures on the capabilities of France's military forces. While technical military matters appeared to be isolated from broader concerns, their application had repercussions far outside the narrow boundaries within which they were addressed. By being prepared in Europe solely for total war, France left no latitude for deft diplomatic maneuvering.

In the broadest sense, France's experience illustrates the dangers of posturing an inflexible military policy that limits the alternatives of political and military leaders. Despite the logic of such a policy and despite the overwhelming evidence in its favor, no single military policy can account for all eventualities. Clausewitz warned about the friction of war; he should also have warned about the friction of policy, especially when it relies upon some aspect of military force.

The mistakes committed by France's political leaders do not excuse or overshadow those of the military. In the particularly crucial area of strategy, France's military leadership must receive the largest share of blame for her unfortunate decisions and actions. Even though her command system provided for the formulation of strategy in committees dominated by civilians, a fairly small group of officers in the Superior Council of War determined its workings and its outlines. Almost from the beginning, the High Command preferred to hold on the right along the northeastern frontier, conduct an economy of force operation in the center along the Ardennes, and defend well forward in Belgium. Since the strategy took advantage of geographic considerations and since it enabled the French to use the strengths—as the army's leaders comprehended them—of the methodical battle, firepower, and the defense, the members of the High Command believed the strategy was logical. They perceived a unity existing between the tactical doctrine and the strategy. Both responded to the strengths of and complemented the other. Later events, however, proved the strategy vulnerable and the tactical doctrine technically deficient.

The consequences of squandering France's major reserves, spreading forces thinly across the entire front, and failing to prepare for the unexpected were disastrous. The military hierarchy made the ill-fated assumption that no major penetration of French defenses could occur. Should a breakthrough take place, they believed they would have time to constitute a reserve and to "sew up" any tear in the defense line. Needless to say, they were wrong. In their analysis of the possible sequence of events, they closed their eyes to the developments made possible by increases in mobility. Though many later stood in line to criticize Gamelin for his strategic decisions, few officers doubted the necessity of those decisions in May 1940. Nevertheless, Gamelin in particular and the High Command in general must bear the brunt of the responsibility for the strategy and its collapse.

As for the inadequate tactical doctrine, the greatest responsibility for its formulation resides with the officer corps as a whole. French doctrine was not issued by fiat from the High Command or developed by politicians; rather, it was formed by a meticulous process in which a wide range and number of officers willingly and agreeably participated. At the same time, no single individual or small group of individuals dominated the formulation and dissemination of doctrine. The French process for formulating doctrine relied more on a consensus than it did on the dictates of the army's leaders. The numerous regulation commissions, field tests, and discussions did not reveal any major dissent among the officer corps. Charles de Gaulle was one of the few to criticize the French solution, but his professional army struck at the core of French republican tradition, and the merits of his argument were subsumed by political rather than military questions. Others, such as General Héring, objected, but only a small and relatively silent minority criticized the doctrine. Hundreds of officers in key positions willingly supported the doctrine and never complained that the French concepts required further change. The doctrine they constructed was a masterpiece of Cartesian logic and bureaucratic compromise. Almost no one doubted the annihilating effects of firepower, and few questioned the necessity of the methodical battle for controlling the delivery of this firepower.

Where imagination was needed, most officers were content with what they considered the obvious solution. The answers one receives to questions of organization, equipment, and doctrine often depend upon the questions one asks. In that sense, most officers failed in their responsibilities, for they failed to ask the hard questions.

Regrettably, there is some truth to the charge made by one officer in 1925 that doctrine was too dominated by the schools and by the staff specialists.[10] Many of those who made the most important contributions to French military thinking had often made their initial marks as superb staff officers, sometimes as chiefs of staff, in World War I and had gone on to higher positions of command. A French officer could sometimes make his way to the highest reaches of the army if he was a superb staff specialist and a moderately good commander; the opposite was not true. Whether a cause or a consequence of their focus on the details of staff work, the French became too pedantic, too theoretical, and not practical enough; their doctrine was more suited for the classroom than for the battlefield. And in their classrooms, officers were not rewarded for being innovative; they were rewarded for absorbing huge amounts of information and learning to apply a series of fairly standard responses (one could almost call them formulas) to particular situations. Sadly for France, memory became a more precious quality for officers than judgment.

In fairness, one has to object to the charge of Charles Serre on behalf of the parliamentary investigating committee after the war that the French army had "retired to its Mount Sinai [after World War I and sat] among its revealed truths and remnants of past glories. . . ."[11] The failure of the French military to formulate a new doctrine cannot be explained simply in terms of "retiring" to a Mount Sinai or in more explicit terms of "stupidity" or "decadence." The simplistic and unfair notion of decadence obscures the workings of the process by which France designed, developed, and employed her forces. Accusations of treason or disloyalty to the republican regime, such as with the "Corvignolles" and the "Cagoulards," also miss the mark badly. Many dutiful, patriotic, and sometimes highly intelligent officers expended countless hours examining alternative approaches that might work best on some future battlefield. And to accuse them of defeatism is to ignore their dedication and their certainty that victory—though bloody—would ultimately belong to France. Their failure was not one of stupidity, decadence, disloyalty, or defeatism; it was one of having decided upon the wrong solution.

The role of General Gamelin is especially tragic, for as Generalissimo of the French army from January 1935 until the defeat in 1940, he was a natural scapegoat for many of the false ideas. After the war, Gamelin attempted to defend himself and to point the finger of blame at others. In his memoirs, he discussed the several conflicting currents of tactical ideas in the French army before 1940 and argued that France had been "obsessed" with theories in 1914 and 1940. In 1914, the dominant theory had been the "offensive at any price," and in 1940 "the strength of the defense." In other comments, he bitterly criticized Marshal Pétain as the source of the ideas on the defense.[12] While Pétain's use of the defense in World War I was obviously important, one must recognize that Gamelin did little to bring an offensive spirit to the forefront in the army, other than add the phrase in the 1936 instructions, "Only the offensive permits the obtaining of decisive results." His published works and his lectures at the Center of Higher Military Studies emphasized the role of the commander, not the importance of the offensive,[13] and his view of the commander as the director of a tightly centralized operation fit perfectly with the methodical battle.

Whether in his comments on French regulations or his comments in the deliberations of the Superior Council of War, Gamelin did little to suggest that he differed dramatically from the remainder of the military hierarchy. As a soldier who enjoyed philosophical discussions and who was always willing to compromise, he hesitated to assume an inflexible position or to fight passionately for a cause. When he altered the army's command structure in January 1940, he chose a solution midway between giving Georges complete control over the northeastern frontier and retaining it completely for himself. When the formation of armored divisions was discussed, Gamelin defended the new unit against its detractors in the Superior Council of War, but his hesitant support was late and might have been more important and successful had it come several years earlier. Clearly, he never supported mechanization as ardently as General Weygand had supported mechanization of the cavalry, but in all fairness, he supported it more sincerely and stronger than most French officers. Ironically, the one difficult and risky decision he apparently made on his own, despite the energetic opposition of several general officers, concerned the "Breda maneuver," and it had disastrous results for France.

When the battle was fought in 1940, France committed the glaring error of trying to impose her way of war on the enemy without having any suitable recourse should this attempt fail. Had the Germans foolishly fought the battle the French desired, the results could have been a French victory. If the Germans had used methodical methods, if they had battered and bloodied themselves against the main French defenses without any attempt to regain the initiative or to exploit a French vulnerability, France may have been able to make a decisive attack. But wars are rarely won by armies who mindlessly do the expected or who surrender the initiative to an enemy; Germany would not docilely permit the French to select the battleground and establish the tempo of battle.

When the attack came on 10 May 1940, the Germans relied upon an imaginative and daring but well-designed plan. They initially struck the allies' left flank in Holland and Belgium; these attacks confirmed the long-held French view that the main thrust would come through the Gembloux gap in central Belgium. As the allied forces rushed forward into Holland and Belgium, certain that the enemy would fight as expected, the Germans unleashed their main attack through the Ardennes and against the weak French center at Dinant, Monthermé, and Sedan. Following the initial crossing of the Meuse River on the night of 12–13 May, German armored forces plunged through the French positions and tore a huge hole in the defensive lines by the evening of the 16th. By striking with speed and surprise, the Germans were able to achieve a massive breakthrough before the French High Command realized what had happened. Thus they outfought the French tactically and outsmarted them strategically.

Events of these and subsequent days demonstrated that the French were extremely vulnerable to a blitzkrieg attack and a *Kesselschlacht* strategy of encirclement and annihilation. While the methodical battle could have succeeded against an opponent using similar or worse tactics, the German style of mobile warfare proved to be markedly superior to the methodical approach. The Germans used their smoothly functioning and highly experienced mobile formations to strike at the lines connecting the French headquarters to subordinate units, and thus to sever the brains of the French army from its tentacles. Once the vital lifelines of command and control were ruptured, the army crumbled into helpless and disconnected fragments. The huge columns of captured Frenchmen testified less to an unwillingness of the soldiers to fight than to the collapse of an archaic and obsolete system. The French were able to establish some hasty defenses along the Somme River after the Dunkirk evacuation and did perform somewhat better in this second phase of the battle. Yet they did not have enough time to adapt completely to the new mode of warfare, and by then they had lost too many soldiers and too much equipment to overcome the habits established by two decades of preparation. When the recognition of the need for change finally came, it came too late.

More than being a victim of German military excellence, France was a victim of her own historical experience, geography, and political and military institutions. With the choices constrained and partially shaped by these influencing factors, her military leaders chose—as the events of 1940 demonstrated—to rely on an inadequate tactical doctrine and to follow a weak and vulnerable strategy. For the military leaders to have altered the doctrine and strategy successfully, France would have had to have abandoned or modified profoundly her doctrine of the methodical battle and firepower; relinquished many important resources crucial to fighting a war against Germany; surrendered a significant portion of her territory to the enemy; ended the fragmentation of her High Command; restructured her army solely on an abstract and unproven relation between new technology and concepts of combat; and rejected many of the lessons, traumas, and experiences of 1914–1918. She might have been able to do some of these. To expect her to have accomplished all, however, is perhaps to expect too much. She made some reforms between 1919 and 1939, but only after the events of May–June 1940 did she recognize that much more extensive changes were necessary.

Notes

ABBREVIATIONS

B.T., C.C.	Bureau technique, Chars de combat
C.C.A.	Conseil consultatif de l'armement
C.H.E.M.	Centre des hautes études militaires
Commission . . . Rapport	Commission d'enquête parlementaire. Rapport.
Commission . . . Témoignages	Commission d'enquête parlementaire. Témoignages et documents.
C.S.D.N.	Conseil supérieur de la défense nationale
C.S.G.	Conseil supérieur de la guerre
D.A.	Direction de l'artillerie
D.C.T.	Direction de la cavalerie et du train
D.D.F.	Documents diplomatiques français, 1932–1939
D.I.	Direction de l'infanterie
E.M.	Etat-major
E.M.A.	Etat-major de l'armée
E.S.G.	Ecole supérieure de guerre
I.C.C.	Inspection des chars de combat
I.G.I.	Inspection générale de l'infanterie
Instruction 1921	Instruction provisoire sur l'emploi tactique des grandes unités, 1921
Instruction 1936	Instruction sur l'emploi tactique des grandes unités, 1936
J.O. Ch. déb.	Journal officiel de la république française: Chambre débats
J.O. Lois et décrets	Journal officiel de la république française: Lois et décrets
J.O. Sén. déb.	Journal officiel de la république française: Sénat débats

199

M.D.N.G.   Ministère de la défense nationale et de la
                                  guerre
M.G.   Ministère de la guerre
P.V., C.S.G.   Procès-verbaux des réunions du conseil
                                  supérieure de la guerre
S.H.A.T.   Service historique de l'armée de terre

PREFACE
1. Col. J. Roger, *Artillery in the Offensive*, trans. J. S. Wood, U.S. Army (typescript, 1922), p. 242.

CHAPTER 1
1. For various interpretations of the fall of France, see John C. Cairns, "Along the Road Back to France 1940," *American Historical Review* 64 (April 1959): 583–603; and Cairns, "Some Recent Historians and the 'Strange Defeat' of 1940," *Journal of Modern History* 46 (March 1974): 60–85. For the latest analysis, see Jean-Baptiste Duroselle, *La décadence, 1932–1939* (Paris: Imprimerie nationale, 1979).
2. For the latest exposition of this thesis, see Jeffery A. Gunsburg, *Divided and Conquered: The French High Command and the Defeat of the West, 1940* (Westport, Conn.: Greenwood Press, 1979).
3. Maj. L. F. Ellis, *The War in France and Flanders, 1939–1940* (London: Her Majesty's Stationery Office, 1953), pp. 358–59, 369–70; and Capt. B. H. Liddell Hart, *The Tanks*, vol. 2, *1939–1945* (New York: Praeger, 1959), pp. 6–7.
4. Charles Chapon, "L'Armée de terre française: le 2 septembre 1939 au 9 mai 1940," *Revue historique des armées* 4 (1979): 164–92; and Lt. Col. Charles de Cossé-Brissac, "Combien de chars français contre combien de chars allemands le 10 mai 1940," *Revue de défense nationale* 5 (July 1947): 75–89.
5. For general works on the battle of France, see Henri Michel, *La seconde guerre mondiale* (Paris: Presses universitaires de France, 1968), vol. 1, *Les succès de l'axe (septembre 1939–janvier 1943)*, pp. 89–92.
6. France, Ministère de la défense, Etat-major de l'armée terre, Service historique, Lt. Col. Henry Dutailly, *Les problèmes de l'armée de terre française (1935–1939)* (Paris: Imprimerie nationale, 1980), p. 289.
7. France, Ministère des armées, Etat-major de l'armée de terre, Service historique, Col. François-André Paoli, *L'Armée française de 1919 à 1939*, 4 vols. (Paris: Société industrielle d'imprimerie, n.d.) vol. 2, *Le phase de fermeté, 1920–1924*, p. 161.
8. Gen. Maurice Gamelin, "Réflexions sur le chef," *Revue d'infanterie* 86 (April 1935): 638–42.
9. Léon Dumoncel, *Essai de mémento tactique: La décision* (Paris: Charles Lavauzelle, 1937), p. xiii.
10. France, M. G., *Règlement provisoire de manoeuvre d'infanterie du 1 février 1920, Deuxième partie* (Paris: Charles Lavauzelle, 1921), p. 8.
11. France, C.H.E.M., Gamelin, "L'Art de la guerre: doctrine et procédés" (April 1937), p. 3.

12. Gen. Eugène Debeney, *La guerre et les hommes* (Paris: Plon, 1937), pp. 264, 282.

13. Marshal Joseph Joffre, *The Personal Memòirs of Joffre, Field Marshal of the French Army*, trans. Col. T. Bentley Mott, vol. 1 (New York: Harper & Brothers, 1932), pp. 33–34; and France, M. G., *Décret du 28 octobre 1913 portant règlement sur la conduite des grandes unités* (Paris: Berger-Levrault, n.d.).

14. *Instruction 1921* and *Instruction 1936*.

15. Gen. Maurice Gamelin, *Servir*, vol. 1 (Paris: Plon, 1946–1947), p. 233. For the distinction between instructions and regulations, see p. 239.

16. *Instruction 1921*, p. 13.

17. Ibid., pp. 11–12, 60–62.

18. Ibid., p. 58.

19. *Instruction 1936*, p. 15.

20. Gamelin, *Servir* 1: 285–88. Gen. Robert-Auguste Touchon made the same point at the Riom trial. See Touchon, *Procès de Riom*, Audience du mardi 24 mars 1942, p. 1178, Fonds Gamelin, carton 2.

21. France, E.S.G., Ecole de perfectionnement des officiers de réserve du service d'état-major, "Le règlement sur le service en campagne," année 1930–1931, p. 1.

22. France, E.S.G., Ecole de perfectionnement des officiers de réserve du service d'état-major, "Le règlement de l'infanterie du 1er mars 1928," année 1930–1931, pp. 41, 1.

23. *J.O. Ch. déb.* (15 March 1935), p. 1025.

24. Gen. André Beaufre, "Liddell Hart and the French Army, 1919–1939," in *The Theory and Practices of War*, ed. Michael Howard (New York: Praeger, 1966), p. 140.

CHAPTER 2

1. *Journal officiel de la république française: documents parlementaires* (1904), p. 148.

2. On the general subject of the French army before 1914, see Douglas Porch, *The March to the Marne: The French Army, 1871–1914* (Cambridge, Eng.: Cambridge University Press, 1981); and David B. Ralston, *The Army of the Republic: The Place of the Military in the Political Evolution of France, 1871–1914* (Cambridge, Mass.: MIT Press, 1967).

3. Cmdt. H. Bouvard, *Les leçons militaires de la guerre* (Paris: Masson, 1920), p. 16. For a more thorough examination of the threat of a long war, see General Serrigny, *Réflexions sur l'art de la guerre* (Paris: Charles Lavauzelle, 1930), pp. 69–75.

4. *J.O. Lois et décrets* (3 April 1928), p. 3808.

5. *Instruction 1921*, p. 9.

6. General Thévenet, "Les forces militaires de la France," *Revue militaire générale* 17 (June 1920): 339.

7. Joffre, *Memoirs* 1: 9.

8. *J.O. Ch. déb.* (25 February 1920), pp. 307–20; (26 February 1920), pp. 338–52.

9. *Journal officiel de la république française* (28 July 1872), p. 5165; and *J.O. Lois et décrets* (27 November 1881), pp. 6571–72; (20 February 1882), pp. 953–54; (5 March 1886), p. 1066.

10. *J.O. Lois et décrets* (25 January 1920), pp. 1300–1301. These responsibilities were included in the 1927 law on the organization of the army (*J.O. Lois et décrets* [27 July 1927], p. 7266).

11. *P.V., C.S.G.*, 31 May 1920, S.H.A.T. carton 50. See also Anonymous, "L'Armée qu'il nous faut," *Revue des deux mondes* 61 (1 January 1921): 12–13.

12. *P.V., C.S.G.*, 2 June 1920, carton 50; 11 December 1920, carton 50; 13 December 1920, carton 50; and 20 February 1922, carton 50.

13. Ibid., 31 May 1920, 13 December 1920, carton 50; and 26 May 1926, carton 50 bis.

14. Following the creation of the air force positions, the Superior Council of National Defense included, among others, the premier, the minister of foreign affairs, the ministers of war, air, and navy, and the three leading generals of the army, navy, and air force.

15. *P.V., C.S.G.*, 30 December 1921, carton 50.

16. *J.O. Lois et décrets* (5 April 1923), pp. 3410–23; (3 April 1928), p. 3825.

17. *J.O. Ch. déb.* (17 March 1922), p. 902; (20 June 1922), p. 1904; (22 June 1922), pp. 1943, 1955–56.

18. Gen. Jean Mordacq, *Le ministère Clemenceau*, vol. 3 (Paris: Plon, 1931), pp. 44–45.

19. *P.V., C.S.G.*, 10 April 1925, carton 50 bis.

20. Ibid., 30 December 1921, carton 50.

21. *J.O. Lois et décrets* (3 April 1928), pp. 3792–3803, 3803–25; (14 July 1927), pp. 7266–70.

22. Gen. Eugène Debeney, *Sur la securité militaire de la France* (Paris: Payot, 1930), p. 28; and Debeney, *La guerre et les hommes* (Paris: Plon, 1937), pp. 181–82. After the war, J. Paul-Boncour argued that "the narrow and backward application [of these laws] contributed to our defeat" (*Entre deux guerres: Souvenirs sur la IIIe république*, vol. 2 [New York: Brentano's, 1946], p. 245).

23. Lucien Souchon, *Feue* [sic] *l'armée française* (Paris: Fayard, 1929). See also Gen. Maurice Duval, "La crise de notre organisation militaire," *Revue de Paris* 32 (15 April 1926): 756–96.

24. Debeney, "Armée nationale ou armée de métier," *Revue des deux mondes* 53 (15 September 1929): 246–48, 258.

25. Paoli, *La phase de fermeté*, p. 169.

26. Figures are taken from France, Ministère des affaires étrangères, Commission de publication des documents relatifs aux origines de la guerre, 1939–1945, *D.D.F.*, 3, no. 214 (28 August 1936), p. 313. Compare Paoli, *L'Armée française de 1919 à 1939* (Paris: Société industrielle d'imprimerie, n.d.), vol. 3, *Le temps des compromis*, p. 141; and vol. 4, *La fin des illusions*, p. 59.

27. *J.O. Lois et décrets* (3 April 1928), p. 3816; *J.O. Ch. déb.* (15 March 1935), pp. 1021–53; *J.O. Sén. déb.* (15 March 1935), pp. 300–301; (20 March 1935), pp. 318–34. The manpower crisis is capably analyzed in Philip Charles Farwell Bankwitz, *Maxime Weygand and Civil-Military Relations in Modern France* (Cambridge, Mass.: Harvard University Press, 1967), pp. 83–115. A description of the adoption of article 40 is included in France, M.D.N.G., E.M.A., *Règlement de l'infanterie, Première partie, Instruction* (Paris: Charles Lavauzelle, 1938), p. 17.

28. General Duval, "L'Armée française de 1938: sa genèse—son avenir," *Revue de Paris* 14 (15 August 1938): 738.

29. Gen. André Prételat, *Le destin tragique de la ligne Maginot* (Paris: Berger-Levrault, 1950), pp. 30–31. Cited in Gunsburg, "'Vaincre ou Mourir': The French High Command and the Defeat of France, 1919–May, 1940" (unpublished Ph.D., diss., Duke University, 1974), pp. 209–10. See Gamelin, *Servir* 3: 446–48. The Superior Council expressed worries about this system on several occasions. See *P.V., C.S.G.*, 1 April 1925, 15 October 1926, carton 50 bis.

30. Jean Vidalenc, "Les divisions de série 'B' dans l'armée française pendant la campagne de France 1939–1940," *Revue historique des armées* 4 (1980): 107–14.

31. Marshal Philippe Pétain, Préface to Gen. Narcisse Chauvineau, *Une invasion, est-elle encore possible?* (Paris: Berger-Levrault, 1939), p. vii.

32. *P.V., C.S.G.*, 14 December 1927, carton 50 bis.

33. For a detailed exposition of this thesis, see France, E.S.G., Lt. Col. Charles Menu, *Application de l'industrie: la leçon d'une guerre*, October 1928–December 1931 (Rambouillet: Pierre Leroy, 1932), passim, S.H.A.T. carton 9N155.

34. C.H.E.M., General Piot, "Préparation de la mobilisation industrielle" (August 1928), pp. 21–22; C.H.E.M., General Gavard, "Conférences sur les fabrications de guerre et la mobilisation industrielle" (1938), pp. 18–20. Gavard's comments on pp. 18–20 are almost exactly the same as those of Piot on pp. 21–22.

35. Chauvineau, *Une invasion*, p. 93.

36. *Règlement de l'infanterie, Instruction*, 1938, p. 36; Cmdt. Henri Laporte, "La défense antichars," *Revue d'infanterie* 93 (December 1938): 1150–51. For an analysis of the earlier antitank weapons, see Chef d'escadrons G. Morel, "Les armes anti-chars," *Revue d'Artillerie* 103 (January 1929): 23–49.

37. Gamelin, *Servir* 1: 167. For an analysis of the effectiveness of the French anti-tank weapons in 1940, see U.S. War Department, Military Intelligence Division, Special Bulletin no. 20, "General Requin's Lessons and Conclusions from Operations of French Fourth Army" (Washington, D.C.: 11 October 1940), p. 7.

38. For a discussion of the effort in the industrial sector, see Richard D. Challener, *The French Theory of the Nation in Arms, 1866–1939* (New York: Russell & Russell, 1965), pp. 184–214.

39. *P.V., C.S.G.*, 1 April 1925, carton 50 bis.

40. *J.O. Lois et. décrets* (3 April 1928), pp. 3817–18.

41. René de Chambrum, *I Saw France Fall. Will She Rise Again?* (London: Jarrolds, 1941), pp. 39–40.

42. *J.O. Ch. déb.* (12 July 1932), pp. 2554–58.

43. Computed from data included in Rapport du M. R. Briat, Instruction de l'armée, 28 février 1942. This report is included as an annex in General Picquendar, chef d'E.M.A., à Monsieur Baraveau, conseiller honoraire à la cour de cassation, n.d., Fonds Gamelin, carton 5.

44. *Règlement de l'infanterie, Instruction*, 1938, pp. 25–26. Cf. France, M.G., E.M.A., *Règlement de l'infanterie, Première partie, Instruction technique* (Paris: L. Fournier, 1928), p. 48.

45. Testimony of General Boris, *Procès de Riom*, Audience du mercredi 25 mars 1942, p. 1277, Fonds Gamelin, carton 2.

46. *J.O. Lois et décrets* (14 July 1927), pp. 7267–68.

47. For an account of this experience, see D. Barlone, *A French Officer's Diary (23 August 1939–1 October 1940)*, trans. L. V. Cass (Cambridge, Eng.: Cambridge University Press, 1942), pp. 2–12.

48. General Brindel, "La nouvelle organisation militaire," *Revue des deux mondes* 51 (1 June 1929): 488–92.

49. The figures given by Daladier were: 1933, 266,000; 1934, 262,000; 1936, 396,000; 1937, 558,000; and 1938, 511,000. He also emphasized that 711,000 reservists were mobilized in 1938 (*Procès de Riom*, Audience du vendredi 27 février 1942, p. 150, Fonds Gamelin, carton 1).

50. Brindel, "La nouvelle organisation," p. 500.

51. M.G., D.I., Général François à M. le Général commandant la 20e région, 9 octobre 1935, 12,714 BT/I.E. , S.H.A.T. carton 9N171.

52. *P.V., C.S.G.*, 14 December 1927, carton 50 bis.

53. Prételat, *Le destin tragique*, pp. 31–36; *The Times*, 1 October 1934, p. 14.

54. Georges Clemenceau, *Grandeur and Misery of Victory*, trans. F. M. Atkinson (New York: Harcourt, Brace, 1930), p. 351.

55. Other repetitive themes were low level of matériel readiness and low morale. See the testimony of Generals Préaud and Conquet, *Procès de Riom*, Audience du 26 mars 1942, Fonds Gamelin, carton 2, dossier 5.

56. *Procès de Riom*, Audience du mardi 24 mars 1942, p. 1178, Fonds Gamelin, carton 2. Touchon's statement is paraphrased in Gamelin, *Servir* 1:297.

57. *Instruction 1936*, pp. 97–98.

58. *Procès de Riom*, Audience du mardi 24 mars 1942, p. 1178, Fonds Gamelin, carton 2.

59. E.S.G., Lt. Col. Voisin, *La division au combat*, Année 1929–1930, pp. 7–9.

60. Gen. Paul-Emile Tournoux, *Défense des frontières. Haut commandement— gouvernement, 1919–1939* (Paris: Nouvelles éditions latines, 1960), pp. 79, 332–35.

61. *The Times*, 16 September 1926, p. 11; 9 September 1927, p. 9; 16 September 1928, p. 11.

62. P.-E. Tournoux, *Défense des frontières*, pp. 335–36.

63. "Manoeuvres en Haute Maurienne," *L'Illustration*, 13 September 1930, pp. 52–53; *The Times*, 6 August 1930, p. 9; 8 August 1930, p. 10; 11 September 1931, p. 12; 14 September 1931, p. 11; 17 September 1931, p. 11.

64. *Règlement de l'infanterie, Instruction, technique*, 1928, pp. 11, 13. Other regulations also emphasized the need for simplification because of the one-year term of service. See France, M.G., *Règlement des unités de chars légers du 1 juin 1929, Deuxième partie, Combat* (Paris: Imprimerie nationale, 1929), p. 11; France, M.G., E.M.A., *Règlement de la cavalerie du 1 février 1934, Première partie, Instruction technique* (Paris: Charles Lavauzelle, 1938), p. 9.

65. *Règlement de l'infanterie, Instruction technique*, 1928, p. 14. The greater emphasis on fire was noted by French military authors. See Cmdt. G. Paille, *Connaissance et emploi des armes et engins de l'infanterie* (Paris: Charles Lavauzelle, 1932), p. 5. Commandant Paille was a member of the commission that wrote the 1938 infantry regulations.

66. *Règlement de l'infanterie, Instruction technique*, 1928, p. 16.

67. Lt. B. H. Liddell Hart, "Etude critique de 'Règlement provisoire de manoeuvres d'infanterie 1920,'" *Revue militaire générale* 19 (15 October 1922): 786. The author's name was mistakenly spelled "Riddell Hart."

68. France, E.S.G., Gen. Lucien Loizeau, *La manoeuvre du corps d'armée* (Courbevoie: P. Chanove, 1932), p. 9.

69. Quoted in Tournoux, *Défense des frontières*, p. 337. In June 1934, in a debate in the Chamber of Deputies, Marshal Pétain (as minister of war) asserted that the building of the Maginot Line did not mean the army was prepared only for the defense; it was also prepared to conduct offensive operations (*J.O. Ch. déb.* [14 June 1934], pp. 1495–96). For the directive concerning a possible offensive between the Rhine and Moselle rivers in 1938, see Gamelin, *Servir* 3: 26–32.

70. Paul-Boncour, *Entre deux guerres* 3: 29–38.

71. Pierre Flandin, *Politique française, 1919–1940* (Paris: Les éditions nouvelles, 1947), pp. 196–205.

72. *D.D.F.*, 1, no. 392 (11 March 1936), p. 504. See also *D.D.F.*, 1, no. 196 (17 February 1936), pp. 290–93; and Gamelin, *Servir* 2: 208–11.

73. *D.D.F.*, 1, no. 525 (28 March 1936), p. 698.

74. *D.D.F.*, 1, no. 392 (11 March 1936), pp. 504–6.

75. *D.D.F.*, 7, no. 446 (15 March 1938), pp. 827–30. France did send one shipment of planes to the republicans, but with increasing domestic pressure from the right and the failure to convince the British of the dangers of a Franco victory, Blum was forced to adopt a policy of nonintervention (Joel Colton, *Léon Blum: Humanist in Politics* [New York: Alfred Knopf, 1966], pp. 234–52).

76. Tournoux, *Défense des frontières*, p. 299.

77. Gen. Maxime Weygand, "L'Etat militaire de la France," *Revue des deux mondes* 29 (15 October 1936): 727.

78. Quoted in Tournoux, *Défense des frontières*, p. 338.

79. Charles de Gaulle, *Vers l'armée de métier* (Paris: Berger-Levrault, 1934), pp. 54–56.

80. Debeney, *Sur la sécurité militaire de la France* (Paris: Payot, 1930); and Debeney, "Encore l'armée de métier," *Revue des deux mondes* 28 (15 July 1935): 279–95.

81. Weygand, "L'Etat militaire de la France," p. 724; and Weygand, "L'Unité de l'armée," *Revue militaire générale* 1 (January 1937): 16, 18–19.

CHAPTER 3

1. France, Institut national de la statistique, *Annuaire statistique* 50 (1934) (Paris: Imprimerie nationale, 1935), pp. 335*, 338*, 341*, 347*.

2. William F. Ogburn and William Jaffe, *The Economic Development of Post-War France: A Survey of Production* (New York: Columbia University Press, 1929), pp. 5, 219; Hilda Ormsby, *France: A Regional and Economic Geography* (London: Methuen, 1931; rev. ed., 1950), pp. 433–35.

3. Computed from *Annuaire statistique*, p. 115.

4. Ogburn and Jaffe, *Economic Development*, p. 279.

5. Computed from *Annuaire statistique*, p. 115.

6. Ibid., p. 372*.

7. Ogburn and Jaffe, *Economic Development*, p. 248.

8. Ratios computed from population figures in Dudley Kirk, "Population and Population Trends in Modern France," in *Modern France: Problems of the Third and Fourth Republics*, ed. Edward Mead Earle (Princeton: Princeton University Press, 1951), p. 317.

9. *J.O. Ch. déb.* (10 December 1929), pp. 599–601.

10. Col. Pierre Rocolle, *2000 ans de fortification française* (Paris: Charles-Lavauzelle, 1973), pp. 265–75.

11. Joffre, *Memoirs* 1: 26, 27–112; and M. G. , E.M. A., *Les armées française dans la grande guerre*, Tome 1, 1er volume, *annexes* (Paris: Imprimerie nationale, 1922), pp. 21–35.

12. France, M.G., E.M.A., *Décret du 28 Octobre 1913 portant règlement sur conduite des grandes unités (Service des armées en campagne)* (Paris: Berger Levrault, n.d.) p. 42.

13. *J.O. Lois et décrets* (25 January 1920), p. 1301.

14. *P.V., C.S.G.*, 17 May 1920, carton 50.

15. Ibid., 22 May 1922, carton 50.

16. Gen. A. M. E. Laure et al., *Pétain* (Paris: Berger-Levrault, 1941), pp. 277–78.

17. *P.V., C.S.G.*, 22 May 1922, carton 50.

18. Tournoux, *Défense des frontières*, pp. 23–47.

19. *P.V., C.S.G.*, 15 December 1925, carton 50 bis.

20. Paoli, *Le temps des compromis*, p. 106.

21. Rapport sur l'organisation défensive du territoire présenté par le maréchal Pétain devant le C.S.D.N. le 4 juin 1928, S.H.A.T. carton 2N6, dossier 8, item 2.

22. *P.V., C.S.G.*, 17 December 1926, carton 50 bis.

23. Séance préparatoire, C.S.G., 15 December 1926, S.H.A.T. carton 50 bis.

24. *P.V., C.S.G.*, 17 December 1926, carton 50 bis.

25. Ibid.

26. Ibid., 1 April 1925, carton 50 bis.

27. Tournoux, *Défense des frontières*, pp. 92–96.

28. Séance préparatoire, C.S.G., 2 July 1927, carton 50 bis.

29. *P.V., C.S.G.*, 4 July 1927, carton 50 bis.

30. Séance préparatoire, C.S.G., 11 October 1927, carton 50 bis.

31. Colonel Tricaud suggested this technical design, which he called an *ouvrage palmé*, to the Guillaumat commission (*P.V., C.S.G.*, 4 July 1927, carton 50 bis).

32. Séance préparatoire, C.S.G., 11 October 1927, carton 50 bis.

33. *P.V., C.S.G.*, 12 October 1927, carton 50 bis.

34. Ibid.

35. See Rapport sur l'organisation défensive du territoire présenté par le maréchal Pétain devant le C.S.D.N. le 4 juin 1928, p. 2; and Laure, *Pétain*, p. 283.

36. Cf. Laure, *Pétain*, pp. 286–87. Laure insists that Pétain was the major force behind the conception of the Maginot Line.

37. *P.V., C.S.G.*, 12 October 1927, carton 50 bis.

38. Rapport sur l'organisation défensive du territoire présenté par le maréchal Pétain devant le C.S.D.N. le 4 juin 1928, p. 1.

39. C.S.D.N., Procès-verbal de la séance du 4 juin 1928, S.H.A.T. carton 2N6, dossier 8, item 3.

40. Pierre Cot, *Triumph of Treason*, trans. Sybille and Milton Crane (Chicago: Ziff-Davis, 1944), p. 218.

41. *J.O. Ch. déb.* (10 December 1929), p. 4235.

42. Cf. Tournoux, *Défense des frontières*, pp. 48–49; and Judith M. Hughes, *To the Maginot Line: The Politics of French Military Preparation in the 1920s* (Cambridge: Mass.: Harvard University Press, 1971), pp. 205–7.

43. *P.V., C.S.G.*, 18 January 1927, carton 50 bis.

44. In the spring of 1938, an exercise was conducted to test the possibility of an *attaque brusquée* by a motorized army through the Ardennes in the direction of Sedan. This exercise demonstrated that the area could be crossed in sixty hours, but there was no change in French thinking. In May 1940, it required fifty-eight hours (Prételat, *Le destin tragique*, pp. 13–14).

45. Quoted in Gamelin, *Servir* 2: 127–29; and Vivian Rowe, *The Great Wall of France* (London: Putnam, 1959), p. 61.

46. Gunsburg, *Divided and Conquered*, p. 22.

47. Jonathan Helmreich, "The Negotiation of the Franco-Belgian Military Accord of 1920," *French Historical Studies* 3 (Spring 1964): 360–78.

48. For a description of the *Parcs mobiles de fortification*, see the comments by André Maginot in *J.O. Ch. déb.* (18 December 1929), p. 4775.

49. *P.V., C.S.G.*, 17 December 1926, carton 50 bis.

50. Ibid., 18 January 1927, carton 50 bis.

51. Ibid., 28 May 1932, carton 50 bis.

52. Ibid., 4 June 1932, carton 50 bis.

53. Ibid., 23 January 1933, carton 50 ter.

54. Ibid., 15 May 1933, carton 50 ter.

55. Ibid., 13 March 1939, carton 50 ter. The minutes for the 13 March and 10 July 1939 meetings are typed summaries. They are not as detailed as the other minutes and are not included in the same book.

56. Ibid., 15 May 1933, carton 50 ter.

57. Dutailly, *Les problèmes de l'armée de terre*, pp. 91–114, 303–6, 353–55, 371–73, 379–83.

58. Gen. Raoul van Overstraeten, *Albert I-Léopold III: Vingt ans de politique militaire belge 1920–1940* (Bruges: Desclée de Brouwer, 1946), pp. 47–49.

59. See Gamelin, *Servir* 1: 84–88.

60. Brian Bond, *France and Belgium, 1939–1940* (Newark, Del.: University of Delaware Press, 1975), pp. 52–56; and Cmdt. Pierre Lyet, *La bataille de France (mai–juin 1940)* (Paris: Payot, 1947), pp. 8–16, 18–21.

61. Quoted in Lyet, *La bataille de France*, p. 22. For a detailed analysis of Gamelin's actions, see Pierre le Goyet, *Le mystère Gamelin* (Paris: Presses de la Cité, 1976), pp. 277–99.

62. *P.V., C.S.G.*, 15 May 1933, carton 50 ter.

63. Jacques Mordal, "Le 'mythe' du front continu," *Revue de défense nationale* (March 1954): 298–302. Mordal's article was in reply to an earlier one by General Ely, "Les leçons qu'il faut tirer des opérations de 1940," *Revue de défense nationale* (December 1953): 563–82.

64. Quoted in Dutailly, *Les problèmes de l'armée de terre*, pp. 94–95.

65. "Note pour le cabinet militaire du ministère (11 juillet 1936)," included in Gamelin *Servir* 3: 519.

66. Debeney, *La guerre et les hommes*, p. 213.

67. Jean-Yves Mary, *La ligne Maginot: ce qu'elle était, ce qu'il en reste* (San Dalmazzo, Italy: L'Istituto Grafico Bertello, 1980), pp. 180–92.

68. *Commission . . . Témoignages* 3: 752.

CHAPTER 4

1. J.P., "Les pertes des nations belligérantes au cours de la grande guerre," *Les archives de la grande guerre* (Paris: Etienne Chiron, 1921), pp. 41, 194, 197, 201–2. The figures are based on the study made by Louis Marin as a member of the army commission in the Chamber of Deputies.

2. *Règlement sur la conduite des grandes unités 1913*, p. 48.

3. For an excellent analysis of the *offensive à outrance*, see Joel A. Setzen, "The Doctrine of the Offensive in the French Army on the Eve of World War I" (unpublished Ph.D., diss., University of Chicago, 1972).

4. Gen. Frédéric Culmann, *Tactique d'artillerie* (Paris: Charles Lavauzelle, 1937), p. 366.

5. *Instruction 1921*, p. 23.

6. Lieutenant Colonel Miguel, *Enseignements stratégiques et tactiques de la guerre de 1914–1918* (Paris: Charles Lavazuelle, 1926), pp. 89–100; and Gen. Emile Alléhaut, *Etre prêts* (Paris: Berger-Levrault, 1935), p. 195.

7. *Instruction 1921*, pp. 10–12, 6.

8. *Règlement sur la conduite des grandes unités 1913*, p. 6.

9. Gen. André Beaufre, *1940: The Fall of France*, trans. Desmond Flower (New York: Knopf, 1968), p. 52.

10. *Table analytique de matières contenus dans les tomes 72 à 91 inclus de la Revue d'infanterie, et Table alphabétique des noms d'auteurs* (Paris: Charles Lavauzelle, 1939). Data from volumes 92 and 93 were gathered from indexes within them. Beginning September 1937, the Spanish Civil War was closely followed in the journal, not in articles but in reviews of other articles and books.

11. Data for the period July 1905 to July 1914 were taken from indexes contained with the individual volumes. If an article was spread through several issues, it was counted as one article.

12. Loizeau, *La manoeuvre du corps d'armée*, pp. 97–129; Loizeau, *Deux manoeuvres* (Paris: Berger-Levrault, 1933), pp. 3–70.

13. Loizeau, *La manoeuvre du corps d'armée*, pp. 92, 67–93. An English translation of Loizeau's lectures was used as an auxiliary text at the U.S. Army Command and General Staff College, at Fort Leavenworth, Kansas, during the mid-1930s.

14. For an analysis of the problems of the Macedonian campaign, see Jan Karl Tanenbaum, *General Maurice Sarrail, 1856–1929: The French Army and Left-Wing Politics* (Chapel Hill: University of North Carolina Press, 1974), pp. 75–172.

15. On the French use of history, see Marc Bloch, *Strange Defeat*, trans. Gerald Hopkins (New York: W. W. Norton, 1968), p. 119; Debeney, *La guerre et les hommes*, pp. 264–65, 44–45; and Lt. Col. Robert Vial, "L'Armée française et l'histoire," *Revue historique*. 217 (April–June 1962): 437–39.

16. A synthesis of Maillard's view can be found in Col. Louis A. G. Maillard, *Eléments de la guerre* (Paris: Librairie militaire de L. Baudoin, 1891).

17. See Gen. Henri Bonnal, *L'Art nouveau en tactique: Etude critique* (Paris: Librairie militaire R. Chapelot, 1904), pp. 57–75.

18. Ferdinand Foch, *Des principes de guerre* (Paris: Berger-Levrault, 1906), passim.

19. Lt. Col. René Tournes, *L'Histoire militaire* (Paris: Charles Lavauzelle, 1922), p. 109; and Debeney, *La guerre et les hommes*, pp. 12, 265, 277–81. For General Weygand's efforts at the War College and the Center of Higher Military

Studies, see his *Mémoires*, vol. 2 (Paris: Flammarion, 1957), pp. 309–14, 326–27, 353.

20. Loizeau, *La manoeuvre du corps d'armée*, p. 4. See France, E.S.G., Lieutenant Colonel Voisin, Cours de tactique générale et d'état-major, *La division au combat* (1929–1930), p. 4; and Gen. Gaston Duffour, "Les exigences et les disciplines actuelles du haut enseignement militaire (Part II)," *Revue de Paris* 11 (15 March 1935): 354–59.

21. Loizeau, *La manoeuvre du corps d'armée*, p. 4.

22. France, E.S.G., Conférences de tactique général et d'état-major, *La division* (1932) (n.p., n.d.), pp. 7–8.

23. Tournes, *L'Histoire militaire*, p. 26.

24. France, E.S.G., Lt. Col. René Prioux, *Cours de cavalerie* (1923–1924) (n.p., n.d.), pp. 325–401, passim; France, E.S.G., Lieutenant Colonel Touchon, *Conférences d'infanterie* (1925–1926), (n.p., n.d.), passim; and France, E . S. G., Col. Paul-Marie Joseph de la Porte du Theil, *Cours d'artillerie* (Courbevoie: P. Chanove, 1930), pp. 197–363.

25. Touchon, *Conférences d'infanterie*, (1925–1926) pp. 7–8, 395–96.

26. France, E.S.G., Col. G. Alexandre, *Cours de tactique d'artillerie* (1925), (n.p., n.d.), pp. 14–18. For a detailed discussion of prewar artillery thought, see Culmann, *Tactique d'artillerie*, pp. 99–115.

27. De la Porte du Theil, *Cours d'artillerie*, p. 64.

28. Alexandre, *Cours de tactique d'artillerie*, pp. 51, 56.

29. Erich von Ludendorff, *Ludendorff's Own Story* (New York: Harper & Brothers, 1919), 1: 326.

30. Cmdt. Marius Daille, *The Battle of Montdidier*, trans. Maj. Walter R. Wheeler, U.S. War Department (typescript), pp. 55, 49. The British to the north had ten heavy and two light battalions of tanks.

31. General Debeney's letter explaining his concept, thought process, and actions are in Daille, *The Battle of Montdidier*, pp. 22–28.

32. See A Graduate (anonymous), "The Ecole Supérieure de Guerre," *Infantry Journal* 21 (October 1922): 402.

33. Daille, *The Battle of Montdidier*, p. 58.

34. Ibid., p. 38.

35. Ibid., pp. 39–44.

36. Gen. Tony Albord, *Pourquoi cela est arrivé, ou les responsabilitiés, d'une génération militaire* (Nantes: Aux portes du large, 1947), passim; Albord, "Appel à l'imagination," *Revue de défense nationale* (August–September 1949): 159–67.

37. *Règlement sur la conduite des grandes unités 1913*, p. 48–49.

38. *Instruction 1921*, p. 14.

39. *Instruction 1936*, pp. 30–31.

40. Some studies have credited Capt. André Laffargue of the French army with suggesting the basic techniques of the infiltration tactics in 1916. The Germans supposedly accepted the ideas of the French captain and applied them with great success against the allies. See Capt. G. C. Wynne, *If Germany Attacks: The Battle in Depth in the West* (London: Faber & Faber, 1940), pp. 53–58; Ludwig Renn, *Warfare: The Relation of War to Society*, trans. Edward Fitzgerald (New York: Oxford University Press, 1939), pp. 110–13; and Capt. Laffargue, *Etude sur l'attaque* (Paris: Plon, 1916).

41. See Ludendorff, *Ludendorff's Own Story*, 1: 200–2; Gen. Wilhelm Balck, *Entwicklung der Taktik im Weltkreige* (2d ed.; Berlin: R. Eisenschmidt, 1922), pp. 352–54; George Bruchmüller, *Die deutsche Artillerie in den Durchschlachten des Weltkrieges* (Berlin: E. S. Mittler & Sohn, 1922); Konrad Krafft von Dellmensingen, *Der Durchbruch* (Hamburg: Hanseatische Verlagsanslatt, 1937), p. 405; and Capt. Timothy T. Lupfer, *The Dynamics of Doctrine: The Changes in German Tactical Doctrine during the First World War*, Leavenworth Papers no. 4 (Fort Leavenworth: Combat Studies Institute, 1981).

42. Alexandre, *Cours de tactique d'artillerie*, p. 49.

43. Daille, *The Battle of Montdidier*, pp. 301–2.

44. France, E.S.G., Lieutenant Colonel Duffour, *Guerre de 1914–1918* (1919–1920), Sixth Lecture (n.p., n.d.), pp. 62–64. For other criticisms of Ludendorff's methods, see Loizeau, *Succès stratégique, succès tactique* (Paris: Berger-Levrault, 1931), p. 140.

45. Gen. A. L. Buat, *Ludendorff* (Paris: Payot, 1921), pp. 193–95; and Buat, *Hindenburg et Ludendorff: Stratèges* (Paris: Berger-Levrault, 1923), pp. 204–12. General Buat did not discuss the tactics used in the breakthrough at Riga.

46. Lt. Col. Auguste Laure, *La victoire franco-espagnole dans le Rif* (Paris: Plon, 1927), p. 50; and Anonymous Officer of the General Staff in Paris, "French Strategy and Tactics in Syria," *The Journal of the Royal United Service Institution* 71 (November 1926): 701–7.

47. Chef de bataillon Goubernard, "Chars au Maroc en 1925," *Revue d'infanterie* 68–69 (May, June, July 1926): 619–49, 749–76, 110–31.

48. Laure, *La victoire*, pp. 50–52, 57–59, 90–93, 266, 268.

49. Captains Loustaunau-Lacau and Montjean, "Au Maroc francais en 1925," *Revue militaire française* 28 (1 April 1928): 36.

50. Anonymous, "French Strategy and Tactics in Syria," p. 711; Lieutenant Colonel Juin, "L'Achèvement de la pacification marocaine: méthodes et programmes," *Revue militaire française* 55 (January 1935): 84–107.

51. General Duchêne, "Le conflit sino-japonais," *Echo de paris*, 21 October 1937, p. 2.

52. Lieutenant Gelot, "Les enseignements de la guerre d'Espagne," *Revue d'infanterie* 93 (November 1938): 1038–39.

CHAPTER 5

1. *Instruction 1936*, p. 69; and *Instruction 1921*, p. 61.

2. *Instruction 1936*, p. 68; and *Instruction 1921*, p. 61.

3. *Instruction 1921*, p. 23. For another elaboration of this theme, see France, M.G., E.M.A., *Règlement de l'Infanterie, Deuxième partie, Combat* (Paris: L. Fournier, 1928), p. 19; and France, M.D.N.G., E.M.A., *Règlement de l'infanterie, Deuxième partie, Combat* (Paris: Charles Lavauzelle, 1938), p. 23.

4. *Règlement de l'infanterie, combat*, 1928, p. 49; *Règlement de l'infanterie, combat*, 1938, p. 25.

5. *Instruction 1921*, pp. 58–61; and *Instruction 1936*, pp. 66–67, 99–100.

6. Loizeau, *La manoeuvre du corps d'armée*, p. 24; and Loizeau, *Deux manoeuvres*, p. 103.

7. *D.D.F.* 3, no. 9 (21 July 1936), p. 22.

8. *Instruction 1921*, pp. 11–12.

9. Chauvineau, *Une invasion,* p. 101.

10. *Instruction 1921,* p. 60; and *Instruction 1936,* p. 100.

11. Alléhaut, *Etre prêts,* pp. 194–96.

12. *Instruction 1936,* p. 31

13. Ibid., pp. 19, 106.

14. Ibid., p. 66.

15. *Commission . . . Témoignages* 2: 446.

16. *Instruction 1936,* p. 70.

17. France, M.G., *Règlement sur le service en campagne de l'artillerie* (Paris: Imprimerie nationale, 1919). For a bibliography of works on artillery in the World War I era, see Mémorial de l'artillerie française, *Bibliographie générale de l'artillerie technique, 1915 à 1926* (Paris: Imprimerie nationale, 1926).

18. Grand Quartier Général des Armées Françaises de l'Est, Maréchal Pétain à M. le Président du conseil, M.G., 24 February 1919, no. 41558, S.H.A.T. carton 16N53, item 161, pp. 6, 3, 4. The study has been reprinted in Paoli, *L'Armée française de 1919 à 1939* (Paris: Société industrielle d'imprimerie, n.d.) vol. 1, *La reconversion,* pp. 151–70. Other technical studies were done by Gen. Sainte-Claire Deville and Gen. F. G. Herr.

19. General Report of General Herr, President of the Central Committee on Artillery, on the Lessons to be Learned from the War in Regard to Artillery, 1 October 1919, pp. 23, 30–32, trans. U.S. Army (typescript).

20. *PV., C.S.G.,* 10 October 1922, carton 50. See the comments by the minister of finance questioning the need for these programs in the 6 December 1922 meeting of the C.S.D.N. Procès-verbal de la séance du C.S.D.N. du 6 décembre 1922, S.H.A.T. carton 2N5, dossier 8, item 3.

21. Commission d'études pratiques de l'infanterie et des chars de combat, Rapport de la commission d'études pratiques de l'infanterie et des chars de combat sur l'emploi du char B-1, 16 January 1932, p. 36, S.H.A.T. carton 9N162, dossier 2.

22. Détachement d'expériences de Sissone, Rapport du Général Delestraint, commandant le détachement, 15 May 1937, vol. 2, p. 30, S.H.A.T. carton 9N164, dossier 2.

23. Col. André Duvignac, *Histoire de l'armée motorisée* (Paris: Imprimerie nationale, 1948), pp. 371–72. For a comparison of average and maximum speeds and distances of motorized and horse-drawn artillery units, see France, M.G., *Règlement de manoeuvre de l'artillerie, 3ème partie, Service en campagne* (25 July 1930), (Paris: Charles Lavauzelle, 1930), pp. 66–67.

24. Déposition du Général Doumenc, 14 janvier 1941, Fonds Gamelin, carton 5.

25. Pétain à M. le Président du conseil, 24 February 1919, p. 8.

26. Report of General Herr, 1 October 1919, pp. 35–37.

27. *P.V., C.S.G.,* 24 February 1936, carton 50 ter.

28. Herr, *L'Artillerie: Ce quelle a été; ce qu'elle est; ce qu'elle doit être* (Paris: Berger-Levrault, 1923), pp. 146–48; Gamelin, *Servir* 1: 180.

29. *P.V., C.S.G.,* 24 February 1936; 2 December 1938; carton 50 ter. See also *P.V., C.S.G.,* 8 December 1939, carton 50 ter. While the 105C model 1934 Schneider and the 105C model 1935 Bourges had a range of 10.6 kilometers, the 105L model 1936 Schneider had a range of 16 kilometers.

30. *P.V., C.S.G.,* 2 December 1938, carton 50 ter.

31. On the number of artillery pieces in the late 1930s, see Gamelin, *Servir* 1: 180; D.A., Situation des matériels, 18 novembre 1938, S.H.A.T. carton 9N198. For the number remaining after World War I, see Herr, *L'Artillerie*, pp. 146–48; and M.G., D.A., Note pour l'E.M.A., 25 July 1919, no. 14,300 A I/3, S.H.A.T. carton 9N185, dossier 1. In comparison, the records on the number of tanks are much more detailed and accurate.

32. Lieutenant Colonel Armengaud, "L'Effort d'armement français," Conférence faite à l'école d'état-major le 15 février 1940, p. 43, S.H.A.T. carton 9N155; Armengaud, "La motorisation et la mécanisation dans l'armée," Conférence faite devant la commission de l'armée de la Chambre des Députés le 14 juin 1939, passim, S.H.A.T. carton 9N155.

33. Herr, *L'Artillerie*, p. 225.

34. France, M.G., E.M.A., *Règlement de manoeuvre de l'artillerie, Deuxième partie, L'Artillerie au combat* (Paris: Charles Lavauzelle, 1926), p. 52.

35. *P.V., C.S.G.*, 4 October 1922, carton 50.

36. *Règlement de manoeuvre de l'artillerie, L'artillerie au combat*, 1926, p. 52.

37. *P.V., C.S.G.*, 28 October 1926, carton 50 bis.

38. Gamelin, *Servir* 1: 181.

39. Centre d'études tactiques d'artillerie, Lieutenant Colonels Fellion et Denys, "Conférences sur la préparation et l'ajustage du tir" (1929) (n.p., n.d.), pp. 6–8.

40. France E.S.G., Chef de Bataillon Martin, "L'Appui de l'infanterie par l'artillerie," 6 December 1927 (n.p., n.d.), pp. 24–25.

41. M.G., *Instruction générale sur le tir de l'artillerie du 7 mai 1936* (Paris): Imprimerie nationale, 1937). For an analysis of the new regulation, see France, E.S.G., Commandant Aizier, Cours d'artillerie, "Note relative à l'instruction générale sur le tir de l'artillerie du 7 mai 1936" (n.p., n.d.).

42. Richard Lee Pierce, "A Maximum of Support: The Development of U.S. Army Field Artillery Doctrine in World War I" (unpublished M.A. thesis, Ohio State University, 1983), pp. 37–39, 42, 65–67, 73, 92–95, 97–98, 112–14, 121–22, 125, 130–31.

43. *P.V., C.S.G.*, 15 October 1926, carton 50 bis.

44. France, E.S.G., Colonel Lemoine, Cours de tactique générale et d'état-major, *Tactique générale* (Rambouillet: Pierre Leroy, 1922), pp. 66, 78; France, E.S.G., Colonel Moyrand, *Cours de tactique appliquée* (1926) (n.p., n.d.), pp. 14, 121; Colonel Alexandre, *Cours de tactique d'artillerie* (1925), pp. 315, 319.

45. *Instruction 1921*, p. 67.

46. *Instruction 1936*, pp. 107, 112.

47. Alexandre, *Cours de tactique d'artillerie* (1925), pp. 137–44, 148–49; de la Porte du Theil, *Cours d'artillerie* (1930), pp. 78–79.

48. France, E.S.G., Commandant du Payrat, Cours d'artillerie, "L'Artillerie divisionaire dans l'offensive: l'attaque" (1936–1937), (n.p., n.d.), p. 23; France, E.S.G., Commandant Charpentier, Cours d'artillerie, "L'Artillerie divisionnaire dans l'attaque: l'emploi de l'artillerie" (1937–1938) (n.p., n.d.), pp. 8–12.

49. France, E.S.G., Chef d'Escadrons Vernoux, Cours d'artillerie, "L'Artillerie dans l'offensive" (1938–1939) (n.p., n.d.), pp. 11–12.

50. France, E.S.G., Lieutenant Colonel Voisin, Cours de tactique générale et d'état-major, *La division au combat* (1929–1930) (n.p., n.d.), p. 36.

51. Moyrand, *Cours de tactique appliquée* (1926), pp. 128, 108–49, 230, 197–260.

52. France, E.S.G., Lieutenant Colonel Curnier, "Conclusion d'ensemble à l'étude de la manoeuvre offensive de la D.I." (20 March 1937) (n.p., n.d.), p. 16.

53. *Règlement de l'infanterie, combat*, 1938, pp. 84–85.

54. France, M.D.N.G., E.M.A., *Règlement des unités de chars de combat, 2ème partie: Combat (projet)* (n.p.: Ecole des chars de combat, 1939), p. 91.

55. Voisin, *La division au combat* (1929–1930), p. 38.

56. France, E.S.G., Cours de tactique générale et d'état-major, *Notes pratiques d'état-major* (1935) (n.p, n.d.), p. 20.

57. France, E.S.G., Lieutenant Colonel Curnier, Cours de tactique générale et d'état-major, "Mouvement des grandes unités motorisées" (1 April 1938) (n.p., n.d.), pp. 44–45; France, E.S.G., Cours de tactique générale et d'état-major, "Mouvement d'une D.I.M. en automobiles, Dossier complémentaire" (1938–1939) (n.p., n.d.).

58. Alexandre, *Cours de tactique d'artillerie* (1925).

59. Lt. H. H. Hunt, "Accompanying Artillery," *Field Artillery Journal* 22 (November–December 1932): 641–64.

60. Germany, Reichswehrministerium, Chef der Heeresleitung, *Führung und Gefecht der verbundenen Waffen*, vol. 1 (Berlin: Offene Worte, 1921), p. 145.

61. Germany, Chef der Heeresleitung, *Truppenführung*, vol. 1 (Berlin: E. G. Mittler & Sohn, 1933), pp. 127–30.

62. De la Porte du Theil, *Cours d'artillerie* (1930), pp. 88–89, 112–15.

63. France, C.H.E.M., Stage de technique d'armée, General Aublet, "L'Artillerie d'armée" (October 1937) (n.p., n.d.), p. 2.

64. Capt. A. -P. Garnier, "L'Artillerie allemande au combat," *Revue d'artillerie* 122 (August 1938): 90, 111. In 1924, an anonymous article reviewed the German artillery regulations and noted the emphasis on decentralization. E.L., "Le nouveau règlement de combat de l'artillerie allemande," *Revue d'artillerie* 93 (June 1924): 607–23; 94 (July 1924): 77–92.

65. *Règlement de l'infanterie, combat*, 1938, pp. 73–74, 128, 136–37.

66. Ibid., pp. 128–29; France, M.G., *Règlement de l'infanterie, Deuxième partie, combat*, 1928 (rev. ed., Paris: Charles Lavauzelle, 1934), passim.

67. *Règlement de l'infanterie, combat*, 1938, p. 135.

68. Touchon, *Conférences d'infanterie* (1925–1926), p. 27. See also pp. 23, 193.

69. France, Ministry of National Defense and War, Bureau of Infantry, *Regulations for Rifle Units* (7 January 1939), trans. U.S. War Department (typescript), pp. 49, 71–72, 83–84, 87, 130–33.

70. Moyrand, *Cours de tactique appliquée* (1925), p. 278.

71. Lemoine, *Tactique générale* (1922), pp. 237, 238; Loizeau, *La manoeuvre du corps d'armées* (1932), p. 76.

72. Chef der Heeresleitung, *Führung und Gefecht* (1921), 1: 140–42; Chef der Heeresleitung, *Truppenführung* (1933), 1: 145–48, 158–59.

73. Chef der Heeresleitung, *Truppenführung* (1933), 1: 127. The contrast can also be seen in some of the military books published between the war. Compare, for example, Colonel Alléhaut, *Le combat d'infanterie* (Paris: Berger-Levrault, 1924) and Erwin Rommel, *Infantry Attacks*, trans. Lt. Col. G. E. Kidde (Washington: The Infantry Journal, 1944).

74. Chef der Heeresleitung, *Führung und Gefecht* (1921), 1: 53–54.

75. Chef der Heeresleitung, *Truppenführung* (1933), 1: 146–48.

76. Von Dellmensingen, *Der Durchbruch*, p. 405.

77. Chef der Heeresleitung, *Truppenführung* (1933), 1: 1.

78. Chef der Heeresleitung, *Führung und Gefecht* (1921), 1: 143; Chef der Heeresleitung, *Truppenführung* (1933), 1: 159, 11. The French were aware of the differences between their doctrine and the German doctrine. In 1938, one French author quoted from a German military journal that the French system was "too methodical and too diagrammatic" (Commandant Carrias, *L'Armée allemande: son histoire, son organisation, sa tactique* [Paris: Berger-Levrault, 1938], p. 193).

79. Chef der Heeresleitung, *Truppenführung* (1933), 1: 121–22, 127, 142–43.

80. France, C.H.E.M. et Stage de technique d'armée, General Audet, "La manoeuvre de l'armée" (September 1938) (n.p., n.d.), pp. 62–65. For a similar description, see France, C.H.E.M., Stage de technique d'armée, General Millet, La manoeuvre d'une armée," deuxième conférence (1934) (n.p., n.d.), pp. 13–17.

81. France, E.S.G., Lieutenant Colonel Curnier, "Conclusions d'ensemble à l'étude de la manoeuvre offensive de la D.I." (20 March 1937) (n.p., n.d.), p. 26.

82. Quoted in U.S. War Department, Military Intelligence Division, Tentative Lessons from the Recent Active Campaign in Europe, Bulletin, no. 24. Training in the French Army, Washington, D.C., 24 July 1940, p. 1.

CHAPTER 6

1. Duroselle, *La décadence*, pp. 14–25.

2. Cmdt. Jean Vial, "La défense nationale: son organisation entre les deux guerres," *Revue d'histoire de la deuxième guerre mondiale* 5 (April 1955): 12–15; Dutailly, *Les problèmes de l'armée de terre*, pp. 134–35; Jean-Paul Cointet, "Gouvernement et haut-commandement en France entre les deux guerres," *Défense nationale* 33 (April 1977): 83–100.

3. Gamelin, *Servir* 1: 54.

4. Vial, "La défense nationale," pp. 15–17; and Duroselle, *La décadence*, pp. 256–57.

5. Le Goyet, *Le mystère Gamelin*, pp. 67–68; Vial, "La défense nationale," p. 15.

6. *J.O. Lois et décrets* (22 January 1938), p. 1020.

7. *J.O. Lois et décrets* (29 July 1911), pp. 6444–45; (20 January 1912), p. 685; Ralston, *The Army of the Republic*, pp. 340, 337. Cf. Porch, *The March to the Marne*, p. 237.

8. General Mordacq, *Le ministère Clemenceau* 4: pp. 40, 48–50, 55–58, 61–62, 95–96, 239, 255, 302–3; quote is from page 302.

9. For a lucid and intelligent description of the problems of the army's High Command, see the testimony of Gen. Pierre Héring at the Riom trial. Héring, *Procès de Riom*, Audience du jeudi 19 mars 1942, pp. 1048–54, Fonds Gamelin, carton 2. On the organization of the office of the minister of war, see Paoli, *La phase de fermeté*, pp. 60–61.

10. Hughes, *To the Maginot Line*, pp. 107–11.

11. Paul Reynaud, *Le problème militaire français* (Paris: Flammarion, 1937), pp. 81–83, 88, 92–93, 102.

12. Weygand, *Mémoires* 2:3 16.

13. Quoted in Pertinax [André Géraud], *The Gravediggers of France* (New York: Doubleday, Doran, 1944), p. 325.

14. *J.O. Lois et décrets* (27 January 1920), p. 1432.

15. *J.O. Lois et décrets* (22 January 1922), pp. 1008–9.

16. *J.O. Ch. Déb.* (19 January 1922), p. 40.

17. Ibid., pp. 57–58.

18. Laure, *Pétain*, p. 246.

19. *J.O. Lois et décrets* (19 January 1935), pp. 628–29.

20. Réquisitoire définitif, *Procés de Riom*, p. 142, Fonds Gamelin, carton 1.

21. *J.O. Lois et décrets* (20 September 1925), pp. 9340–41.

22. See *P.V., C.S.G.*, 31 May 1920; 10 September 1920; 11 December 1920; 23 March 1922; carton 50.

23. Ibid., 3 April 1925; 10 April 1925; carton 50 bis; quote is from 3 April.

24. Ibid., 8 November 1926, carton 50 bis.

25. Ibid., 10 April 1925; 30 March 1925; 19 March 1926; carton 50 bis.

26. Ibid., 21 January 1924, carton 50.

27. Ibid., 15 May 1933, carton 50 ter.

28. Rapport d'ensemble du Général Dufieux, I.G.I., pour l'année 1935, No. 150/IGI/S, p. 75. S.H.A.T. unnumbered carton entitled "Inspection générale de l'infanterie, Rapports d'ensemble, etc."

29. Weygand, *Memoires*, 2:348, 383.

30. Ibid. 2:43. See the comments by General Weygand in *P.V., C.S.G.*, 15 January 1935, carton 50 ter; and *Commission . . . Rapport* 1: 122–24.

31. Gamelin, *Servir* 2: 199.

32. *Commission . . . Témoignages* 1: 236.

33. Weygand, *Mémoires* 2: 366.

34. Robert Jacomet, *L'Armement de la France, 1936–1939* (Paris: Editions de la jeunesse, 1945), p. 36n.

35. Mordacq, *Le ministère Clemenceau* 4: 303.

36. *J.O. Lois et décrets* (3 February 1929), pp. 1212–13; Jacomet, *L'Armement de la France*, p. 32: Paoli, *La phase de fermeté*, p. 66.

37. *J. O. Lois et décrets* (19 January 1935), pp. 629–30.

38. Jacomet, *L'Armement de la France*, p. 36.

39. *J.O. Lois et décrets* (2 July 1938), p. 7765; Gamelin, *Servir* 1: 195.

40. *J.O. Lois et décrets* (23 May 1926), p. 5799; (27 April 1924), pp. 3817–19.

41. *P.V., C.S.G.*, 19 March 1926, carton 50 bis.

42. Ibid., 11 March 1932, carton 50 bis.

43. Ibid., 19 March 1926, carton 50 bis.

44. Ibid., 15 October 1926, carton 50 bis.

45. Ibid., 10 April 1925, carton 50 bis.

46. Ibid., 15 December 1925, carton 50 bis.

47. *Procès de Riom*, Audience du vendredi 27 février, samedi 28 février, et mardi 3 mars 1942, Fonds Gamelin, carton 1; *Commission . . . Témoignages* 1: 22–23.

48. M.D.N.G., E.M.A. *Règlement des unités de chars de combat, 2ème partie: Combat (Project)* (n.p.: Ecole des chars de combat, 1939); Remarques des membres consultatifs et nouvelle rédaction proposée aux membres de la commission (n.d.), pp. 5–11. S.H.A.T. carton 9N165.

49. General Georges, C.S.G., Remarques faites sur le *Règlement des unités de chars de combat, 2ème partie—combat*, 10 January 1939, S.H.A.T. carton 9N165: Georges,

C.S.G. Avis sur *Règlement des chars de combat, 2ème partie—combat*, 16 January 1939, S.H.A.T. carton 9N165.

50. General Georges, C.S.G., Avis sur *Règlement des unités de chars de combat, 2ème partie—combat*, 3 April 1939, S.H.A.T. carton 9N165. For an analysis of the points accepted and rejected, see E.M.A., D.I., Note relative aux observations importantes, 10 March 1939, S.H.A.T. carton 9N165.

51. General Gamelin, vice-président du C.S.G., 7 April 1939, No. 1965/A, S.H.A.T. carton 9N165.

52. While Lieutenant Colonel Perré indicated the regulation was not published, Gamelin stated that it was finally made available in the spring of 1940. Testimony of Col. Jean P. Perré, *Procès de Riom*, Audience du mercredi 1 avril 1942, p. 1504, Fonds Gamelin, carton 2; Gamelin, *Servir* 1: 288.

53. See Gen. Joseph-L.M. Maurin, *L'Armée moderne* (Paris: Flammarion, 1938), p. 28.

54. Testimony of General Rinderknech, *Commission . . . Témoignages* 5: 1479; Testimony of General Happich, *Commission . . . Témoignages* 7: 1717.

55. Paoli, *La reconversion*, pp. 126–27; and *La phase de fermeté*, p. 64.

56. M.G., D.C.T., Note pour l'E.M., Objet: Organes d'études, 14 January 1921, No. 178/4/2, S.H.A.T. carton 9N172.

57. Weygand, *Mémoires* 2: 369.

58. Testimony of General Dassault, *Commission . . . Témoignages* 5: 1460.

59. Weygand, *Mémoires* 2: 370.

60. *Commission . . . Témoignages* 5: 1459–60.

61. Testimony of General Rinderknech, *Commission . . . Témoignages* 5: 1480.

62. Ibid.

63. *J.O. Lois et décrets* (4 July 1935), pp. 7112–15. For an analysis of the problems of this bureaucratic structure and a diagram showing the relationships between the numerous offices, see D.I., B.T., C.C., Lieutenant Colonel Perré, Note no. III, Etude et réalisation des matériels automobiles de combat, n.d., S.H.A.T. carton 9N158.

64. Testimony of General de Sablet, *Commission . . . Témoignages* 6: 1580–81.

65. Testimony of General Rinderknech, *Commission . . . Témoignages* 5: 1480.

66. *J.O. Lois et décrets* (4 July 1935), p. 7112.

67. *Commission . . . Témoignages* 2: 371.

68. Ibid. 2: 374. See also Gamelin, *Servir* 1: 185–86.

69. Testimony of General Rinderknech, *Commission . . . Témoignages* 5: 1488; testimony of Daladier, *Procès de Riom*, Audience du samedi 28 février 1942, p. 235, Fonds Gamelin, carton 1; Cour suprême de justice, Rapport général No. 155–3 presenté à Monsieur le président de la cour suprême de justice par le contrôleur général de l'armée M. Cunin sur les crédits d'armement et leur emploi de 1935 à 1940, 3 November 1940, p. 86, Fonds Gamelin, carton 3; and Gamelin, *Servir* 1: 185–86.

70. *Commission . . . Témoignages* 7: 2160.

71. See Gamelin, *Servir* 1: 67–77. The standard reference is Jacques Minart, *P. C. Vincennes, Secteur 4*, 2 vols. (Paris: Berger-Levrault, 1945).

72. *Commission . . . Témoignages* 3: 675–79.

73. Jean Verzat, "A propos du P. C. Gamelin," *Revue historique des armées* 2 (1982): 100.

CHAPTER 7

1. M.G., La 3° direction—Artillerie d'assaut à l'E.M.A., 27 March 1920, no. 2346 AS/3, S.H.A.T. carton 9N158; M.G., Tableau joint à la lettre no. 0150 du 14 mars 1922 de l'inspecteur général des fabrications de guerre à la mobilisation, Plan de fabrication, Chars de combat, tableau 1, S.H.A.T. carton 9N198.

2. France, M.G., E.M.A., *Instruction provisoire sur l'emploi des chars de combat comme engins d'infanterie du 23 mars 1920* (Paris: Charles Lavauzelle, 1920), pp. 5, 8–9.

3. France, M.G., *Règlement provisoire de manoeuvre d'infanterie du 1er février 1920, Deuxième partie* (Paris: Charles Lavauzelle, 1921), pp. 31–32.

4. *Instruction 1921*, pp. 24–25.

5. Ibid., p. 25. *Instruction provisoire sur l'emploi des chars de combat du 23 mars 1920*, p. 5.

6. Paoli, *La reconversion*, p. 125.

7. Grand quartier générale des armées françaises de l'est, Etude sur les missions des chars blindés en campagne, 8 July 1919, S.H.A.T. carton 9N157.

8. See Perré, "Naissance et évolution du char de combat en France durant la guerre 1914–1918," *Revue d'infanterie* 86 (January 1935): 13–30; Le Goyet, "Les chars de combat pendant la première guerre mondiale," *Revue historique de l'armée* 24 (1968): 119–41.

9. General Estienne, *Conférence faite le 15 février 1920 sur les chars d'assaut* (Paris: Librairie de l'enseignement technique, 1920), p. 44.

10. In addition to Estienne, the commission included Colonel Chedeville, Lieu-tenant Colonel Corap, Major Bloch, Major Hallez, Major Keller, Captain Bruneau, and others.

11. M.G., E.M.A., Commission chargée de la rédaction d'un programme de chars de combat, Programme arrêté par la commission, n.d., S.H.A.T. carton 9N158; M.G., Commission chargée de la rédaction d'un programme de chars de combat, Procès-verbal de la réunion du 15 janvier 1921, and Procès-verbal de la réunion du 13 janvier 1921, S.H.A.T. carton 9N158.

12. Note relative au système de chars de combat à l'étude, 10 October 1925, p. 5, S.H.A.T. carton 9N158.

13. *P.V., C.S.G.*, 19 March 1926, carton 50 bis; M.G., le M.G. (Paul Painlevé) à M. le Général inspecteur des chars de combat, Objet: Programme des chars de combat, 2 April 1926, no. 0382-3/11-2, S.H.A.T. carton 9N158. The program also included a light colonial tank. A copy of the program is included in M.G., D.A., le M.G. à M. le Général Estienne, chargé des études de chars de combat, 11 October 1926, no. 79670 2/3, S.H.A.T. carton 9N158.

14. Jeffrey Johnstone Clarke, "Military Technology in Republican France: The Evolution of the French Armored Force, 1917–1940" (unpublished Ph.D. diss., Duke University, 1969) p. 83.

15. M.G., D.I., Note pour l'E.M.A., Objet: Fabrication des chars de combat, 31 May 1929, no. 398 CC/1/2, S.H.A.T. carton 9N158.

16. France, M.G., *Règlement des unités de chars légers du 1 juin 1929, Deuxième partie: Combat* (Paris: Imprimerie nationale, 1929), p. 11.

17. France, M.G., E.M.A., *Instruction sur l'emploi des chars de combat* (Paris: Imprimerie nationale, 1929), pp. 9, 12.

18. *Règlement des unités de chars légers*, 1929, 2: 13.

19. *Instruction sur l'emploi des chars de combat, 1929*, p. 12.

20. France, M.G., *Règlement des unités de chars légers, Première partie: Instruction technique* (Paris: Imprimerie nationale, 1929), p. 11.

21. E.M.A., Rapport fait au ministère le 4 juillet 1930, Analyse: Au sujet d'un programme de motorisation dans l'armée, no. 01380 bis 3/11-1; Séance d'études, C.S.G., 25 June 1930, S.H.A.T. carton 50 ter.

22. Char léger fortement blindé, char rapide (Projet du Capitaine Deygas), 23 January 1930, S.H.A.T. carton 9N158.

23. Note relative au système de chars de combat à l'étude, 10 October 1925, p. 2; M.G., D.A., le M.G. à M. le Général inspecteur des études et expériences techniques de l'artillerie, Objet: Char de bataille, 7 November 1930, no. 78200 2/3, p. 2; M.G., D.I., Note pour l'E.M.A., Objet: Programme de chars, 18 May 1931, no. 740/CC1 S. Both are in S.H.A.T. carton 9N158.

24. I.C.C., General Bezu, Avis du général inspecteur des chars de combat sur le nouveau projet de programme de chars de combat de la Ière direction, 15 June 1931, no. 26/ICC, pp. 3–4, 7, S.H.A.T. carton 9N158.

25. M.G., D.I., Note pour l'E.M.A., Objet: Programme de chars, 18 May 1931, no. 740/CC1 S, pp. 5, 8, S.H.A.T. carton 9N158.

26. Rapport du Colonel Touchon, commandant l'école d'application de l'infanterie et des chars de combat, chargé de l'arbitrage du détachement mécanique de combat aux exercices combinés de 1932, 18 October 1932, pp. 18–20, S.H.A.T. carton 9N166.

27. General Dufieux, I.G.I., relatif aux enseignements à tirer des exercices combinés de 1932, 12 December 1932, no. 97/IGI/S, S.H.A.T. carton 9N166. Dufieux's report is reprinted in *Commission . . . Témoignages* 4:1056–59. Weygand, Mémoires 2: 407–8.

28. Colonel Martin, détachement d'expériences d'emploi d'engins blindés, Rapport du Colonel commandant le détachement, camp de Coëtquidan, 25 July 1933, pp. 31, 33, 37, S.H.A.T. carton 9N164.

29. Commission d'expériences des matériels de chars, Exemplaire no. 8, Etude du char B-1, note no. 2, Essais exécutés sur le champ de tir de Bourges, 14 August 1930, p. 15, S.H.A.T. carton 9N162.

30. Commission d'études pratiques de l'infanterie et des chars de combat, Rapport de la commission d'études pratiques de l'infanterie et des chars de combat sur l'emploi du char B-1, 16 January 1932, pp. 28, 31–32 , 36, 49, S.H.A.T. carton 9N162.

31. *P.V., C.S.G.*, 4 June 1932, carton 50 bis.

32. Lieutenant Colonel Perré and Captain [illegible], "Evolution du char du combat en France de 1915 à 1934" (typescript), pp. 111–117, S.H.A.T. carton 9N155.

33. C.C.A., Note relative à l'étude d'un nouveau modèle de char léger, 15 June 1933, pp. 1, 3–5, S.H.A.T. carton 9N158.

34. C.C.A., Projet de résolution, 2 June 1934, S.H.A.T. carton 9N158; *P.V., C.S.G.*, 24 March 1934, S.H.A.T. carton 50 ter.

35. General Estienne, Section technique de l'artillerie, Résumé de mes convictions sur la politique des chars de combat exposée hier au Général Corap, 20 October 1933, S.H.A.T. carton 9N157.

36. General Estienne, Note du Général Estienne sur l'importance du tonnage des chars de combat, 15 November 1933, p. 3, S.H.A.T. carton 9N157.

37. France did not have fifty D-2 tanks until February 1937 (C.C.A., Figure no. 1). This chart shows the monthly output and total number of French tanks from 1929 until January 1939. It is included with the résumés of the council's meetings on 3 May 1937, and 1 June 1938, in an unnumbered S.H.A.T. carton entitled "Inspection des chars de combat, Rapports d'inspection d'unités."

38. *P.V., C.S.G.*, 24 March 1934, carton 50 ter; Document ayant servi au Général Velpry, lors de son exposé relatif au matériel de 6 tonnes, devant le C.S.G., le 24 mars 1934, unnumbered S.H.A.T. carton entitled "Inspections des chars de combat, Rapports d'inspection d'unités"; and note du Général Velpry, matériel chars, 1934, p. 16, S.H.A.T. carton 9N158.

39. *P.V., C.S.G.*, 24 March 1934, carton 50 ter.

40. M.G., D.I., Note pour l'E.M.A., Objet: Plan de fabrication du matériel chars, 18 juin 1936, no. 1881 BT/1-CCS, S.H.A.T. carton 9N158.

41. C.H.E.M., Conférence du Général Martin au C.H.E.M. le 17 janvier 1936 sur l'emploi des chars, n.d., pp. 9, 18–20, 26, 32, 42, S.H.A.T. carton 9N157.

42. Inspection des chars de combat, le Général Velpry à M. le Général, chef d'état-major général de l'armée, 23 March 1936, no. 46/ICC/S, p. 2, unnumbered S.H.A.T. carton entitled "Inspections des chars de combat."

43. Clarke, "Military Technology in Republican France," p. 148; J.P., "Chars légers," n.d., pp. 7–8, S.H.A.T. carton 9N158.

44. The H-35 tank was very similar to the R-35, but it had a maximum speed of 35 kilometers per hour and a weight of 10.9 tons. The F.C.M.-36 was also very similar, but its diesel engine gave it a cruising range of more than 300 kilometers. M.D.N.G., *Silhouettes d'engins blindés*, August 1936, S.H.A.T. carton 9N156.

45. M.G., E.M.A., *Notice provisoire sur l'emploi des chars D en liaison avec l'infanterie du 3 août 1935* (Paris: Imprimerie nationale, 1935), p. 4; conférence du Général Martin au C.H.E.M. le 17 janvier 1936 sur l'emploi des chars, p. 20.

46. *Instruction 1936*, pp. 44, 105–6.

47. Général Delestraint, Détachement d'expériences de Sissone, Rapport du Général Delestraint commandant le détachement, Sissone, 15 May 1937, 1: 78, 101, 120–22, 124–25; 2: 30–31, S.H.A.T. carton 9N164.

48. M.D.N.G., E.M.A., Synthèse des rapports des généraux Dufieux, Velpry, et Delestraint sur les expériences de chars modernes, executées à Sissone en avril 1937, p. 8, S.H.A.T. carton 9N164.

49. *Instruction sur l'emploi des chars de combat*, 1929, p. 33.

50. Rapport du Colonel Touchon, chargé de l'arbitrage du détachement mécanique de combat aux exercices combinés de 1932, 18 October 1932, pp. 16, 18; General Dufieux, relatif aux ensignements à tirer des exercices combinés de 1932, 12 December 1932.

51. Colonel Martin, Rapport du colonel commandant le détachement, camp de Coëtquidan, 25 July 1933, pp. 53–55.

52. Note relative à l'emploi des chars et des moyens anti-chars, résumant les remarques faites par le général directeur de l'infanterie, en particulier au cours des manoeuvres de la 6ème région, 9 October 1936, pp. 5–7, S.H.A.T. carton 9N165.

53. Rapport du Général Delestraint commandant le détachement, Sissone, 15 May 1937, 1: 124–25, 101, 120.

54. E.M. du Général Georges, Procès-verbal de la réunion de la commission chargée de l'étude de l'emploi des chars de combat, 13 October 1937, S.H.A.T. carton 9N163.

55. France, M.D.N.G., E.M.A., *Notice provisoire sur l'emploi des chars modernes* (15 December 1937) (Paris: 1937), pp. 3, 7, 8, 13. Earlier drafts of the manual and summaries of the criticisms made by Generals Georges, Dufieux, and Limasset are in S.H.A.T. carton 9N157.

56. I.G.I., le Général Dufieux à M. le président du Conseil, M.D.N.G., Objet: Situation actuelle des chars de combat, 19 May 1938, no. 76 IGI, pp. 1–2, S.H.A.T. carton 9N158.

57. I.C.C., le Général Velpry à M. le Général Dufieux, Objet: Expérience de Sissone, 28 May 1937, no. 121/ICC/S, p. 19, unnumbered S.H.A.T. carton entitled "Inspection générale de l'infanterie (organisation)."

58. France, M.D.N.G., E.M.A., *Règlement des unités de chars de combat, Deuxième partie: Combat (projet)* (n.p.: Ecole des chars de combat, 1939), pp. 10, 14–15.

59. Remarques des membres consultatifs et nouvelle rédaction proposée aux membres de la commission, n.d., S.H.A.T. carton 9N165.

60. *Règlement des unités de chars de combat, Combat*, 1939, pp. 56–57; General Georges, Remarques faites sur le *Règlement des unités de chars de combat, Deuxième partie: Combat*, 10 January 1939, pp. 3–4, S.H.A.T. carton 9N165.

61. General Georges, Remarques, 10 January 1939, pp. 6–7. See *Règlement de l'infanterie, Combat*, 1938, pp. 33–44.

62. *Règlement des unités de chars de combat, Combat*, 1939, pp. 91, 42; General Georges, Avis sur *Règlement des unités de chars de combat, Deuxième partie: Combat*, 3 April 1939, p. 2, S.H.A.T. carton 9N165.

63. *Règlement des unités de chars de combat, Combat*, 1939, pp. 22–24, 30.

64. Ibid., p. 95.

65. Chef der Heeresleitung, *Truppenführung* 1: 133.

66. Lt. Col. D. Braun, "Deutsche und französische Grundsätze fur den Kampfwageneinsatz," *Militär-Wochenblatt* 122 (22 October 1937): 1035.

67. Ibid., p. 1036.

68. Chef der Heeresleitung, *Truppenführung* 1: 133.

69. Ibid.

70. Lieutenant Colonel Braun, "Deutsche und französische Grundsätze," p. 1038.

CHAPTER 8

1. Estienne, *Conférence faite le 15 février 1920*, pp. 42–43.

2. J.-R. Tournoux, *Pétain et de Gaulle* (Paris: Plon, 1964), pp. 155; Weygand, *Mémoires* 2: 353.

3. Lieutenant Colonel Keller, Etude sur la division mécanique, 1930, S.H.A.T. Carton 9N158. Keller became inspector general of tanks in August 1939.

4. De Gaulle, *Vers l'armée de métier*, passim.

5. C.C.A., fig. 1. This chart shows the monthly output and total number of French tanks (except for the SOMUA S-35) from 1929 until January 1939. It is included with the résumés of the council's meetings on 3 May 1937, and 1 June 1938, in an unnumbered S.H.A.T. carton entitled "Inspection des chars de combat, Rapports d'inspection d'unités."

6. Char B-1 bis, Note sur un dispositif de fortune destiné à augmenter le rayon d'action et applicable rapidement, 6 June 1940, S.H.A.T. carton 9N158.

7. Perré, *Evolution du char de combat*, pp. 111–17; M.G., D.I., Note pour l'E.M.A., Objet: Char de bataille, 3 January 1936, no. 9 BT/ICC; M.G., D.I., Note pour la direction des fabrications d'armement, Objet: Char de 20 tonnes, 1 February 1938, no. 456 BT/ICC; D.I., Note pour l'E.M.A. (S.A.E.T.), Objet: Char lourd, dit "de 45 tonnes," 21 February 1938, no. 782 BT/ICC/S/. All are in S.H.A.T. carton 9N158.

8. For a discussion of tank production problems see C.C.A. et des matériels de guerre, Procès-verbal de la réunion du 10 mai 1936 de la commission chargée de l'établissement d'un programme de char lourd, unnumbered S.H.A.T. carton entitled "Inspection générale de l'infanterie"; and Renseignements donnés par le Général Velprey à la suite de la séance du C.C.A. du 4 mai 1936, 6 May 1936, unnumbered S.H.A.T. carton entitled "Inspection des chars de combat, Rapports d'inspection d'unités."

9. *P.V., C.S.G.*, 29 April 1936, carton 50 ter.

10. Robert Frankenstein, "A propos des aspects financiers du réarmement français (1935–1939)," *Revue d'histoire de la deuxième guerre mondiale* 26 (April 1976): 3.

11. MacGregor Knox, *Mussolini Unleashed, 1939–1941* (Cambridge, Eng.: Cambridge University Press, 1982), pp. 294–95.

12. Jacomet, *L'Armement de la France*, pp. 121–26; Gamelin, *Servir* 1: 261–62.

13. *Commission . . . Témoignages* 1: 23.

14. *Procès de Riom*, Audience du mardi 31 mars 1942, p. 1431, Fonds Gamelin, carton 2, dossier 7.

15. *P.V., C.S.G.*, 15 December 1937, S.H.A.T. carton 50 ter.

16. Général Martin commanded the ill-fated XI Corps in May 1940, and after his corps was driven off the Meuse and decimated by Gen. Erwin Rommel's 7th Panzer Division, he was relieved by Gamelin.

17. I.C.C., Rapport sur le groupement d'instruction: Son fonctionnement, les résultats obtenus, l'organisation proposée, n.d., pp. 2, 5, unnumbered S.H.A.T. carton entitled "Inspection des chars de combat."

18. I.C.C., Général R. Martin, Notice provisoire à l'usage des unités de la division cuirassée, 19 October 1938, no. 257/ICC/S; and I.C.C., le Général R. Martin à M. le président du Conseil, M.D.N.G., 19 October 1938, no. 261/ICC/S, p. 1. Both are in an unnumbered S.H.A.T. carton entitled "Inspections des chars de combat."

19. *P.V., C.S.G.*, 2 December 1938, S.H.A.T. carton 50 ter.

20. *Procés de Riom*, Audience du mercredi 1er avril 1942, pp. 1510–11, Fonds Gamelin, carton 2, dossier 8.

21. De Cossé-Brissac, "Combien de chars français," p. 78.

22. France, M.D.N.G., D.I., *Notice provisoire à l'usage des unités de la division cuirassée* (mimeographed) (n.p., n.d.), pp. 1–4, 8–9, 13, 58, 61, 56.

23. De Cossé-Brissac, "Combien de chars français," p. 79. The third light mechanized division was very similar to the first two, except it used the H-39 tank (instead of the S-35) and light reconnaissance tanks.

24. France, M.G., E.M.A., *Règlement de la cavalerie du 19 avril 1930, Deuxième partie: Emploi de la cavalerie* (Paris: Imprimerie nationale, 1930), pp. 1, 5–7, 28–29, 89.

25. Weygand, *Mémoires* 2: 408; M.G., D.C.T., le Général Flavigny, Note pour l'E.M.A., Objet: Mise sur pied d'une division légère motorisée, 9 November 1933, no. 2651 S 4/2, S.H.A.T. carton 9N172; Question des chars, March 1934, (handwritten note, marked "Vu par le Général Weygand"), S.H.A.T. carton 9N158; M.G., D.C.T., le général directeur Flavigny, Programme des specifications d'une automitrailleuse de cavalerie type combat, 26 June 1934, S.H.A.T. carton 9N177. In 1931, the cavalry expressed an interest in studying the new D-1 tank but apparently found it to be unsatisfactory. M.G., D.C.T., Note pour le 1ère direction, Objet: Exercice de motorisation, 6 Jun 1931, no. 1064 4/2, S.H.A.T. carton 9N175.

26. Section technique de la cavalerie, Etat des études intéressant la cavalerie, 1936, Additif du 1er trimestre; Section technique de la cavalerie, Etat des études intéressant la cavalerie, 1936, Additif du 2ème trimestre, 15 July 1936. Both are in S.H.A.T. carton 9N177.

27. France, M.G., E.M.A., *Notice provisoire sur l'emploi des unités motorisées et mécaniques de la cavalerie* (Paris: Imprimerie nationale, 1935), pp. 19–21, 92–106.

28. M.G., D.C.T., Général Flavigny, Note sur la division légère motorisée: Son role—sa composition, 2 February 1935, no. 3972 S 4/2, p. 3, S.H.A.T. carton 9N172.

29. France, E.S.G., Chef d'Escadrons Mariot, Cours de cavalerie, "La division légère mécanique: Organisation et emploi" (1935–1936) (n.p., n.d.), p. 10.

30. *Instruction 1936*, p. 203.

31. France, C.H.E.M., et Stage de technique d'armée, Chef d'Escadrons du Vigier, "La cavalerie actuelle" (October 1938) (n.p., n.d.), pp. 24, 26; France, E.S.G., Lieutenant Colonel de Lassus, cours de cavalerie, "Notes sur la manoeuvre offensive des D.C. et D.L.M." (November 1938) (n.p., n.d.), p. 37.

32. France, C.H.E.M., General Flavigny, "Les divisions légères mécaniques" (September 1938) (n.p., n.d.), p. 10.

33. Ibid., pp. 37, 54.

34. France, M.D.N.G., E.M.A., *Règlement de la cavalerie, Première partie: Emploi de la cavalerie* (Saumur: Imprimerie de l'Ecole militaire, 1939), pp. 3, 7, 80, 114–21, 16, 8, 85–86, 33–34, 118–19.

35. M.D.N.G., la D.C.T. à l'E.M.A., 29 November 1939, no. 827 4/2, S.H.A.T. carton 9N173.

36. *P.V., C.S.G.*, 13 March 1939, 10 July 1939, carton 50 ter.

37. De Cossé-Brissac, "Combien de chars français," pp. 78–80.

CHAPTER 9

1. *Procès de Riom*, Audience du mardi 31 mars 1942, pp. 1490–91, Fonds Gamelin, carton 2.

2. Ibid., Audience du mardi 24 mars 1942, pp. 1185–88.

3. Lt. Col. Jacques M. Vernet, "L'Armée d'armistice, 1940–1942: Une petite armée pour une grande revanche?" paper presented at the International Military History Symposium, Carlisle Barracks, Pennsylvania, 1–4 August 1982.

4. Cited in Robert O. Paxton, *Parades and Politics at Vichy: The French Officer Corps under Marshal Pétain* (Princeton: Princeton University Press, 1966), p. 51.

5. *Procès de Riom*, Audience du jeudi 19 mars 1942, p. 1041.

6. Bloch, *Strange Defeat*, p. 120.

7. Robert Frankenstein, *Le prix du réarmement français, 1935–1939* (Paris: Publications de la Sorbonne, 1982), p. 303; Anthony Adamthwaite, *France and the Coming of the Second World War, 1936–1939* (London: Frank Cass, 1977), p. 164; Robert Frank, "Le front populaire a-t-il perdu la guerre?" *L'histoire* (July–August 1983), pp. 58–6.

8. J.P., Financement des commandes d'engins blindés (chars et autosmitrailleuses) de 1920 au 1.9.39, n.d., p. 1, S.H.A.T carton 9N158.

9. *Commission . . . Témoignages* 1: 8.

10. Lieutenant Colonel Reboul, "Le malaise de l'armée," *Revue des deux mondes* 26 (5 March 1925): 389.

11. *Commission . . . Rapport* 1: 67.

12. Gamelin, Servir 1: 241–42; *Commission . . . Témoignages* 2: 446–47. In a manuscript included in his papers at the S.H.A.T., General Gamelin concluded, "The essential cause of our reverse in May 1940 was then, outside the superiority of the German combat aviation, the continued long-lived influence of the ideas of Marshal Pétain" (Fonds Gamelin, carton 7).

13. See Gamelin, "Hier et demain," *Revue militaire générale* 1 (January 1937): 25–28; "Réflexions sur le chef," *Revue d'infanterie* 86 (April 1935): 633–61; and C.H.E.M., General Gamelin, "L'Art de la guerre: Doctrine et procédés" (April 1937), année 1938–1939.

Select Bibliography

BIBLIOGRAPHIES

Mémorial de l'artillerie française. *Bibliographie générale de l'artillerie technique, 1915 à 1926.* Paris: Imprimerie nationale, 1926.

Ministère des armées. Etat-major de l'armée de terre. Service historique. *Guide Bibliographique sommaire d'histoire militaire et coloniale française.* Paris: Imprimerie nationale, 1969.

Probobysz, Cmdt. A. Favitski de. *Répertoire bibliographique de la littérature militaire et coloniale française depuis cent ans.* Paris: G. Thone, 1935.

UNPUBLISHED DOCUMENTS

France. E.M.A. S.H.A.T. Archives for the period 1919–1940.

France. E.M.A. S.H.A.T. Fonds Gamelin

France. C.H.E.M. Lectures for the period 1921–1939.

France. E.S.G. Lectures for the period 1921–1939.

OFFICIAL DOCUMENTS AND PUBLICATIONS

France. Assemblée nationale. Commission d'enquête sur les événements survenus en France de 1933 à 1945. *Rapport fait au nom de la commission d'enquête parlementaire par M. Charles Serre.* 2 vols. Paris: Presses universitaires de France, 1952.

———. Assemblée nationale. Commission d'enquête sur les événements survenus en France de 1933 à 1945. *Annexes. Témoignages et documents recueillis par la commission d'enquête parlementaire.* 9 vols. Paris: Presses universitaires de France, 1951–1952.

———. Ministère des affaires étrangères. Commission de publication des documents relatifs aux origines de la guerre, 1939–1945. *Documents diplomatiques francais, 1932–1939.* 2d série (1936–1939). 15 vols. Paris: Imprimerie nationale, 1963–1981.

———. Ministère des armées. Etat-major de l'armée de terre. Service historique. Col. François-André Paoli. *L'Armée française de 1919 à 1939.* 4 vols. Paris: Société industrielle d'imprimerie, n.d.

———. Ministère de la défense. Etat-major de l'armée de terre. Service historique. Lt. Col. Henry Dutailly. *Les problèmes de l'armée de terre française (1935–1939).* Paris: Imprimerie nationale, 1980.

France. M.G. E.M.A. *Décret du 28 mai 1895 portant règlement sur le service des armées en campagne.* Paris: Berger-Levrault, n.d.

———. *Décret du 28 octobre 1913 portant règlement sur la conduite des grandes unités (Services des armées en campagne).* Paris: Berger-Levrault, n.d.

———. *Instruction provisoire sur l'emploi tactique des grandes unités.* Paris:Charles Lavauzelle, 1922.

———. *Instruction sur l'emploi tactique des grandes unités.* Paris: Berger-Levrault, 1937.

Germany. Reichswehrministerium. Chef der Heeresleitung. *Führung und Gefecht der Verbundenen Waffen.* 2 vols. Berlin: Offene Worte, 1921.

Germany. Chef der Heeresleitung. *Truppenführung.* 2 vols. Berlin: E. G. Mittler & Sohn, 1933.

Journal officiel de la république français, 1870–1940. Paris: Imprimerie des journaux officiels, 1870–1940.

MEMOIRS, DIARIES, AND PERSONAL ACCOUNTS

Barlone, D. *A French Officer's Diary (23 August 1939–1 October 1940).* Trans L. V. Cass. Cambridge, Eng.: Cambridge University Press, 1942.

Bloch, Marc. *Strange Defeat.* Trans. Gerald Hopkins. New York: W. W. Norton, 1968.

Chambrun, René de. *I Saw France Fall. Will She Rise Again?* London: Jarrolds, 1941.

Clemenceau, Georges. *Grandeur and Misery of Victory.* Trans. F. M. Atkinson. New York: Harcourt, Brace, 1930.

Cot, Pierre. *Triumph of Treason.* Trans. Sybille and Milton Crane. Chicago: Ziff-Davis, 1944.

Flandin, Pierre. *Politique française, 1919–1940.* Paris: Les éditions nouvelles, 1947.

Foch, Marshal Ferdinand. *The Memoirs of Marshal Foch.* Trans. Col. T. Bentley Mott. London: William Heinemann, 1931.

Gamelin, Gen. Maurice. *Servir.* 3 vols. Paris: Plon, 1946–1947.

Gauché, Gen. Maurice. *Le deuxième bureau au travail, 1935–1940.* Paris: Amiot-Dumont, 1953.

Jacomet, Robert. *L'Armement de la France, 1936–1939.* Paris: Editions de la jeunesse, 1945.

Joffre, Marshal Joseph. *The Personal Memoirs of Joffre, Field Marshal of the French Army.* Trans. Col. T. Bentley Mott. 2 vols. New York: Harper and Brothers, 1932.

Ludendorff, Gen. Erich von. *Ludendorff's Own Story.* New York: Harper & Brothers, 1919.

Overstraeten, Gen. Raoul van. *Albert 1–Léopold III: Vingt ans de politique militaire belge 1920–1940.* Bruges: Desclée de Brouwer, 1946.

Paul-Boncour, Joseph. *Entre deux guerres: souvenirs sur la IIIe république.* 3 vols. New York: Brentano's, 1946.

Pertinax [André Géraud]. *The Gravediggers of France.* New York: Doubleday, Doran, 1944.

Prételat, Gen. André. *Le destin tragique de la ligne Maginot.* Paris: Berger Levrault, 1950.

Reynaud, Paul. *Mémoires.* 2 vols. Paris: Flammarion, 1960–1963.

———. *Au coeur de la mêlée, 1930–1945.* Paris: Flammarion, 1951.

Weygand, Gen. Maxime. *Mémoires.* 3 vols. Paris: Flammarion, 1950–1957.

BOOKS, PAMPHLETS, AND DISSERTATIONS

Adamthwaite, Anthony. *France and the Coming of the Second World War, 1936–1939.* London: Frank Cass, 1977.

Albord, Gen. Tony. *Pourquoi cela est arrivé, ou les responsabilités d'une génération militaire.* Nantes: Aux portes du large, 1947.

Alerme, Colonel. *Les causes militaires de notre défaite.* Paris: Centre d'études de l'agence "Inter France," 1941.

Alexander, Martin S. "Maurice Gamelin and the Defence of France: French Military Policy, the U.K. Land Contribution, and Strategy towards Germany, 1935–1939." Unpublished Ph.D. diss., Oxford University, 1982.

Alléhaut, Gen. Emile. *Le combat d'infanterie.* Paris: Berger-Levrault, 1924.

———. *Etre prêts.* Paris: Berger-Levrault, 1935.

Balck, Gen. Wilhelm. *Entwicklung der Taktik im Weltkrieg.* 2nd ed. Berlin: R. Eisenschmidt, 1922.

Bankwitz, Philip Charles Farwell. *Maxime Weygand and Civil-Military Relations in France.* Cambridge, Mass.: Harvard University Press, 1967.

Beaufre, Gen. André. *1940: The Fall of France.* Trans. Desmond Flower. New York: Knopf, 1968.

———. "Liddell Hart and the French Army, 1919–1939." In *The Theory and Practice of War,* Michael Howard, ed. New York: Praeger, 1966.

Bond, Brian. *France and Belgium, 1939–1940.* Newark, Del.: University of Delaware Press, 1975.

Bonnal, Gen. Henri. *L'Art nouveau en tactique: Etude critique.* Paris: Librairie militaire R. Chapelot, 1904.

Bouvard, Cmdt. H. *Les leçons militaires de la guerre.* Paris: Masson, 1920.

Bruchmüller, George. *Die deutsche Artillerie in den Durchschlachten des Weltkrieges.* Berlin: E. S. Mittler & Sohn, 1922.

Bruge, Roger. *Histoire de la ligne Maginot.* 2 vols. Paris: Fayard, 1973–1975.

Buat, Gen. A. L. *Hindenburg et Ludendorff. Stratèges.* Paris: Berger-Levrault, 1923.

———. *Ludendorff.* Paris: Payot, 1921.

Carrias, Eugéne. *La pensée militaire française.* Paris: Presses universitaires de France, 1960.

Carrias, Cmdt. *L'Armée allemande: son histoire, son organisation, sa tactique.* Paris: Berger-Levrault, 1938.

Challener, Richard D. *The French Theory of the Nation in Arms, 1866–1939.* New York: Russell & Russell, 1965.

Chapman, Guy. *Why France Fell.* New York: Holt, Rinehart & Winston, 1969.

———. "The French Army and Politics." In *Soldiers and Governments,* Michael Howard, ed. London: Eyre & Spottiswoode, 1957.

Chauvineau, Gen. Narcisse. *Une invasion, est-elle encore possible?* Paris: Berger-Levrault, 1939.

Clarke, Jeffrey Johnstone. "Military Technology in Republican France: The Evolution of the French Armored Force, 1917–1940." Unpublished Ph.D. diss., Duke University, 1968.

Cole, Ronald Harvey. "'Forward with the Bayonet!' The French army prepares for Offensive Warfare, 1911–1914." Unpublished Ph.D. diss., University of Maryland, 1975.

Colton, Joel. *Léon Blum: Humanist in Politics.* New York: Knopf, 1966.

Conquet, General. *L'Enigme de notre manque de divisions blindées (1932–1940)*. Paris: Nouvelles éditions latines, 1956.

Corda, Marie L.V.H. *L'Evolution des méthodes offensives de l'armée française (1914–1918)*. Paris: Villars, 1921.

Daille, Cmdt. Marius. *The Battle of Montdidier*. Trans. Major Walter R. Wheeler. U.S. War Department, typescript.

Debeney, Gen. Eugène. *Sur la securité militaire de la France*. Paris: Payot, 1930.

———. *La guerre et les hommes*. Paris: Plon, 1937.

Delmensingen, Konrad Krafft von. *Der Durchbruch*. Hamburg: Hanseatische Verlagsanslatt, 1937.

Dumoncel, Léon. *Essai de mémento tactique: la décision*. Paris: Charles Lavauzelle, 1937.

Duroselle, Jean-Baptiste. *La décadence, 1932–1939*. Paris: Imprimerie nationale, 1979.

Duval, General. *Les leçons de la guerre d'Espagne*. Paris: Plon, 1938.

Duvignac, Col. André. Histoire de l'armée motorisée. Paris: Imprimerie nationale, 1948.

Ellis, Maj. L. F. *The War in France and Flanders, 1939–1940*. London: Her Majesty's Stationery Office, 1953.

Estienne, Gen. Jean. B. *Conférence faite le 15 février 1920 sur les chars d'assaut*. Paris: Librairie de l'enseignement technique, 1920.

Foch, Ferdinand. *Des principes de guerre*. Paris: Berger-Levrault, 1906.

France. Institut national de la statistique. *Annuaire statistique*. vol. 50 (1934) Paris: Imprimerie nationale, 1935.

Frankenstein, Robert. *Le prix du réarmement français, 1935–1939*. Paris: Publications de la Sorbonne, 1982.

Gaulle, Charles de. *Vers l'armée de métier*. Paris: Berger-Levrault, 1934.

Girardet, Raoul. *La société militaire dans la France contemporaine, 1815–1939*. Paris: Plon, 1953.

Gorce, Paul-Marie de la. *The French Army*. New York: George Braziller, 1963.

Goutard, Col. A. *The Battle of France, 1940*. Trans. A. R. P. Burgess. New York: Ives Washburn, 1959.

Gunsburg, Jeffery A. *Divided and Conquered: The French High Command and the Defeat of the West, 1940*. Westport, Conn.: Greenwood Press, 1979.

Herr, Gen. Frédéric G. *L'Artillerie: ce quelle a été; ce qu'elle est; ce qu'elle doit être*. Paris: Berger-Levrault, 1923.

Hughes, Judith M. *To the Maginot Line: The Politics of French Military Preparation in the 1920s*. Cambridge, Mass.: Harvard University Press, 1971.

Kirk, Dudley. "Population and Population Trends in Modern France." In *Modern France: Problems of the Third and Fourth Republics*, Edward Mead Earle, ed. Princeton: Princeton University Press, 1951.

Kirkland, Faris R. "The French Officer Corps and the Fall of France, 1920–1940." Unpublished Ph.D. diss., University of Pennsylvania, 1983.

Knox, MacGregor. *Mussolini Unleashed, 1939–1941*. Cambridge, Eng.: Cambridge University Press, 1982.

Laffargue, Capt. André. *Etude sur l'attaque*. Paris: Plon, 1916.

Laure, General Auguste M.E., et al. *Pétain*. Paris: Berger-Levrault, 1941

Laure, Lt. Col. Auguste M.E. *La victoire franco-espagnole dans le Rif*. Paris: Plon, 1927.

Le Goyet, Pierre. *Le mystère Gamelin*. Paris: Presses de la Cité, 1976.

Lemoine, General. *L'Enseignement du combat dans les petites unités d'infanterie*. 4th ed. Paris: Charles Lavauzelle, 1931.

Liddell Hart, Capt. Basil H. *The Tanks*. 2 vols. New York: Praeger, 1959.

Loizeau, Gen. Lucien. *Deux manoeuvres*. Paris: Berger-Levrault, 1933.

————. *La manoeuvre du corps d'armée*. Courbevoie: P. Chanove, 1932.

Lucas, Lieutenant Colonel. *L'Evolution des idées tactiques en France et en Allemagne pendant la guerre de 1914–1918*. Paris: Berger-Levrault, 1925.

Lupfer, Capt. Timothy T. *The Dynamics of Doctrine: The Change in German Tactical Doctrine during the First World War*. Leavenworth Paper 4. Fort Leavenworth: Combat Studies Institute, 1981.

Lyet, Cmdt. Pierre. *La bataille de France (mai–juin 1940)*. Paris: Payot, 1947.

Maillard, Col. Louis A.G. *Eléments de la guerre*. Paris: Librairie militaire de L. Baudoin, 1891.

Mary, Jean-Yves. *La ligne Maginot: ce qu'elle était, ce qu'il en reste*. San Dalmazzo, Italy: L'Istituto Grafico Bertello, 1980.

Maurin, Gen. Joseph-L.M. *L'Armée moderne*. Paris: Flammarion, 1938.

Menu, Lt. Col. Charles. *Application de l'industrie: la leçon d'une guerre*. Rambouillet: Pierre Leroy, 1932.

Michel, Henri. *Le second guerre mondiale*. 2 vols. Paris: Presses universitaires de France, 1968.

Minart, Jacques. *P. C. Vincennes, Secteur 4*. 2 vols. Paris: Berger-Levrault, 1945.

Miquel, Lt. Col. *Enseignements stratégiques et tactiques de la guerre de 1914–1918*. Paris: Charles Lavauzelle, 1926.

Monteilhet, J. *Les institutions militaires de la France (1814–1932)*. Paris: Felix Alcan, 1932.

Mordacq, Gen. Jean. *Le ministère Clemenceau*. 4 vols. Paris: Plon, 1931.

Mysyrowicz, Ladislas. *Autopsie d'une défaite: Origines de l'effondrement militaire français de 1940*. Lausanne: L'Age d'homme, 1973.

Ogburn, William F. and William Jaffe. *The Economic Development of Post-War France: A Survey of Production*. New York: Columbia University Press, 1929.

Ormsby, Hilda. *France: A Regional and Economic Geography*. London: Methuen, 1931; rev. ed. 1950.

Paille, Cmdt. G. *Connaissance et emploi des armes et engins de l'infanterie*. Paris: Charles Lavauzelle, 1932.

Paxton, Robert O. *Parades and Politics at Vichy: The French Officer Corps under Marshal Pétain*. Princeton: Princeton University Press, 1966.

Pierce, Richard Lee. "A Maximum of Support: The Development of U.S. Army Field Artillery Doctrine in World War I." Unpublished M.A. thesis, Ohio State University, 1983.

Porch, Douglas. *The March to the Marne: The French Army, 1871–1914*. Cambridge, Eng.: Cambridge University Press, 1981.

Ralston, David B. *The Army of the Republic: The Place of the Military in the Political Evolution of France, 1871–1914*. Cambridge, Mass.: MIT Press, 1967.

Remond, René and Janine Bourdin. *Edouard Daladier, chef de gouvernement, avril 1938–septembre 1939*. Paris: Presses de la fondation nationale des sciences politiques, 1977.

Renn, Ludwig. *Warfare: The Relation of War to Society*. Trans. Edward Fitzgerald. New York: Oxford University Press, 1939.

Reynaud Paul. *Le problème militaire français*. Paris: Flammarion, 1937.

Rocolle, Col. Pierre. *2000 ans de fortification française*. Paris: Charles Lavauzelle, 1973.

Roger, Col. J. Artillery in the Offensive. Trans. J. S. Wood. U.S. Army, typescript, 1922.

Rommell, Erwin. *Infantry Attacks*. Trans. Lt. Col. G. E. Kidde. Washington: The Infantry Journal, 1944.

Rowe, Vivian. *The Great Wall of France*. London: Putnam, 1959.

Ryan, Stephen. *Pétain the Soldier*. New York: A. S. Barnes, 1969.

Schneider, Lt. Col. Fernand. *Histoire des doctrines militaires*. Paris: Presses universitaires de France, 1957.

Serrigny, General. *Réflexions sur l'art de la guerre*. Paris: Charles Lavauzelle, 1930.

Setzen, Joel A. "The Doctrine of the Offensive in the French Army on the Eve of World War I." Unpublished Ph.D. diss., University of Chicago, 1972.

Souchon, Lucien. *Feue* [sic] *l'armée française*. Paris: Fayard, 1929.

Tanenbaum, Jan Karl. *General Maurice Sarrail, 1856–1929: The French Army and Left-Wing Politics*. Chapel Hill: University of North Carolina Press, 1974.

Tournes, Lt. Col. René. *L'Histoire militaire*. Paris: Charles Lavauzelle, 1922.

Tournoux, J.-R. *Pétain et de Gaulle*. Paris: Plon, 1964.

Tournoux, Gen. Paul-Emile. *Défense des frontières. Haut commandement-gouvernement, 1919–1939*. Paris: Nouvelles éditions latines, 1960.

Wynne, Capt. G. C. *If Germany Attacks: The Battle in Depth in the West*. London: Faber & Faber, 1940.

Young, Robert J. *In Command of France: French Foreign Policy and Military Planning*. Cambridge, Mass.: Harvard University Press, 1978.

ARTICLES

Albord, Gen. Tony. "Appel à l'imagination." *Revue de défense nationale* (August–September 1949): 159–67.

Anonymous. "L'Armée qu'il nous faut." *Revue des deux mondes* 61 (1 January 1921): 5–15.

Anonymous officer of the General Staff in Paris. "French Strategy and Tactics in Syria." *The Journal of the Royal United Service Institution* 71 (November 1926): 699–711.

Bonnefous, Edouard. "Les responsabilités politiques et militaires de la défaite de 1940." *Revue politique et parlementaire* (May 1967): 27–38.

Brindel, General. "La nouvelle organisation militaire." *Revue des deux mondes* 51 (1 June 1929): 481–501.

Cairns, John C. "Some Recent Historians and the 'Strange Defeat' of 1940." *Journal of Modern History* 46 (March 1974): 60–85.

———. "Along the Road back to France 1940." *American Historical Review* 64 (April 1959): 583–603.

Chapon, Charles. "L'Armée de terre française: le 2 septembre 1939 au 9 mai 1940." *Revue historique des armées* 4 (1979): 164–92.

Cointet, Jean-Paul. "Gouvernement et haut-commandement en France entre les deux guerres." *Défense nationale* 33 (April 1977): 83–100.

Coox, Alvin D. "General Narcisse Chauvineau: False Apostle of Prewar French Military Doctrine." *Military Affairs* 37 (February 1973): 15–19.

Cossé-Brissac, Lt. Col. Charles de. "Combien de chars francais contre combien de chars allemands le 10 mai 1940." *Revue de défense nationale* (July 1947): 75–89.

Debeney, Gen. Eugène. "Armée nationale ou armée de métier." *Revue des deux mondes* 53 (15 September 1929): 241–76.

———. "Encore l'armée de métier." Revue des deux mondes 28 (15 July 1935): 279–95.

Doughty, Robert A. "French Antitank Doctrine, 1940: The Antidote that Failed." *Military Review* 56 (May 1976): 36–48.

———"De Gaulle's Concept of a Mobile, Professional Army: Genesis of French Defeat?" *Parameters: The Journal of the U.S. Army War College* 4 (1974): 23–34.

———. "The Enigma of French Armored Doctrine, 1940." *Armor* 83 (September–October 1974): 39–44.

Duchene, General. "Le conflit Sino-Japonais." *Echo de Paris* (21 October 1937), p. 2.

Duffour, Gen. Gaston C.G.A. "Les exigences et les disciplines actuelles du haut enseignement militaire." *Revue de Paris* 42 (1 March 1935): 99–112; (15 March 1935): 339–59.

Duval, Gen. Maurice. "La crise de notre organisation militaire." *Revue de Paris* 33 (15 April 1926): 756–96.

Ely, General. "Les leçons qu'il faut tirer des opérations de 1940." *Revue de defense nationale* (December 1953): 563–82.

Frank, Robert. "Le front populaire a-t-il perdu la guerre?" *L'histoire* (July–August 1983): 58–66.

Frankenstein, Robert. "A propos des aspects financiers du réarmement français (1935–1939)." *Revue d'histoire de la deuxième guerre mondiale* 26 (April 1976): 1–20.

Gamelin, Gen. Maurice. "Hier et demain." *Revue militaire générale* 1 (January 1937): 25–28.

———. "Réflexions sur le chef." *Revue d'infanterie* 86 (April 1935): 633–61.

Garnier, Capt. A.-P. "L'Artillerie allemande au combat." *Revue d'artillerie* 122 (July 1924): 77–92.

Gaulle, Capt. Charles de. "Doctrine à priori ou doctrine des circonstances." *Revue militaire française* 95 (1925): 306–28.

Gelot, Lieutenant. "Les enseignements de la guerre d'Espagne." *Revue d'infanterie* 93 (November 1938): 1038–39.

Goubernard, Chef de bataillon. "Chars au Maroc en 1925." *Revue d'infanterie* 68–69 (May, June, July 1926): 619–49, 749–76, 110–31.

Goyet, Colonel Pierre le. "Les chars de combat pendant la première guerre mondiale." *Revue historique de l'armée.* 24 (1968): 119–41.

Gunsburg, Jeffery A. "Coupable ou non? Le rôle du général Gamelin dans la défaite de 1940." *Revue historique des armées* 4 (1979): 145–63.

Helmreich, Jonathan. "The Negotiation of the Franco-Belgian Military Accord of 1920." *French Historical Studies* 3 (Spring 1964): 360–78

D'Hoop, Jean-Marie. "La politique française du réarmement." *Revue d'histoire de la deuxième guerre mondiale* 4 (April 1954): 1–26.

Hunt, Lt. H. H. "Accompanying Artillery." *Field Artillery Journal* 22 (November–December 1932): 641–64.

Juin, Lieutenant Colonel. "L'Achèvement de la pacification marocaine: méthodes et programmes." *Revue militaire française* 55 (January 1935): 84–107.

Laporte, Cmdt. Henri. "La défense antichars." *Revue d'infanterie* 93 (December 1938): 1140–87.

Liddell Hart, Lt. B. H. "Etude critique de 'Règlement provisoire de manoeuvres d'infanterie 1920.'" *Revue militaire générale* 19 (15 October 1922): 783–93; (15 April 1923): 292–99; (15 September 1923): 675–81.

Loustaunau-Lacau, Captains and Montjean. "Au Maroc français en 1925." *Revue militaire française* 28 (1 April 1928): 22–37.

Mordal, Jacques. "Le 'mythe' de front continu." *Revue de défense nationale* (March 1954): 298–302.

Morel, Chef d'escadrons G. "Les armes antichars." *Revue d'artillerie* 103 (January 1929): 23–49.

Perré, Lt. Col. J. "Naissance et évolution du char de combat en France durant la guerre 1914–1918." *Revue d'infanterie* 86 (January 1935): 13–30.

Stolfi, R. H. S. "Equipment for Victory in France in 1940." *History* 55 (February 1970): 1–20.

Thévenet, General. "Les forces militaires de la France." *Revue militaire générale* 17 (June 1920): 337–56; (July 1920): 400–23; (August 1920): 496–514; (September 1920): 577–85.

Vernet, Lt. Col. Jacques M. "L'Armée d'armistice, 1940–1942: Une petite armée pour une grande revanche?" Paper presented at the International Military History Symposium, Carlisle Barracks, Pennsylvania, 1–4 August 1982.

Verzat, Jean. "A propos du P. C. Gamelin." *Revue historique des armées* 2 (1982): 99–109.

Vial, Lt. Col. Robert. "L'Armée française et l'histoire." *Revue historique* 217 (April–June 1962): 437–44.

———. "La défense nationale: son organisation entre les deux guerres." *Revue d'histoire de la deuxième guerre mondiale* 5 (April 1955): 11–32.

Vidalenc, "Les divisions de série 'B' dans l'armée française pendant la campagne de France 1939–1940." *Revue historique des armées* 4 (1980): 107–14.

Weygand, Gen. Maxime. "L'Etat militaire de la France." *Revue des deux mondes* 29 (15 October 1936): 721–36.

———. "L'Unité de l'armée." *Revue militaire générale* 1 (January 1937): 15–19.

Young, Robert J. "Preparation for Defeat: French War Doctrine in the Interwar Period." *Journal of European Studies* 2 (June 1972): 155–72.

Index

Page numbers in italics indicate maps

Alexandre, Col. M. N. G., 106, 107
American Expeditionary Force (AEF),
    105
antitank mines, 138
antitank weapons, 27–28, 149
Ardennes. *See* frontier defense,
    Ardennes
armored units. *See* division, armored
army. *See* French army; German army
artillery
    American doctrine for, 105
    doctrine for use of, 102–106, 107
    German deployment compared to
        French, 103–104, 110, 111
    mechanization of, 99
    in methodical battle strategy, 98–99,
        106–107
    mobility of, 99, 100
    tanks supported by, 159–161, 163
    types of, 100–102
    in World War I, 83–84
attaque brusquée, 26–27, 29, 53, 55, 56

Barthou, Louis, 20
bataille conduit. See methodical battle
Belgium
    German attack through, 197
    northern frontier defense and,
        62–66, 68, 71
blitzkrieg, 4, 90, 186, 197
Blum, Léon, 2, 12, 119
Bonnal, Col. Henri, 80
Breda maneuver, 70, 71, 196
Buat, Gen. Edmond A. L., 50, 51, 63,
    89, 117, 124
budget, military, 170, 190–191

cavalry
    doctrine for, 178–182

frontier defense and, 71–72
    light mechanized, 178–180
    light mechanized divisions and,
        175–176
Center of Higher Military Studies, 80,
    81, 84, 115
citizen-soldier, 17
civil-military relations, 117–119
    French army failure associated with,
        192
    problems in, 125–126
Clemenceau, Georges
    army training problems noted by,
        33
    civilian control of army and, 121
    length of service and, 21
Colson, Gen. L. A., 172
Condé, Gen. Charles M., 130, 160
conscription, 16
    length of service and, 23
    size of army and, 19
Consultive Council on Armament,
    136, 137, 153, 157
Cot, Pierre, 60
covering force, 26–27
    frontier defense strategy and, 55
    mobilization of, 39
    size of, 29
Culmann, Gen. Frédéric, 77

Daille, Maj. Marius, 85–86
Daladier, Edouard
    armored divisions and, 170
    military budget and, 67
    as minister of war, 117, 120, 122,
        133
    responsibility of, for French defeat,
        192
    at Riom trial, 2, 32, 170

Dassault, General, 136
de Gaulle, Gen. Charles, 167
  criticisms of ideas of, 12
  French doctrine criticized by, 194
  professional army concept from, 40
Debeney, Gen. Eugéne
  at Battle of Montdidier, 84–85
  as Chief of General Staff, 117
  flexibility in French doctrine pro-
    posed by, 8
  French doctrine and, 6
  length of service and, 21–22
  opposition to professional army
    from, 41
  at War College, 80
defense
  emphasis on, 35–36
  in French doctrine, 187
  of frontiers, 43–74
  importance of, 96
  nation in arms concept for, 15–18
Dégoutte, Gen. Jean M. J., 57–58
Department of the Fabrication of
    Armaments, 136–137, 138
division, armored, 167–184
  creation of, 173–174
  organization of tanks in, 173–175
division, light mechanized, 175–176
  armored division compared to, 180
  mission of, 177, 178–182
doctrine, French
  for artillery deployment, 102–106,
    107, 110–111
  for cavalry, 177
  communication in, 8
  confusion of authority over,
    133–134
  definition of, xi
  development of, 5–7
  evolution of, 186–187
  failures of, 185–186, 188–189,
    191–192, 193–194
  framework of, 1–13
  German doctrine compared to,
    114–115
  government and military institu-
    tions and, 117–140
  incorporation of technology into,
    135
  infantry, 36–37

  inflexibility of, 11–12
  for light mechanized division,
    178–182
  Marshal Pétain as author of, 6
  regulations for, 9
  reliance on historical analysis for,
    93
  role of tanks in, 141–142, 144–148,
    157–158, 161, 164–166
  World War I impact on, 75–76, 80,
    82–83, 87
doctrine, German, 4
  for artillery deployment, 110–111
  continuous battle in, 114–115
  role of tanks in, 165–166
Doumenc, Gen. André, 139, 140, 167
Doumergue, Gaston, 51–52
du Picq, Col. Ardant, 76
Duffour, Lt. Col. Gaston C. G. A., 89
Dufieux, Gen. J. C. M. S., 93, 129, 130,
    150–151, 160
Dyle Plan, northern frontier defense
    and, 69–70

Escaut Plan, northern frontier
    defense and, 69
Estienne, Gen. Jean-B., 167
  armored units promoted by, 167
  criticism from, 153–155
  as "father" of French armor,
    143–144
  as inspector of tanks, 144
  tank building and, 145, 147,
    155–156, 181

Fabry, Col. Jean, 18, 30, 117
Fillonneau, Gen. Etienne, 57–58
firepower
  emphasis on, 13, 53, 77, 82
  methodical battle and, 95–116
Flandin, Pierre, 38
Flavigny, Gen. J. A. L. R., 176, 177,
    178
Foch, Marshal Ferdinand, 6
  artillery doctrine criticized by, 103
  covering force and, 29
  frontier defense strategy from,
    48–50, 51, 52
  offensive strategy proposed by, 80
foreign policy, military policy and, 193

fortifications
    frontier defense and, 47, 51–53, 61
    German attacks against, 72–73
    for northern frontier defense,
        65–66, 67
    technical design of, 54, 56, 58, 59
France
    battle of (1940), 1–2, 185–186,
        190–192, 196–197
    government ministries in, 117
French army
    changes in, from 1919 to 1939,
        187–188
    civilian leadership of, 121, 133
    collapse of (1940), 3, 4–5
    conscription and, 19
    doctrine of, after World War I, 5–13
    as dominant French military body,
        120
    failure of, 188–192
    General Staff of, 130–131
    inspector general of, 123
    Laws of 1927–1928 and, 22–25
    length of service and readiness of,
        125–126
    length of service and size of, 21–22
    nation in arms concept and, 15–17
    preparedness of (1940), 2–4
    readiness of, 29, 125–126
    size of, 20, 23, 24
    training of, 22–23, 29–31
    training problems of, 33
    World War I success of, 84–85
frontier
    French natural resources located
        by, 43–44
    northeastern, vulnerability of, 26
    safety of, mobilization and, 26
frontier defense, 43–74
    Ardennes, 61–62
    fortifications for, 61
    northeastern
        after 1871, 46–47
        fortifications for, 61
        map of, 49
    northern, 46–47
        Belgium as key to, 62–66, 68, 71
        complications of, 62–63
        fortifications for, 65–66, 67
        map of, 64

Gamelin, Gen. Maurice
    armored divisions and, 169–170,
        171, 172–173
    artillery deployment and, 101–102
    as Chief of General Staff, 117, 120,
        124
    as commander in chief, 139, 140
    French defeat blamed on, 185, 193
    French doctrine and, 6, 7
    northern frontier defense and, 66,
        68
    relieved of command, 140
    responsibility of, for French defeat,
        139–140, 194, 195–196
    Rhineland remilitarization and,
        38–39
    at Riom trial, 2, 185
Georges, Gen. Alphonse
    artillery and, 160, 162–163
    in control of northeastern frontier,
        139, 196
    criticisms from, 134
    as deputy commander in chief, 139,
        140
    Dyle plan and, 69–70
    Maginot Line and, 73
German army
    infiltration tactics of, 88, 89, 112,
        113, 186
    revival of, in 1920s, 26
    storm battalions in, 88
    World War I tactics of, 89–90
Germany, France invaded by (1940),
        1–2
Gerodias, Gen. Henri, 185–186
Giraud, Gen. Henri H., 145, 146
Gouraud, Gen. H. J. E., 67–68
Guillaumat, Gen. Marie L. A.
    fortifications recommended by, 51,
        52–53
    frontier defense strategy and,
        54–55, 63, 65

Hellot, Frédéric E. A., 50
Héring, Gen. Pierre, 172–173, 188,
        194
Herr, Gen. F. G., 101
High Command
    armored divisions and, 170
    army training and, 32, 34

failures of, 189
frontier defense strategy and, 62–63
lack of authority of, 133
leadership of, 117
organization of, 117–118, 139
responsibility of, for French military failure, 185, 193–194
structure of, 127–128
High Military Committee, 119
Huntziger, Gen. Charles, 1, 186

industry, German threat to, 45
infantry
formations of, 36–37
in methodical battle, 111
motorized, 71–72, 109–110
movement of, in methodical battle, 106–109
tanks used with, 142, 146, 147, 161–162
vulnerability of, 45
infiltration tactics, German, 88, 89, 112, 113, 186
Instructions on the Tactical Employment of Large Units (1936), 9, 11
approach to battle in, 97
firepower emphasized in, 95–96
methodical battle in, 34, 93, 97
offense *versus* defense in, 97–98
principles of war in, 88
total war in, 40

Jacomet, Robert, 129
Joffre, Marshal Joseph
as Chief of General Staff, 121
French doctrine regulations and, 9
frontier defense strategy and, 48, 50, 51

Keller, Lt. Col. Marie J. P., 167, 185

Laval, Pierre, accusations against, 2
Laws of 1927–1928
adoption of, 21–22
frontier defense strategy and, 55
military failures associated with, 188
size of army affected by, 22–25
Lefèvre, André, 20, 123

Lemoine, Col. Felix A., 106
length of military service, 16–17, 18, 19
after World War I, 125
one-year, 21, 125–126
size of army and, 20, 21–22
training problems associated with, 33
Loizeau, Gen. Lucien, 37, 79, 96, 162
Ludendorff, Gen. Erich von, 84, 89
Lyautey, Marshal Louis, 90

Maginot, André, 51, 60
Maginot Line, 188
construction of, 29
Debeney's influence on, 6
emphasis on defense and, 35
German attack against, 72–73
northern frontier defense and, 62, 67, 70, 71
resources protected by, 191
Maglinse, Gen. Henri, 63
Maillard, Col. Louis A. G., 80
Malmaison, Battle of, 87
Mandel, Georges, 38
Martin, Col. Julien F. R.
armored divisions and, 171–172
artillery support for tanks proposed by, 159
tank tests conducted by, 151
tanks supported by, 155–156
Maurin, Gen. Joseph L. M., 59, 117, 152
methodical battle
artillery role in, 98–99, 106–107
in beginning of Battle of France, 34–35
description of, 4, 10, 115–116
emphasis on, in 1930s, 97
failure of, 186, 197
French army focus on, 13
infantry in, 111–112
Maginot Line and, 70–72
nation in arms and, 41
reliance on firepower and, 77, 95–116
in total war concept, 93
World War I lessons and, 77–78

Ministry of War, 18, 30, 66, 117, 120–124, 128–129
mobility
  of artillery, 99, 100
  in colonial campaigns, 91–92
mobilization
  centers for, 31–32
  French response to German remilitarization and, 39–40
  of industrial resources, 26–28
  system for, 24, 25
Montdidier, Battle of, 84–85, 86
Mordacq, Gen. Jean, 21, 121, 128
Mordal, Jacques, 70
motorization
  of French army, 71–72
  of infantry, 109–110
Moyrand, Col. A. E. M., 108
Munich crisis, 39–40

nation in arms, 15–16, 17, 18
natural resources
  protection of, 43–44
  vulnerability of, 45
Niessel, Gen. Henri-A., 32
Nollet, Gen. Charles, 57

offense
  decline in emphasis on, 35–36
  emphasis on, in French doctrine, 187
  importance of, 96
offensive à outrance, 9, 76, 82, 88

Painlevé, Paul, 52, 147
Paul-Boncour, Joseph, 18, 38
Permanent Committee of National Defense, 119
Perré, Col. Jean, 173
Pétain, Marshal Philippe
  accusations against, 2
  covering force and, 29
  French doctrine associated with, 6
  frontier defense strategy and, 50, 51–52, 54, 56–59
  as inspector general of army, 123, 124
  as minister of war, 117
  northern frontier defense and, 68

Provisional Instructions written by, 10
  in Rif campaign, 91
  in Superior Council of War, 117
  on war council, 122
Plan D, northern frontier defense and, 69–70
Plan E, northern frontier defense and, 69
Plan XVII, 47, 71
Porte du Theil, Col. Paul M. J. de la, 82, 107, 110
Prételat, Gen. André, 24, 33
principles of war, 87–88
Prioux, Lt. Col. René J. A., 82
Provisional Instructions on the Tactical Employment of Large Units (1921), 9–11, 36, 76
  approach to battle in, 96–97
  firepower in, 77, 95–96
  nation at arms, 17
  principles in, 88

reserve forces, 15–42
  readiness of, 31
  training of, 29–30
Revue d'infanterie, 78–79
Reynaud, Paul, 2
Rhineland
  French presence in, 35
  German remilitarization of, 38–39
  offensive movement into, 37
  withdrawal from, 188
Rif campaign (1925–1926), 90–91
Riga, Battle of, 89–90
Riom trial, 2, 3, 32–34, 124, 170, 173, 185
Roger, Col. J., ix

Seré de Rivières, Gen. Raymond A., 45–46
Spanish Civil War, 39, 92–93
Superior Council of National Defense, 20, 118
Superior Council of War
  armored divisions and, 169–170, 171
  army readiness and training and, 32
  establishment of, 18–19

frontier defense strategy from, 48,
    52, 57, 61
influence of, 131–133
leadership of, 117
length of military service and,
    20–21, 125
responsibility of, for French mili-
    tary failure, 193–194
tank program discussed in, 148,
    152, 154–155, 172
vice president of, 123

tanks
    in armored divisions, 173–175
    artillery support for, 159–161, 163
    B-1, 99–100, 148, 151–155, 159,
        167–168
    2C, 148
    D-2, 153, 154, 155, 159
    development of, 141–166, 168–169,
        182–183
    French versus German views of,
        165–166
    FT-17, 141–142, 148
    infantry supported by, 161–162
    R-35, 157, 159, 168
    in Rif campaign, 91
    role of, in French doctrine,
        141–142, 144–148, 157–158, 161,
        164–166
    S-35, 176–177
    types and numbers of, 141,
        146–147, 153, 167–168
    in World War I, 141–142
Technical Cabinet, 136
technology, military, 135
total war
    French preparation for, 17, 25,
        38–40
    methodical battle in, 93
Touchon, Gen. Robert-Auguste, 34,
    82, 112, 150, 159
Tournoux, Gen. P. E., 35, 37
training
    limits of, 22–23
    problems in, 33
    of reserve forces, 29–31

universal military service, 17

Velpry, Gen. G. M., 154, 156
Vichy regime, 2
Vuillemin, Gen. Joseph, 140

war, principles of, 87–88
War College
    criticism of, 80
    doctrine taught at, 80–81, 83–84
War Committee, 119
war plans, 69–70, 187
weaponry, adequate, 27–28
Weygand, Gen. Maxime
    accusations against, 2
    cavalry mechanization promoted
        by, 181
    as Chief of General Staff, 117, 124
    as commander in chief, 140
    criticism of civilian leadership from,
        126–127
    French army division of authority
        and, 122
    French doctrine and, 6
    as inspector general of army, 124
    northern frontier defense and, 66,
        68
    professional army criticized by, 40,
        41
    tank doctrine and, 152
World War I
    artillery used in, 102–106
    casualties from, 75
    French doctrine based on, 80,
        82–83, 87
    impact of, on French doctrine,
        75–76
    tanks used in, 141–142